Technology and society

handbook
for social research in
urban areas

Edited by Philip M. Hauser

Professor and Chairman, Department of Sociology,
University of Chicago

unesco

301.364
H 376

Published by the United Nations
Educational, Scientific and Cultural Organization
Place de Fontenoy, Paris-7e
1st impression September 1965
2nd impression August 1967
3rd impression August 1970
Printed by Beugnet S.A., Paris

Foreword

At the eleventh session of the General Conference of Unesco, Paris 1960, 'the Director-General was authorized, in co-operation with the United Nations, the Specialized Agencies and competent non-governmental organizations . . . (b) to continue to promote the application of the social sciences to the problems of rural life, of balanced social and economic development, of urbanization, including housing, and of the social implications of technological change'. Following the organization in earlier years of a series of regional conferences and seminars on the social aspects of urbanization (see below, 'Introduction and Overview') it was decided to have a handbook prepared for social research in urban areas, the scope of which is described in detail by the editor in that chapter. It is a particular pleasure that Professor Philip M. Hauser has agreed to act as editor of the present handbook since Unesco had earlier enlisted his co-operation in the scientific organization of the last two seminars—one in Latin America and one for Asia and the Far East. The handbook thus benefits from his wide experience, not only as a distinguished demographer and urban sociologist, but also as a specialist in the urbanization problems of the developing world of today.

Unesco wishes to express to Professor Hauser its sincere appreciation for his long-standing contribution to research work sponsored by the Organization,

as well as to the other contributors, Professors
P. H. Chombart de Lauwe (France), Gino Germani
(Argentina), Judah Matras (Israel), Giuseppe Parenti
(Italy) and Z. Pioro (Poland) who have succeeded
in establishing an international team and over-
coming the obstacles inherent in long-distance communications, with a view to preparing the present
handbook.

Contents

Preface

This handbook was initiated in discussions by an expert working group in Paris at Unesco House in October 1961. Participating in the meeting were: Professor P. H. Chombart de Lauwe, Groupe d'Ethnologie Sociale, Centre National de la Recherche Scientifique, Paris; Professor Philip M. Hauser, Department of Sociology, University of Chicago; Professor Giuseppe Parenti, University of Florence; and Professor Z. Pioro, Urban and Architectural Institute, Warsaw. Representing Unesco were P. Lengyel, J. D. N. Versluys and H. M. Phillips. Attending the meeting, in part, as observers, were Mr. Lambert-Lamond, United Nations European Office, and Mr. Ernest Weissman, Bureau of Social Affairs, United Nations.

Physical, social, economic and administrative planning are dependent on sound facts. But the developing areas usually experience a shortage both of data and experienced personnel for research purposes. Although trained and experienced social science personnel should be utilized whenever possible to conduct social research, this is not always feasible. In consequence, this handbook is addressed to social scientists who, although not widely experienced in the conduct of research, are nevertheless called upon to conduct urban studies as a preliminary to policy formation and administrative action. It is hoped that this handbook, together with the bibliographical references which it contains, will provide such social scientists with effective help in designing and conducting research into urban problems. Moreover, the handbook should be useful to administrators in indicating types of studies that may be helpful to them in dealing with urban problems.

When it is necessary to collect data by means of a survey operation the United Nations *Handbook of Household Surveys: a Practical Guide for Inquiries on Levels of Living*, New York, 1964, will be found indispensable. It is an excellent guide to the design and conduct of household surveys which may be a prerequisite to the types of research to which reference is made in

11

this volume. This handbook is concerned more with research objectives and the analysis of data for use than with data collection. The two handbooks may, therefore, be viewed as complementary.

This handbook has many deficiencies for which the editor must assume major responsibility. Some subjects intended for inclusion are not covered by reason of various problems which prevented the intended authors from completing their tasks. Problems of communication have been encountered because of the wide dispersion of the authors. Unanticipated and pressing matters of high priority have badly interfered with time schedules of the editor as well as of the authors. Despite its defects, however, this handbook, it is felt, may nevertheless serve a useful function.

The editor gratefully acknowledges his indebtedness to the contributors to this volume and to the officials of Unesco, all of whom have shown extraordinary patience and who have been most gracious in their co-operation throughout the enterprise. Special appreciation must be expressed to Dr. Judah Matras who, during his year of residence as Research Associate (Assistant Professor) at the University of Chicago, materially assisted in the task of bringing this work to completion.

List of contributors

CHOMBART DE LAUWE, P. H. Director of Studies of the École Pratique des Hautes Études, Groupe d'Ethnologie Sociale, Sixième Section, Sorbonne, Paris.

GERMANI, Gino. Director, Institute of Sociology, University of Buenos Aires.

HAUSER, Philip M. Professor and Chairman, Department of Sociology, and Director, Population Research and Training Center, University of Chicago.

MATRAS, Judah. Instructor in Social Sciences, Kaplan School, Hebrew University, Jerusalem, and Research Associate (Assistant Professor of Sociology) at the Population Research and Training Center, University of Chicago (1963-64).

PARENTI, Giuseppe. Professor of Statistics, School of Economics and Trade, University of Florence.

PIORO, Z. Connected with the Urban and Architectural Institute, Warsaw.

Introduction and overview

Philip M. Hauser

Accelerating rates of urbanization, especially in Asia, Latin America and Africa (see Chapter 5) have worsened both chronic and acute urban problems and intensified national and international efforts to cope with them. Unesco, with the active co-operation of the United Nations Bureau of Social Affairs and the International Labour Organisation (ILO), the World Health Organization (WHO) and others, has organized a number of seminars and conferences focusing on the problems of urbanization. Among these were: the Conference on the Social Impact of Industrialization and Urban Conditions in Africa, held in Abidjan from 29 September to 27 October 1954; the Seminar on Urbanization in Asia and the Far East, held in Bangkok from 8 to 18 August 1956; the Seminar on Urbanization in Latin America, held in Santiago (Chile) from 6 to 18 July 1959; the Urbanization and Survey Mission in the Mediterranean Region, November-December 1959; and the North American Conference on the Social Implications of Industrialization and Technological Change, held in Chicago from 15 to 22 September 1960.

Each of these activities resulted in reports, four of which have been published (see the bibliography in Chapter 5).

It was the consensus of the participants in these various meetings that many problems in the developing nations may be better understood and ameliorated if viewed as functions of accelerating urbanization. The problem areas include adequate housing and urban amenities, adjustment and acculturation of in-migrants, accommodation to rapid social change, effective economic organization and growth, and efficient local government.

Clearly the remediation of urban problems requires, first, an understanding of their origin, magnitude and characteristics. Only with a sound foundation of facts can responsible agencies, public and private, determine policy, make plans and design programmes to cope with the frictions of rapid urbanization. Physical, social and economic planning are necessarily dependent on facts about specific urban problems as a prerequisite for effective action.

Yet, despite the need for sound facts, the developing areas generally are characterized by the absence of adequate census, administrative and other forms of data. There is a great gap in such areas between the need for knowledge and its availability. The purpose of this handbook is to help to fill this gap. It is designed to serve as a guide to public and private agencies desiring to study urban problems, especially in the developing areas where there is a great shortage of trained research personnel as well as of basic data.

Structure of the handbook

This handbook is divided into two major parts. Following this 'Introduction and Overview' is Part I, entitled 'Social Research Data and Procedures'. It contains a discussion of the areal units for urban analysis, the sources of data for social research in urban areas, the use of field and case studies, and the usefulness of various types of research approaches.

Part II, entitled 'Types of Studies', deals with specific areas of urban social research. General studies of urbanization, demographic studies, the study of social organization, the study of social and personal disorganization and the study of the urban physical plant and administration are considered.

In greater detail, Chapter 1, 'Areal Units for Urban Analysis', by Hauser and Matras, considers the problem of definition and delineation of basic geographic units of analysis. Alternative approaches to definition of 'urban' and of 'urban locality' are reviewed, and it is seen that the criteria of 'urban' may vary considerably among the different countries. To overcome, in part, the problems of comparability posed by the variety of approaches and definitions employed in different countries, the United Nations has recommended that statistical data be tabulated and presented by size of locality or number of inhabitants in the agglomeration, as well as by the respective national urban and rural definitions.

Combinations or sets of urban localities, e.g., cities or urban places grouped by population size, or classified by region, topographic, historical or economic criteria, are often useful in analysis of urban characteristics. Another type of combination of urban localities is the 'metropolitan area' or 'urbanized area', ordinarily defined in terms of contiguity of smaller or satellite urban areas to a major or central city or metropolis. This type of combination of areal units is often useful both for description and analysis of a single such 'metropolitan area' or 'urbanized area', or for the study of metropolitan areas or metropolitan population of a country taken as a whole.

Finally, within a city or urban locality, sub-areas are often delineated and used in description and analysis of physiographic, demographic or socio-economic differentiation within the city. Primary analytical areal units, consisting of city blocks, 'census tracts' or 'enumeration districts', or other more or less permanent small areal units comprising a framework in which data are collected and grouped, may themselves be studied and compared; or, alternatively and more commonly, primary analytical units may be combined into larger areal units within the larger urban locality, e.g., community area, neighbourhoods, quarters, wards, etc., which, in turn, are to be studied and compared.

In Chapter 2, 'Basic Statistics and Research', Parenti lists the chief sources of statistical data available for social research in urban areas, indicates their scope and, also, their limitations, and points to their potential uses and exploitation in urban planning, administration and evaluation.

The national population census is a fundamental statistical source in many countries; and, in particular, the census typically seeks to identify inhabited localities and to relate population to detailed territorial units. Within urban or larger areas, census data relating to primary analytical units may often be combined to yield data for smaller areal units such as neighbourhoods, public health zones, school districts, economic regions and other administrative or natural sub-areas. In addition to numbers of inhabitants of specified territorial units, population censuses ordinarily include data on biological, demographic and ethnic characteristics, as well as on social and economic characteristics of the population.

A second category of statistical sources is that of administrative statistics. This category includes registration data, licence and permit data, data from public institutions and administrative data from non-government sources. Births, deaths, marriages and divorces are in many countries subject to registration procedures. Persons who would vote must often register or be included in lists of eligible voters. Individuals and institutions must often seek licences and permits for certain activities, such as owning or operating motor vehicles, owning or operating certain types of property or businesses, building construction, etc. School systems, labour exchanges, welfare centres and tax agencies typically maintain records concerning the volume of their activities, the volume of clientele served and, often, the characteristics of the clientele. Finally, business, religious or voluntary private organizations may similarly maintain records of their activities, membership, customers and clientele. Any or all of these sources of statistical data may be of value in social research in urban areas.

A third category of statistical sources is that of recurring or of special single-instance investigations, surveys and reports. Often these special-purpose investigations have objectives quite apart from urban research; but data from such studies often can, nevertheless, be profitably drawn upon and used. In general, both administrative and special-purpose statistics can be exploited most effectively in urban research when used in conjunction with the census statistics.

In Chapter 3, 'Field and Case Studies', Chombart de Lauwe stresses the need in social research for interpretation, comparison and experimentation in addition to simple observation. Observation of social life is properly an interdisciplinary undertaking: the theories and methods of ethnology, linguistics, sociology and social psychology are of direct bearing, and the findings of historical, geographic and economic studies must also be taken into account, in the planning and implementation of sociological field studies.

Field studies may be carried out both for quite large urban areas as a whole, e.g., for cities, conurbations or metropolitan areas, or for quite specific sub-areas within the urban setting, e.g., the neighbourhood, quarter, city ward or sector. Similarly case studies can concern formally organized groups, e.g., youth movements, women's associations, political parties and the like; but case studies of broad non-organized groups, such as social classes, occupational sectors, etc., are held to be even more significant.

Observation can be direct or indirect, controlled or uncontrolled, with advantages and disadvantages associated with each type of combination. A large variety of aids, such as questionnaires, maps, audio-visual materials, etc., are available to researchers for use in field and case observation. The reliability of observation is always to be subject to question and critique. Means must be sought for verification, the primary means being the personal stock-taking of the observer. Collaboration of teams of observers and the evolvement of collective judgements or evaluations increases reliability.

Case materials on individuals and on groups of individuals are extremely useful, especially in qualitative interpretation of broader field and statistical studies. Field and case materials may be used in plotting the networks of social relationships in the urban milieu.

The social milieu in the urban setting is typically an aggregate of human beings, not necessarily characterized by group ties, but sharing nevertheless certain bonds of common attitudes, styles and content of communications and forms of behaviour. These urban social milieux increasingly replace the more structured groups which characterize life in smaller, more isolated, societies; and, though difficult to plot and trace, their influence on the individual is not less.

In the final chapter in Part I, Chapter 4, 'Other Social Research Approaches', Matras looks at six alternative approaches to social research in the urban setting. These include, respectively, historical studies, economic studies, geographic studies, ecological studies, content analysis and experimental studies.

The objectives of historical studies of the urban area include description of the development through time of the urban area, identification and description of key events and personalities in this development, and analysis of the influence of these events and personages.

The purpose of economic studies of the urban area is description of the economy of the area, including major economic activities and units of economic activity, and analysis of the relationship of the urban area's economy to the larger regional or national economy. Special attention attaches to analysis of urban locality's 'economic base', i.e., the goods and services produced in the area which are sold outside or 'exported' elsewhere rather than consumed locally.

Geographic studies of the urban locality are oriented to description of the physical characteristics of the area, its topographical, geological and climatological features, and the relationship of these to land population distribution and economic activities. Classification of sub-areas within the urban locale and analysis of geographic differentiation are also included in such studies.

The analysis of interrelationships between population, environment, level and modes of technology, and social organization is the subject matter of ecological studies of urban areas. Ecological studies view both social and economic organization as influenced by interrelationships obtaining between population, environment and technology; and the structure and growth of population as influenced by the other factors—environment, technology and social organization—as foci of their investigations. Spatial distributions of population, economic activities and social institution in the urban locale are viewed as indicators of social and economic relationships and orders obtaining in the area.

Content analysis is applied to all areas of inquiry and all institutions and activities embodying verbal expression or communications content of any form. Content analysis seeks to render quantitative descriptions of communications content. As such, it may be applied to analysis of urban media of communication as objects for study themselves, or, alternatively, as reflecting the views, attitudes or behaviour of urban groups, individuals or institutions.

Finally, experimental studies may be applied to all areas of inquiry but depend upon the possibility of either laboratory or field manipulation of all or part of the situations or variables being studied.

In Chapter 5, 'Comprehensive Urban Studies', Hauser describes three types of comprehensive urban research. The first of these is general study of urbanization, the purpose of which is to throw light on the factors associated with the development of cities and the consequences of urbanization— physical, economic, social and political. The available literature of this type is briefly reviewed with the recommendation that it be consulted as a guide to similar or more specific urban researches.

The second type of comprehensive study considered is the study of individual cities. References are given to such investigations of cities in the developing areas as well as in economically advanced nations. The table of contents of these works may be utilized as outlines for similar studies of cities. Such comprehensive analyses of individual places provides essential background for general planning purposes and for more specific studies of urban problems.

Finally much of the chapter is devoted to the discussion of urban problems under the following headings: economic, physical, social, and governmental and administrative. The discussion is designed to point to the kinds of problems which research should illuminate and to indicate the types of questions for which answers must be sought.

In Chapter 6, 'Demographic Trends in Urban Areas', Matras outlines how to conduct demographic studies. The extent of urbanization in a country, the rate and structure of urban population growth, and urban population distribution are subjects for demographic analysis. Similarly, the relationships between urbanization and urban social institutions and the vital processes of nuptiality, fertility and mortality are also subject matters for investigation. Sources of data include censuses, vital registration systems, surveys, and, sometimes, administrative statistics.

Analysis of population growth calles for measurement of total population growth, mortality, fertility and migratory movements. These are related to one another in a 'balancing equation' and, also, may be measured separately. Measures of mortality include crude death rates, age-sex-specific mortality rates, standardized summary death rates, and measures derived from life tables such as 'life expectancy'. Fertility measures include crude birth rates, the general fertility rate, age-specific fertility rates, standardized birth rates, and gross and net reproduction rates, all based upon vital registration data. Fertility measures not dependent upon vital registration data include the effective fertility rate and the fertility ratio, and these have been widely used to measure fertility in the absence of detailed or comparable vital statistics data.

Analysis of population composition is seen as representing an inventory of the community's resources. Measurements used in its analysis include the sex ratio, the dependency ratio and percentage distributions by age and by marital status. Marriages represent formation of new families, and crude and refined rates are employed to measure the frequency both of marriage and divorce.

In Chapter 7, 'Social Organization in an Urban Milieu', Chombart de Lauwe sets up a model consisting of a hierarchy of increasingly complex networks of social relationships in the large urban centre, with traditional social attachments both in primary and secondary groups retaining much more of their significance and psycho-sociological hold upon individuals than is commonly recognized. Family and kinship relationships, neighbour-hood and work groupings, and local voluntary associations continue—even in long-established urban centres, but particularly in urban centres of newly developing countries—to keep the individual in touch with the individual norms and values. On the other hand, certain social units are declining while other less homogeneous units and wide varieties of voluntary social, econo-mic and political units emerge. Not less important is the emergence of social categories and types, without formal membership bonds, but with certain common interests, values and behaviour patterns. Examples include age groups, social classes, ethnic groups, occupational groups, trade unions, religious groupings and political parties and supporters.

Increasingly, efforts are made to organize and plan the urban environs with the needs of individuals in mind. Central governments and local, municipal and regional governmental institutions are obvious agents of planning and decision-making. However, private and semi-public organiza-tions and institutions serve as intermediaries between individuals and governments, and accordingly they are also concerned with planning. Similarly, public, semi-public, and private social and cultural institutions, e.g., schools, welfare organizations, etc., are also involved with planning and decision-making.

A number of examples citing research carried out and practical uses to which research results lend themselves are cited. Likewise methodological approaches to research are mentioned.

Gino Germani, in Chapter 8, 'Migration and Acculturation', sets forth conceptual schemes for the study of migration and of the adjustment and acculturation of migrants. He considers three processes or stages in the analysis of migration: the decision to emigrate, the actual transfer and the process of acculturation. He calls attention to three levels of analysis: an objective level, a normative level and a psycho-social level, and elaborates various types of analytical problems involved. He points also to the types of data needed for research on migration and acculturation and discusses types of models that may be employed for analytical purposes.

In Chapter 9, 'Social and Personal Disorganization', Matras defines 'social disorganization' as failure or inability of a social system, group or institution to attain its goals because of conflicts, inconsistencies or absence of co-ordination among component elements; and 'personal disorganization' as failure or inability of the individual to accept the values or follow the behaviour norms of the social group of which he is a member. Moreover, both social and personal disorganization are viewed as social processes rather than simply situations or attributes of institutions or individuals.

Historically, research in social disorganization stimulated by social reform movements has been the forerunner of modern empirical social research. Methods of research include controlled or non-controlled field observation, case studies, and sample surveys.

Finally, in Chapter 10, 'Research on Urban Plant and Administration', knowledge of the material, physical and technological dimensions of urban life is seen by Pioro as basic for the understanding of urban social structure and process. The geographic environment is the natural basis of urban artifacts and patterns of human settlement, land use and communication are dependent upon geological and climatological characteristics. Accordingly, physiographic research in the urban environment is basic both to analysis of the community's ecological structure and to town-planning.

The land use survey is employed to plot, analyse, catalogue and classify types of settlement, exploitation and use of urban land. Very extensive use is made of maps for plotting historical and current data, and for planning future land use.

Many communities have experienced very serious housing shortages or deterioration of housing and entire neighbourhoods. Urban research must consider the housing problem in its physical, socio-economic, and legal and administrative aspects. Zoning regulations and building codes must be ascertained as a first step in such research. Practices of the building industry, procedures for public control and inspection, and arrangements for financing must also be studied. Housing research must provide, also, information concerning the number and condition of housing units; size, value, and rentals of units; and characteristics of inhabitants of housing of the various types and categories. Sources of data include censuses, administrative records of financial and government institutions, and special housing surveys.

Land use and relationships of industry to other aspects of urban life are viewed as fundamental factors in urban growth and over-all physical setup. Types of industry, their locations, patterns of concentration, segregation or dispersal; relationship to costs of transport; and social, physical and biological implications of industrial expansion should all be included in the study of urban plant. Recreational uses and facilities are called 'the lungs of a city' and the importance of preservation of such areas is stressed. Water supply, sewerage and drainage, and refuse disposal facilities must likewise be inventoried and evaluated.

Provision of facilities for intra-urban area transport and traffic, on the one hand, and control of the huge flows of private and mass transportation vehicular traffic, on the other hand, constitute one of the most difficult of modern urban problems. Dealing with it demands research on traffic flows including their classification by type, purpose and mode, direction, volume and routes.

Analysis of major power sources and patterns of power consumption is basic to improvement both of technological exploitation and private use of energy.

Finally, attention should be directed to careful study of urban administration with a view to rationalizing it and enhancing its efficiency as far as possible. Such study includes the nature of government and its constitutional and historical bases; the manner in which officials are recruited; and the scope of competence and authority of the city administration. Additional topics include budgeting and financial arrangements for administration and publicly initiated activities, the mechanics of government and administration, and the relationship of the administration to workers, to voluntary organizations, and to other governmental organizations, institutions and structures.

Part I   Social research data and procedures

1   Areal units for urban analysis

Philip M. Hauser and Judah Matras

The very first problem to be confronted in social research in urban areas is that of definition and delineation of adequate and meaningful geographic units of analysis. As is well known the very concept of urban locality or urban place is defined in many different ways in different countries. Moreover, for many purposes a single urban locality concept is not adequate for description or analysis of the variations occurring between the types of urban places nor, indeed, of the variation occurring within a given urban locality. This chapter outlines some of the main types of areal units employed in urban analysis, their definitions or the criteria for their determination, the manner in which they are delineated in practice and their utilization in social research.

Administrative units and urban localities

The two fundamental types of areal units of urban analysis are administrative units and urban localities. Administrative units may or may not coincide with geographic or 'natural' areal units. A given country may contain quite large administrative sub-areas (states, provinces, cantons, departments, etc.) or smaller administrative sub-areas (counties, townships, municipalities). Often larger administrative units overlap the smaller ones, and there may be a hierarchy of area of jurisdiction, e.g., national, state, county, and township, municipal or other local jurisdictions. Administrative areal units are basic to social research in that they are usually identifiable, bounded and relatively permanently delineated areas, ordinarily with some legal status and jursdiction, and data concerning population size, composition and characteristics as well as data bearing upon the physical and economic characteristics may often be obtained with reference to such areas.

Urban localities may or may not be administrative units, depending usually upon the definition of locality employed and sometimes upon the definition of urban. The United Nations has classified the definitions of locality employed by the various countries into three types:

1. Population agglomerations identified without regard to fixed boundaries. For example, in the Iceland census carried out in 1950, forty-three localities or agglomerations of 300 or more inhabitants are listed; and in the 1946 census carried out in Ireland, 827 towns or villages of twenty houses or more are listed. India's census of 1951 identifies 561,107 agglomerations, including 380,020 localities with fewer than 500 inhabitants.

2. Places with fixed boundaries, commonly under the jurisdiction of local or urban forms of government. In Aden sixteen such places were listed in the 1946 census; and in the United States 18,548 incorporated and unincorporated places of 1,000 or more inhabitants, and 9,827 places of less than 1,000 inhabitants, were recorded in the 1950 census.

3. Relatively small, or the smallest, administrative sub-divisions having fixed boundaries, which together comprise the entire country. Thus Egypt was divided into 3,981 such localities at the time of the 1947 census; Greece was divided into 5,975 municipalities and communes in 1951; and France was divided into 37,983 communes at the time of the 1954 census.

The United Nations has recommended that a locality be defined as a 'distinct and indivisible population cluster (also designated as agglomeration, inhabited place, populated centre, settlement, etc.) of any size, having a name or a locally recognized status and functioning as an integrated social entity'. Localities so defined may coincide with the smallest administrative divisions of a country. However, this need not be the case: even the smallest administrative division may contain two or more localities, whereas some localities such as large cities or towns may contain two or more administrative divisions.

The concept of urban is almost universally understood to have reference to relatively large and relatively densely settled populations engaged primarily in non-agricultural economic pursuits. By contrast, the concept of rural ordinarily is understood to refer to relatively small and relatively sparsely settled populations, typically with large proportions engaged in agriculture. The broad consensus about the nature of the difference between urban and rural not withstanding, in actual practice the designation of localities as urban or rural varies widely and is often dependent upon administrative, political, cultural and historical as well as upon demographic or economic considerations. Definitions of urban place or locality have been classified by the United Nations into three major types:

1. Classification of minor civil divisions in accordance with some specified criteria such as: type of local government, number of inhabitants, or proportion of the population engaged in or directly dependent upon agriculture.
2. Designation of administrative centres of minor civil divisions as urban, the remainder of each division being classified rural.
3. Designation of localities or agglomerations of some specified minimum size as urban regardless of administrative arrangements or boundaries.

In practice rural places are ordinarily not defined at all, but comprise rather a residual category including all the non-urban places.

Within each of the categories of definitions, the specific definitions of urban may vary broadly from country to country. Thus, as the United Nations has observed, urban status is granted to places with 250 or more inhabitants in Denmark, whereas in Korea localities with fewer than 40,000 inhabitants are classified as rural. The United Nations has not recommended a uniform definition of urban, recognizing that such a definition would not be practicable at the present. But to overcome in part the problems occasioned by differences in definition of urban and to promote international comparability, the United Nations Population Commission has recommended that, in addition to urban-rural classifications as defined by the individual countries, statistical data be tabulated and presented classified also by size of locality or agglomeration. In this manner international comparability could be assured even though the precise definitions of urban and rural continue to vary from country to country.

Within any given country the definition of urban locality tends to be standardized, so that there are no problems of comparability. In a given administrative unit, or in the country as a whole, the urban population is usually the total number of inhabitants of urban localities. In some countries, however, the populations of localities not themselves designated urban but having some specified geographic or socio-economic relationship to urban localities are also designated as urban populations. For example, in the United States census usage, the urban population comprises all persons living in urban places (localities of 2,500 or more inhabitants) and in other places located within urbanized areas (areas containing at least one city of 50,000 or more inhabitants and surrounding incorporated places and unincorporated areas meeting specified criteria). (See below under the heading 'The Urbanized Area and Standard Metropolitan Statistical Area'.) Thus there is sometimes a distinction between the total population of urban localities and the urban population of a given area or country. But if the urbanized area, conurbation, or other similarly defined areas are specified in addition to the urban localities it is always possible to analyse the total urban population in terms of its geographically separate parts and to reconstruct the total urban population as a sum of the various parts in urban localities and in the various specially defined urban areas.

Combinations of urban localities and administrative units

It would appear self-evident that the dichotomous classification of localities and of population as urban and rural does not exhaust the possibilities for description and analysis of differentiation by type of residence. In particular, the twofold classification does not allow study of differentiation within the urban locality category although clearly there are many types of urban places, e.g., large cities and small towns, financial centres and mining hamlets, river and seaport cities and inland and mountain towns, etc.

Very often it is of interest in social research to classify urban localities in terms of various characteristics and criteria. It is then possible both to investigate the distribution of the urban population with respect to the several types or classes of urban localities and to study the demographic, social and economic differentiation which may be associated with the various classes of urban places. For example, size of locality is an obviously interesting criterion for classification of urban places; and it has been noted that in, say, Switzerland and Sweden the sex ratio (the number of males per 100 females) diminishes with increasing size of locality, i.e., there are fewer males per 100 females in the larger cities than in smaller cities and rural places. By contrast, in India and Egypt the reverse is true: the ratio of males to females increases with increasing size of locality. In the United States it has been found that families are smaller in larger localities than they are in smaller localities, and separation or divorce are more common the larger the locality.

In each case such results are obtained by grouping localities of a given size, say (a) cities of more than 100,000 inhabitants, (b) those with between 50,000 and 99,999 inhabitants; (c) those with between 25,000 and 49,999 inhabitants, and so on, and measuring the sex ratio (i.e., total males divided by total females in all cities of group (a), in all cities of group (b), in all cities of group (c), and so on; or obtaining fertility or divorce and separation measurements for the total population of each size-group of urban localities.

In addition to size it is often possible to classify urban localities with respect to other criteria. For many purposes it is of interest to compare urban places in the different geographic locations in a country, e.g., by regions or major administrative areal units such as states, provinces, cantons, departments, etc. Another criterion for classification of urban localities is the physiographic or topographic criterion: cities and towns are sometimes grouped in terms of distance from or access to water routes, height, climate, soil characteristics, etc. Cities and towns have been grouped according to date of settlement or foundation and, often, urban localities are classified with respect to major types of economic activities carried on. Finally, localities may be classified or grouped in terms of characteristics of the populations inhabiting them. For example, cities have been classified by ethnic, racial or religious group composition of their populations, by income composition or by average or median income, by industrial or occupational compositions of their employed persons, and so on.

Another type of combination of areal units often employed in urban analysis is the combination of adjacent and interrelated administrative units and urban localities, e.g., metropolitan areas, conurbations, urbanized areas, etc. Specification of the exact proximity or interrelationships defining such combinations varies in the different countries and according to the particular combination being used. However, in all cases such combinations are used in recognition of the fact that the political boundaries of administrative units or of urban localities may not reflect faithfully the boundaries of a socially and economically integrated urban area.

For example, in a county containing a large city many residents, both of the suburbs outside the city which are designated urban and of the rest of the county not designated urban, may be employed in the city, study in the city, seek their recreation in the city, shop or bank in the city, etc.

On the other hand, stores, banks, etc., of the city may have branches in the surrounding suburbs. Thus, if the activities of the city and its surrounding area form an integrated social and economic system it is often useful to consider the entire area and its population as a unit. Accordingly both individuals engaged in research and official data-producing agencies often delineate broader combinations of urban localities and administrative areas for study as a single urban area. For example, a city and its immediately adjacent townships, or a city and the county in which it is located, may comprise such a combination.

In addition to studying the growth, composition and characteristics of a given such urban area, combinations similarly defined but located in different parts of a country are often compared, e.g., in the comparative study of metropolitan areas. Sometimes the parts of such combinations or urban areas are studied separately and compared, as in comparative studies of cities and suburbs, etc.

Typically, the criteria for determining association of a given locality with the nearby urban area or metropolitan area is some specified distance from the major or central city in the area, a specified population density, some specified economic relationship with the city, and/or some specified social relationship with the city. For example, in the United States the county containing a city of 50,000 or more inhabitants is automatically included in that city's standard metropolitan statistical area. Moreover a county adjacent to the county containing the large city is also considered part of that city's standard metropolitan statistical area if at least 75 per cent of the labour force of the county is in the non-agricultural labour force, and either (a) half or more of the county's population lives in contiguous minor civil divisions with a density of at least 150 persons per square mile, in an unbroken chain of such minor civil divisions radiating from the central city in the area; or (b) the number of non-agricultural workers employed in the county must equal at least 10 per cent of the number of non-agricultural workers employed in the county containing the largest city in the area, or the county must be place of employment of 10,000 or more non-agricultural workers; or (c) the non-agricultural labour force living in the county must equal at least 10 per cent of the number of the non-agricultural labour force living in the county containing the largest city in the area, or the county must be the place of residence of a non-agricultural labour force of 10,000.

Very often such combinations of urban localities or administrative units must be delineated for a given research undertaking in the absence of current data, and it may not be established that the area in question in fact meets the criteria of the type of combination specified and defined. Nevertheless there may often be good reason to suppose, say on the basis of earlier data, that the area does meet the criteria. In such cases a preliminary objective of the investigation is to establish whether or not a given area or set of localities and administrative units does in fact meet the criteria of the specified combinations.

Very often the delineation of such combinations of urban localities or administrative units is a matter of interest to a large variety of public and private institutions. In particular, to the extent that data may be collected and published for such urban areas or combinations of localities, the manner in which these areas or combinations are delineated is often a matter of concern to the agencies and institutions which might utilize or consume such data. Thus very often the agencies and institutions which consume or are potential consumers or users of areal data are consulted and participate in the delineation of such areas, and both the definition or specification of criteria for such areas or combinations of localities and administrative units and the actual delineation of these areas may be a joint undertaking of both agencies responsible for collecting and publishing areal data and agencies and bodies utilizing and consuming such data.

Once such combinations of urban localities or urban areas are delineated it is possible to study their size, patterns of growth, population composition and characteristics, land use, transportation patterns, government and political interrelationships, and so on. In many instances it is of considerable interest to investigate and compare the growth and characteristics of parts of urban areas or combinations. Probably the most common type of comparison is that investigating differences and similarities of a city as compared to its suburbs within, say, a given metropolitan area. Another type of comparison frequently found is that between urban and rural subareas within a metropolitan area. Such comparative studies or specialized investigations of parts of areas demand careful definition and delineation of the sub-areas. Usually it is important to avoid overlapping of sub-areas in order to permit reconstruction of the whole area from addition of results obtained for the separate parts.

Very often in national or international studies of urban areas it is of interest to group areas of a given type or to compare areas of a given type, for example, in the world-wide study of metropolitan areas. In such studies it is of considerable importance to assure comparability of definitions and criteria for delineation of the areas or combinations being studied and compared. For example, international comparison of characteristics of urban places as variously defined in the different countries would have but little validity in view of the very broad divergence of definitions and criteria. On the other hand, comparison of characteristics of localities having 20,000 or more inhabitants—while far from perfect—holds much more promise of yielding valid as well as interesting results. Similarly international and even national comparative studies of urban areas or of combinations of urban localities or administrative areas must first be concerned with comparability of the combinations in question and standardization of definitions and criteria of delineation. More specifically, the parts of such combinations must also be defined and delineated in a standardized or comparable manner if comparison of parts is to be carried out over several such combinations.

The urbanized area and standard metropolitan statistical area

The urbanized area and standard metropolitan statistical area (the latter often abbreviated simply SMSA) are two examples of combinations of urban localities and administrative units employed in research in urban areas. Briefly, the urbanized area consists of a central city and all the urban, densely settled, area contiguous to that central city or radiating from the city, whether or not such areas are incorporated or have other legal or political status (see Figure 1). The standard metropolitan statistical area includes a central city and the surrounding territory, whether urban or rural, deemed by certain specified criteria to be economically and socially integrated with the central city. More specifically the SMSA includes a central city, the county which contains it, and such adjoining counties which, by various criteria of employment and residential relationships to it, are considered dependent upon the central city (see Figure 1).

In the United States the evolvement of the concept of urbanized area grew especially from the need for adequate definition and enumeration of the urban population (as distinct from the total population of all urban places). Previously persons living in what were to all intents and purposes urban areas, and who were engaged in non-agricultural economic activities and resembled urban populations in every respect, were enumerated as rural population in the census due to the fact that places in which they resided usually were too small to be considered urban places in accordance with census criteria. Delineation of urbanized areas has permitted inclusion of such persons in the urban population, the latter now being defined as those residing either in urban places or in urbanized areas.

Development of the concept of standard metropolitan statistical area evolved in connexion with recognition that the partially arbitrary political boundaries of urban places do not coincide with the boundaries of the socio-economic entity represented by the central city, satellite cities, suburbs and adjacent rural area and the need to develop a statistical representation of such a geographic and socio-economic entity.

The urbanized area is defined as a central city and its contiguous or radiating densely settled territory. As additional contiguous territory becomes densely settled, e.g., as adjacent agricultural land is converted to residential use, such territory becomes part of the urbanized area. Thus the territory or area of the urbanized area is not fixed but rather is typically extended from year to year as additional adjacent areas become heavily settled. By contrast the SMSA is defined as a county containing a city of 50,000 or more inhabitants plus adjacent counties meeting the specified demographic and socio-economic criteria. The number of SMSA counties may change in one of two ways: counties containing large cities may become SMSA counties by virtue of the fact that the population of the city reaches 50,000; or, counties adjacent to SMSA counties may themselves become SMSA counties when and if they meet the same criteria regarding their demographic and socio-economic relationships with the central city of the SMSA.

The major sub-areas of the urbanized area are usually defined by the boundaries of the central city: the part of the urbanized area outside the central city is called the urban fringe, and it may include incorporated or unincorporated communities, large or small localities, whether or not classified as urban. Localities in the urban fringe are, however, all characterized by relatively high population density and all are linked to the central city by a continuous band or chain of similarly high-density areas. The major sub-areas of the standard metropolitan statistical area are likewise defined by the boundaries of the central city: the part of the SMSA outside the central city is called the SMSA ring or the metropolitan ring. The ring includes all localities in the SMSA counties but outside the central city, regardless of density and regardless of contiguity to built-up areas. The metropolitan rings of SMSAs are frequently divided into urban and rural places. Other classifications of localities within SMSAs are possible, including, for example, size of place, distance from central city, population composition, and composition of the labour force. The study of sub-areas of urbanized areas or of standard metropolitan statistical areas is often of direct interest in a given urban area, e.g., the study of communities of a specified size range within a given SMSA. In addition the parts of the area are frequently compared, as in the case of comparison of larger with smaller suburbs, or comparison of urban with rural areas, within a given standard metropolitan statistical area. Finally the sub-areas are often grouped over a set of urbanized areas or SMSAs, as in the study of urban fringe areas as compared to central cities, in a country as a whole.

If the criteria and definitions of urbanized area and standard metropolitan statistical area are fixed for an entire country, minimal standards of comparability are, of course, assured within that country. However, even where standardized criteria and definitions obtain in an entire country certain problems of comparability may arise. For example, in the United States certain metropolitan areas are the only metropolitan areas in their respective regions while others are located virutally side by side. Similarly, while all SMSAs must include at least one city of 50,000 or more inhabitants, many include only one such city and the county containing it, while others may include a number of cities, millions of inhabitants and many more counties.

When criteria and definitions of urbanized area and standard metropolitan statistical area are fixed locally or for individual research projects, comparability is naturally even more problematic. The International Urban Research project has used standard criteria for delineation of metropolitan areas, and it is likely that acceptance and following of these criteria will prove very beneficial in promoting international and even within-country comparability.

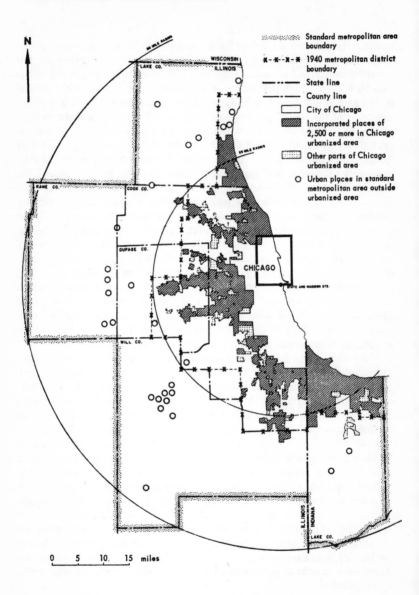

Fig 1. Chicago standard metropolitan area, as of 1950. In 1960 the name of the area was changed to standard metropolitan statistical area and the Chicago area restricted to counties in Illinois.

Areal units for urban analysis

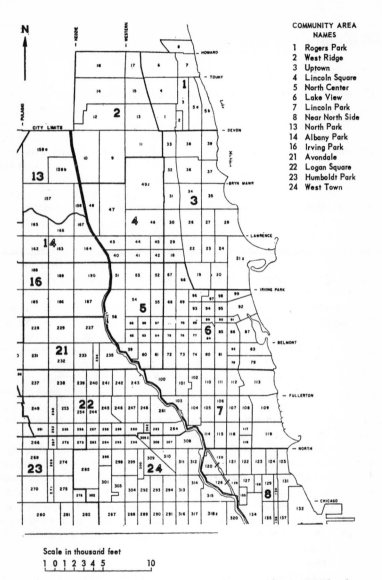

COMMUNITY AREA
NAMES

1 Rogers Park
2 West Ridge
3 Uptown
4 Lincoln Square
5 North Center
6 Lake View
7 Lincoln Park
8 Near North Side
13 North Park
14 Albany Park
16 Irving Park
21 Avondale
22 Logan Square
23 Humboldt Park
24 West Town

Scale in thousand feet
1 0 1 2 3 4 5   10

Fig. 2. Community areas and census tracts, 1960 census
of housing and population (city limits as of May
1960). (Enlarged detail from Fig. 1.)

——— Community area boundary
——— Census tract boundary
342 Census tract number
33 Community area number

35

Within-urban area analysis

PRIMARY ANALYTICAL UNITS

Cities or other urban areas are very often characterized by distinct sections, quarters, neighbourhoods or other smaller sub-areas, each having its own peculiar history, land use, population density and composition, and social and economic activities. It is very often of great interest to study such neighbourhoods, etc., separately. When it is possible to obtain data concerning the population and physical characteristics of small areas within urban areas, such as for blocks, enumeration districts, tracts or neighbourhoods such data may be used both to describe and analyse within-area differentiation at any moment in time and to analyse urban changes occurring over time but differently in the separate small areas. For example, it is known, on the basis of such data, not only that the different areas within cities are inhabited by different ethnic, racial, occupational or age groups, but also that the different neighbourhoods and sub-areas may be characterized by varying rates of fertility, of mortality, of delinquency and of morbidity.

For purposes of analysis of differentiation within urban areas it is useful to employ some set of small areal units as primary analytical units. Sometimes it is convenient to use city blocks as primary analytical units. In countries which have more or less permanent census-taking or population survey arrangements it may be most convenient to use enumeration districts or census tracts as the primary areal units of analysis. Such primary analytical units should be more or less permanent or, at least, fixed over several censuses or other investigations; and they should be relatively homogeneous with respect to characteristics of the population residing in them at any moment in time. It is usually useful to delineate such areas in terms of physical characteristics or distinguishing aspects of land utilization, e.g., natural boundaries such as rivers and streams, or relatively permanent man-made boundaries such as railroads or major traffic arteries. If the same primary areal analytical units are to be used for data collected and published in the framework of national censuses or surveys, it is essential that national and local authorities and agencies co-operate in delineating the areas to be employed in order to assure most advantageous use both at local and at national levels.

Once a network of such primary analytical units is established, identified and delineated, it is essential to make provision for carrying out subsequent analyses, studies or investigations within the urban area with reference to the primary analytical units. In other words, it is necessary to make some more or less permanent arrangements for relating new data and information to the system of primary areal analytical units. This may usually by achieved by identifying the primary analytical unit associated with each datum, i.e., by assigning each datum a co-ordinate or location in terms of the network of primary analytical units using maps or coding guides.

The primary analytical units may be indicated and numbered or otherwise identified on a map of the urban area being studied (see Figure 2). Data referring to persons residing in a given primary analytical areal unit, or working in a unit, or to businesses, schools, institutions, factories, or other activities carried out in a given primary analytical unit may be identified and located on the map and grouped in terms of the number or other identification symbol of the unit. In larger or more complex urban areas, coding guides relating street addresses to primary analytical unit numbers or identification symbols may be employed to relate new data to the network of primary areal units. A coding guide gives the primary analytical areal unit code number which corresponds to each possible street address in the area so that, if the street address associated with a given individual or institutional datum is given, the primary analytical unit code number or identification symbol may be readily found. Thus data bearing upon population, social and economic institutions, land use and values, transportation, recreational facilities, etc., may be classified by individual primary areal analytical units or by groups or classes of such units.

Primary analytical areal units may be most readily employed for analyses within urban areas in a wide variety of research problems, but their uses may also be limited by problems of comparability. In particular variations the size of the areal units delineated may affect results of analyses of distributions of population and activities within an urban area. For example, if a given urban area be divided into, say, two primary analytical units, it may be found that both units contain both business and residential land use, whence it is concluded that there is no discernible concentration either of business or of residential land use. If, however, the same area were divided into, say, four primary analytical units, it might just as correctly be found that two such units contain only residential land use and two only business land use. The latter finding is not necessarily inconsistent with the former, but in the latter case it might well be concluded that the urban area being studied is characterized by complete concentration of business and of residential land use in distinctly separate parts of the urban area.

Primary analytical areal units have enjoyed very wide use in social scientific research in urban areas for many decades. Early examples of the use of such units include the comparative studies of living conditions in the various sections of London, studies of differential mortality and infant mortality in the Paris *arrondissements* grouped by relative affluence, and studies of delinquency and of mental illness in American cities. More recently, use of primary analytical units in social research within urban areas has expanded to a much wider range of subjects. In most instances the general approach of such analyses calls for grouping the primary analytical units within an urban area in terms of some characteristic of the areal unit, e.g., distance from centre, median income of families, average age of residential structures, percentage of land devoted to manufacturing, proportion of adult population foreign-born, etc. Characteristics of the population, of people, or of activities in the respective groups of primary analytical units may then be measured and compared.

FUNCTIONAL COMBINATIONS OF PRIMARY ANALYTICAL UNITS

Collection and analysis of data on a primary analytical unit basis lends itself to a very wide variety of uses in social research and, in particular, such primary analytical unit data are useful when units are grouped in meaningful or significant classes or categories. One special case of grouping of primary analytical units is the grouping of adjacent or contiguous primary analytical units into larger areal units. This may be carried out when larger units have some special historical, political, economic, administrative or social significance and data are available on a primary analytical unit basis. For example, the primary analytical units comprising the historically delineated quarters or boroughs of a city, a waterfront or manufacturing sub-area, an administrative ward, a school district, etc., may be combined for investigation, study or comparison with areal units of larger size.

A second type of grouping of primary analytical units ignores contiguity entirely and considers only characteristics of the primary areal unit or of its population. Thus, units characterized by high socio-economic levels and by low socio-economic levels of the population respectively have been grouped and been compared with respect to such characteristics as fertility, mortality, health, educational levels, labour force participation, type of housing, etc. Such groupings or combinations of primary analytical units are based not upon areal contiguity but rather upon homogeneity with respect to some specified characteristic. In order to form the groupings or combinations, it is necessary first to have basic data available concerning the characteristics in question for each primary unit. While maps and coding guides are particularly useful in delineating combinations based upon areal contiguity and physiographic considerations in the urban area, they do not ordinarily suffice for grouping the primary units on the basis of homogeneity of characteristics.

Statistical and other data collected, organized and presented by primary analytical units are most helpful in delineating such groupings of primary units. Such data are often found in publications of censuses and governmental agencies, in city or administrative unit fact books, and so forth. Using such aids, it is usually possible to determine the categories of primary analytical units in terms of a given variable (e.g., percentage of housing units valued over a specified amount, or percentage of adult females gainfully occupied) and array all the primary analytical units in terms of the variable in question.

Particular care must be taken in relating the results of one study based upon combinations of primary analytical units to results of other studies based upon combinations of primary units, for often the combinations are not identically defined or delineated. For example, in two studies primary analytical units may be grouped as 'high' and 'low' income categories respectively, but the cutting point at which a given primary unit is classified either 'high' or 'low' may not be identical in the two studies. Accordingly when both carrying out and using urban analyses based upon functional combinations of primary analytical units, it is of great importance to ascertain the exact method of forming or delineating the combinations and groupings employed.

The maps of the city of Chicago (Figures 1 and 2) illustrate the various areal units discussed. Thus the city, the urbanized area and the standard metropolitan statistical area are shown. Also shown are primary analytical units, census tracts, and combinations of these units into community areas. A series of publications for each decade since 1920 has been made available to permit analysis of area changes over time. The latest of these is the *Local Community Fact Book, Chicago Metropolitan Area, 1960* (Evelyn M. Kitagawa and Karl E. Taeuber, editors) prepared by the Chicago Community Inventory of the University of Chicago.

Bibliography

BOGUE, D. J. *The structure of the metropolitan community: a study of dominance and subdominance.* Ann Arbor, Mich., University of Michigan Press, 1949.

DICKINSON, R. E. *City region and regionalism.* London, Routledge & Kegan Paul, 1956.

DUNCAN, O. D. *et al. Metropolis and region.* Baltimore, Md., Johns Hopkins Press, 1960.

GIBBS, J. P. *Urban research methods.* Princeton, N.J., Toronto, London and New York, D. Van Nostrand, 1961.

HOYT, H. *The structure and growth of residential neighbourhoods in American cities.* Washington, D.C., Federal Housing Administration, 1939.

INTERNATIONAL URBAN RESEARCH. *The world's metropolitan areas*. Berkeley and Los Angeles, Calif., University of California Press, 1959.

KITAGAWA, E.; TAEUBER, K. E. (eds.). *Local community fact book for the Chicago metropolitan area: 1960*. Chicago, Ill., Chicago Community Inventory, University of Chicago, 1963.

UNITED NATIONS. *Demographic yearbook*. New York, 1955.

UNITED STATES BUREAU OF THE BUDGET. *Standard metropolitan area definitions*. Washington, D.C., United States Government Printing Office, 1950.

UNITED STATES BUREAU OF THE CENSUS. *U.S. census of population: 1960*. Vol. I: *Characteristics of the population. Part A: Number of Inhabitants*, Washington, D.C., United States Government Printing Office, 1961.

2   Basic statistics and research

Giuseppe Parenti

The study of the data and problems connected with the urbanization of a region almost always requires special surveys. Before embarking on these surveys, all the available statistics already existing must be identified and carefully examined. In fact, as will be shown more clearly farther on, these statistics make it possible to respond immediately to particular requirements of research (to define the degree of urbanization of the region or of certain of its sub-areas; to determine the characteristics of areas with different degrees of urbanization; to follow the gradual development of the process of urbanization, etc.) and are at all events useful to make a proper programme for eventual *ad hoc* surveys.

In the following paragraphs summary and exemplificative information will be given on the kind of statistics available even in developing countries and from which useful suggestions can be drawn for the study of urbanization. In each case the purpose for which the statistics are usually taken, the information they supply and the precautions which must be taken in order to make proper use of them will be discussed. Of course, as urbanization is a process which is determined in relation to a specific territory, the statistics must be drawn from an exact local area.

The collection of the statistical data available for a given territory meets with difficulties which differ according to the type of statistical system in operation. Where a major operating office for compiling general statistics exists one can apply to it for the full range of available data.

With a completely decentralized system in which various offices either national or local attend to the collection, compilation and publication of statistics, each in its own field, there is almost always a co-ordinating office or commission through which one can discover which statistics to consult, or which offices to contact.

For the collection of administrative statistics, in particular, it is necessary first of all to examine the whole structure of the administrative system both on a national and local level and to study the procedure according to which public services are carried out, as it is this procedure which determines the form of the administrative records on which statistics are based.

The census

The population census constitutes the basic statistical operation in each country. In view of its importance for administrative purposes, too (national electoral distribution, legal and administrative status of provinces and cities, etc.), a census of population is carried out in most countries. The United Nations *Demographic Yearbook* for 1961 gives data for the aggregate population of 262 separate geographic units (countries, territories and component parts of collective territories).

For more than two-thirds of these geographic units these data are drawn from complete census operations and taken together refer to over 2,000 million people. The usefulness of the census for purposes of research on the subject of urbanization is made clear in the discussion of this operation in the United Nations *Handbook of Population Census Methods*.

A census of population may be defined as the total process of collecting, compiling and publishing demographic, economic and social data pertaining at a specified time or times to all persons in a country or delimited territory.

The essential features of an official national census are: (a) the sponsorship by the national government, sometimes with the co-operation of provincial and local governments; (b) the coverage, relating to a precisely defined territory; (c) the universality of the enumeration to include every member of the community within the scope of the census without omission or duplication and with reference to one well-defined point of time; (d) the recording of separate data for each individual by direct enumeration and not by registration, although the mechanics of collection may make it possible to record information common to all members of a household or family for the group as a whole; (e) the compilation and publication of data by geographic areas and by basic demographic variables as an integral part of the census.

It must be noted that not all 'censuses'—especially in the case of developing countries—fulfil exactly all the conditions laid down above. For some areas or for some population clusters the enumeration is often made by groups (for example, by inviting the headmen of villages or the tribal chiefs to declare the number of persons subject to their authority), a method which does not allow of reference to individual characteristics. Usually, however, in the case of areas classified as urban, census data in the proper sense are available.

It may also be remarked that many countries have established regular intervals for their censuses which, for one thing, makes it possible to follow the demographic development of particular territories and to calculate the prospects for the future.

In any case, even if we can only make use of a single census and even if it is not a very recent one, the relative data, properly elaborated, always enable us to discover interesting facts about the 'state' of urbanization and about the differential features of the economic-social structure of the urban and rural populations, this being due to the slow and gradual evolution of such features. The census will also furnish interesting data for the study of the movement of population.

It must next be noted that in the enumeration of persons in relation to the territory two different concepts may be utilized: on a *de facto* basis, all persons in the country are counted in the area where they are physically present at some precise time of the census day; in a *de jure* count, the population of each area is defined as persons who usually or legally reside in the area, regardless of their actual location within the country or their absence from the country at the date of enumeration. In practice, strict adherence to either of these concepts is rarely found. What is usually used is some sort of modification or a combination of the two concepts.

In some countries other censuses, too, are taken at the same time as the population census, or at least by the help of the organization set up for this. Such other censuses present the same essential features as those just illustrated. They usually relate to housing, agriculture, distribution and industry. About four-fifths of the countries which carried out demographic censuses in the decade 1945 to 1954 carried out a housing, industrial or agriculture census also, either separately or conjointly; only about two-fifths gathered data concerning distribution.

The data on an area basis drawn from these censuses too and utilized in conjunction with those of the demographic census or drawn from other surveys, offer much that is interesting for studies on the subject of urbanization.

It has been said that one of the features of the census is the exact reference of the population data to the territory. This requires the carrying out of some preliminary topo-geographical operations intended to determine and recognize on the site the internal boundaries separating the various territorial divisions for which information is required. These divisions are usually administrative or political in nature, such as provinces, departments, districts or municipalities, which usually have legal boundaries. Some countries, however, present census information for other types of areas, such as economic regions, public health zones, school districts or metropolitan areas. These may include parts of different large administrative or political divisions, or cover more administrative units, so that a second set of boundaries is superimposed upon the more usual ones.

One next proceeds to the sub-division of the territorial divisions into enumeration areas (also called enumeration districts or census areas), that is, the smallest territorial divisions established for census purposes.

Finally one proceeds to the identification of inhabited localities. This last operation is of particular importance for the population census, for it makes it possible to discover the characteristics of the area distribution of the population and provides elements for assessing the degree of urbanization of a territory. The concepts utilized by various countries are, however, different. Chapter 1 contains a discussion of the problems of definition of 'urban'.

Some countries confuse 'locality' with the smallest administrative division. This creates difficulties for studies on urbanization, as administrative units are seldom homogeneous from the point of view of the human settlement and as administrative boundaries may alter in course of time. On the other hand, some large cities or towns may contain two or more administrative divisions, which should be considered only as segments of a single locality rather than as separate localities.

All the topo-geographical materials collected on the occasion of a census with reference to localities also constitute a valuable source of information for studies on urbanization.

The individual characteristics of the census units vary from one country to another. For the demographic census both data for families, households, etc. (structure, housing, etc.) and those of the individuals counted in the census are usually collected. For the latter there are the personal data (sex, age, civil status, place of birth), economic data (type of activity, occupation, etc.), cultural and educational data (ethnic group, language, literacy, level of education, etc.).

For a housing census, note is taken of each dwelling of each type and size as well as of the inside and public services to which it is linked (water, light, gas, sewerage). For an industrial and distribution census account is taken of the features of local units (factories, shops, offices, etc.): branch of activity, number of persons employed, motive power installed, etc.

In all censuses the units utilized (families, persons, factories, dwellings, etc.) are given for the locality or district in which they are located. This allows the tabulation of data by territorial, administrative or statistical units, and, in due course, the analysis of the structural features of the units belonging to particular areas or to particular types of areas.

For the definition of their urban population different countries follow different concepts, often making use of them jointly. On the whole they are concepts applicable not so much to the population as to the areas in which they live and which are considered as possessing the character of urban areas: (a) by reason of their administrative status; (b) by reason of their population size; (c) by reason of particular economic and social characteristics of the area or of its population.

Often use is made of a mixed concept, which it is necessary to know and examine carefully before embarking on studies on the degree of urbanization of a territory. Still, a comparison between successive censuses makes it possible to follow the development of the 'urbanization process' even when the urban areas are defined in relation to administrative boundaries, provided it is possible to take the variations of the latter into account in some way or other.

MIGRATION DATA

Among the separate data collected and tabulated in the population census, those on place of birth assume particular importance. In fact, a classification of the population of a given area by place of birth makes possible a crude measure of the volume and sources of migration into the area during an indefinite number of prior years. The classification by country of birth shows the number of surviving immigrants born in each foreign country, while the figures on place of birth within the country where the census is taken show the residuum of internal migration to each geographical subdivision from other parts of the country.

The measures of immigration and internal migration obtained in this way are very crude because they do not take account of migrants having died between the time of migration and the date of the census, of those having returned to their places of birth or moved on to other areas after migrating to the area in question, nor of previous migrations between the time of birth and the time of entering the given area. Thus they do not show the amount of migration to or from any particular area within any given time.

Migration measures from this source may be refined if data are available from a series of censuses. In that case, the change between two successive censuses in the number of natives of a given area living in another area (interpreted with allowance for mortality) gives an indication of the amount of migration from the former to the latter area during the interval. The allowance for mortality can be made most accurately if the statistics on place of birth are classified by sex and year of birth or age groups. Even with this refinement, however, the migration measures thus obtained are imperfect because return movement of persons having previously migrated between the two areas cannot be taken into account.

Data on place of birth can also provide some measure of information on the ethnic composition of the population in certain areas in so far as ethnic groups can be identified solely on this basis.

CO-OPERATION WITH THE CENSUS

The census authorities generally publish, together with the census results, a methodological and administrative report which provides all the information needed for a correct interpretation of the data, including specimens of the questionnaires, the instructions for the enumeration and the indication of the composition of the tabulated categories.

This material, even when not published, is always available at the census offices and, if necessary, can be enlarged and completed by information obtained directly from those responsible for the census operations.

Collaboration with the census offices is useful for other purposes besides a correct interpretation of the results tabulated. Untabulated material is equally useful for anyone wishing to carry out preliminary researches into urbanization, whether on a national or local level. In cases where the results are only published for administrative divisions which do not correspond exactly with the urban areas which are to be studied, the data relating to enumeration districts or to localities make it possible to determine the population of these areas or sub-areas. This offers the further advantage of connecting the population checked in several successive censuses with unchanging areal units, even if changes in administrative boundaries have taken place.

Another kind of useful collaboration which the census offices can offer students of urbanization is that of including questions of particular interest in the plan for future censuses. Quite often the addition of a single question, thanks to the possibility of cross-tabulating the answers with other characteristics usually discovered by the census, can provide an interesting mass of information. For example, in several censuses, in order to discover data on internal migrations, the question on place of birth has been supplemented by one on place of work, or of place of residence on some fixed date, or of date of arrival in the place of present residence. These and other questions may also be included in supplementary questionnaires, to be used only in particular areas.

Administrative statistics

Whatever may be the politico-administrative set-up of a country there always exist public functions involving records which can be checked statistically. Some of these functions depend on local authorities, others on central authorities. But in both cases, owing to the peripheral flexibility of national services, there is the possibility of obtaining data relative to the administrative divisions of the territory. It must, however, be borne in mind that these divisions change according to the administrations and often fail to coincide with those of the census, and they may change with time. As regards the data to be drawn from administrative statistics, their significance and their completeness depend on the nature of the operation or of the administrative functions which produce them. This may invalidate their comparability and almost always involves the employment of special expedients.

The public functions carried out by the central administration and by local authorities may be divided into politico-administrative, educational, health, public assistance, fiscal and so on. Special services, records or procedures, and therefore special types of statistics, correspond to each group of these functions.

The politico-administrative functions of local authorities, for example, create the services of the registry office, of electoral machinery, and of the office dealing with the granting of special licences and permits.

REGISTRATION DATA

The registry-office service, where it exists, collects birth, marriage and death certificates and keeps track of the movement of the population by recording changes of residence. It is the source of the vital statistics which provide, *inter alia*, the statistical classification of events by their most important characteristics, including that connected with territorial dislocation.

This makes it possible to gather data on the natural and social movement of the population in each administrative unit and, in many cases (towns and metropolitan areas), for statistical sub-divisions of these units which may also correspond to the enumeration districts of the census.

The registry office, besides recording the movements of persons within the territory, issues on occasion identity cards and must then keep a name-roll recording this issue. Such rolls constitute a subsidiary source for obtaining information on the numbers of the population, or of a part of it. The service of electoral rolls keeps track of the change of residence of the voters, in accordance with the requests for election certificates on occasion of political and administrative meetings. The statistics drawn from them, in default of registry records, constitute a good indicator of internal migrations, even if only with reference to a fraction of the whole population. On the other hand, the exclusion of certain categories of the population from the body of voters corresponds to concepts closely connected with the politico-administrative set-up of the country, which it thus becomes necessary to know.

LICENCE AND PERMIT DATA

In almost all countries the carrying on of any economic, commercial or industrial activity is dependent on the granting of appropriate licences and compliance with prescribed bureaucratic formalities. It is thus possible to collect statistical data on the commercial and industrial concerns and on the changes they present (opening of new business and closing-down of others). This source *inter alia*, is particularly useful as showing the economic structure of the urban zones and of the metropolitan areas which are characterized by the existence of particular types of business (large stores, supermarkets, production and distribution chains, etc.). It is to be noted, however, that these surveys have a drawback: i.e., in some cases they take the permit or licence for the manufacture and sale of particular articles as the survey unit and in others the business, and also that the lists of business are usually inflated by reason of the incomplete record of those closing down.

To this group of statistics belong, too, those relative to permits for the construction of buildings to be used as dwellings or otherwise. The granting of these permits or licences is generally due to needs of various kinds, such as those connected with town-planning, health services, etc., and thus it may happen that they refer only to sections of the administrative divisions of the country, or only to particular categories of subjects (e.g., to private individuals).

EDUCATION

The functions performed by the public administration in the field of education provide the statistical records known as school, cultural, etc., statistics. From these records data may be obtained on the availability and location of schools, class-rooms, pupils and teachers, as well as on cultural events affecting the whole population in particular areas (shows, radio-television programmes, book publishing and so on). The availability of this kind of information is closely linked with the degree of development reached by the country, the organization of public school and cultural activities and the degree of control exercised by public authorities over private enterprise in these fields.

Similar considerations apply to the statistical records of the public functions performed in the matter of public health and hygiene, i.e., the investigations into morbidity (diseases and in particular infectious diseases), the health service organization (hospitals, doctors, pharmacies, etc.), causes of death, etc.

LABOUR DATA

The functions performed by public bodies in the labour field produce an important body of statistical information such as, for example, statistics on compulsory insurance, generally concerned with sickness, accident and unemployment. The territorial distribution of the number of contributors or of the contributions paid provides a measure of the number of persons employed and thus serves up to a point to determine the employment situation. It must, however, be remembered that the coverage of these statistics is determined by the system of social insurance in force and by the degree of efficiency in the offices responsible for it.

Of the same type are the statistics taken from the records of the labour force; for instance, those kept by the employment services for the purpose of finding suitable employment.

The regulation regarding the employment service determines the field covered by the statistics and their degree of completeness; moreover, their validity depends on the interest the unemployed feel in having their names entered on the lists and on the range, distribution and geographical density of the labour exchanges.

FISCAL DATA

Finally we must mention the statistics due to the administrative functions connected with the collection of public revenue and the provision of public services. The revenue collection involves assessment operations which furnish lists or statistics of taxable subjects (property, business, taxpayers, etc.) or of specific sources of revenue (incomes, inheritances, excisable articles). Expenditure on public services (directly managed or controlled by the administration) involves assessments on important activities, especially in urban centres, such as, for instance, the building of houses for the working class, transport of persons or goods, urbanization work (road, water, sewerage networks, etc.).

4

NON-GOVERNMENT SOURCES

It must not be forgotten that in many countries some of the functions mentioned above are performed wholly or partly by private bodies and organizations. These bodies also maintain statistical records which may profitably be consulted.

Separate mention should be made of the statistics kept by some religious communities which, besides recording any work carried out in the fields of education, welfare, recreation, etc., sometimes also record the number of their followers and the changes in their civil status when these correspond to facts having importance from the religious point of view.

Finally we must mention the internal statistics of trade unions (of workers or employers) and of other associations which set themselves particular aims.

Of course, all these statistics of private bodies must be used with the circumspection already explained in the case of administrative statistics. It must especially be borne in mind that the data regarding the number of adherents, of those present at services, etc., vary in accordance with the degree of development of the bodies and with their possibility of making proselytes.

Recurrent and special statistical reports

The student of urbanization problems may find useful information in a series of statistical surveys which are carried out in many countries on a national or local level for various purposes, as well as in censuses and in statistics collected as by-products of administrative operations.

In this case the list can only be exemplificative. In the first place we may mention the surveys into production, occupation and wages which are carried out where there are no censuses on these questions, or in the intervals between one industrial census and the next; the surveys into new construction, which aim at ascertaining the features of the new dwellings and the demographic and socio-professional characteristics of their tenants (usually carried out only in urban areas); the labour force sample surveys or other sample surveys into employment; the health surveys carried out on special occasions or recurrently in particular areas, etc.

Various countries collect data and publish reports on the subjects of nutrition, consumption or family budgets—data which are almost always tabulated separately for urban districts or for large metropolitan areas.

In some cases surveys are carried out on the traffic of the average road (goods or people), which, taken in conjunction with the administrative traffic statistics, make it possible to estimate the exchanges between the different districts of the territory. The special surveys made in order to discover the commuting between the urban centres and the surrounding areas belong to the same type. There are also countries which regularly carry out multi-purpose sample surveys on an areal basis, in the course of which a quantity of information of a demographic, economic or social nature is collected. These surveys are made in successive rounds, the programme of which is laid down beforehand by the body responsible for the scheme. This, *inter alia*, makes it possible to obtain information of particular interest, by means of slight modifications or enlargements of the survey plans.

Use of basic statistics

The researches of which we shall speak in the following chapters aim at penetrating more deeply into the process of urbanization now taking place and at suggesting the methodological means suitable for formulating the diagnoses or forecasts indispensable for a proper urbanization policy—a policy which may be imposed both on a national and local level.

But there is no doubt that for a first definition of the problems to be tackled, for a choice of the aspects which will require specific surveys, as well as for the planning of these surveys, for the identification of the type of society in which to operate, for a first directive layout of the urbanization policy, the utilization of the statistical sources of which we have spoken earlier is essential.

First of all the census makes it possible to discover the salient characteristics of the distribution of population and of the economic activities in the territory, to delineate and describe (either alone or taken together with other sources of information) the urbanized areas, to define the type of urbanization characteristic of each area, to discover (provided there exist data on the population distributed according to place of residence and of birth) the contribution made by the geographical mobility of the population to the territorial settlement achieved.

The data collected in the course of the census often make it possible to compare, with some exactitude, the structural characteristics of the urban zones and of the rural zones from the most varied points of view, offering a more complete idea of 'urbanization' and a preliminary identification of the problems to be tackled with priority. If in addition we find available a series of censuses taken at regular intervals, the comparison of their results —by itself or taken together with other surveys of an administrative character (demographic records, etc.)—makes it possible to isolate the present tendencies and thus to formulate projections useful for planning in advance the required actions or at least to pin-point definitely the aims of planning.

The other administrative statistics of which we have spoken—which exist to a greater or lesser degree in all countries, whatever may be their state of development—may in part make up for the lack of census statistics, or else, taken together with the latter, may permit a preliminary picture of the process of urbanization in its complexity, stressing the relationships and discrepancies between the growth of the population and that of the public services and economic activities.

The basic statistics of which we have spoken, besides being directly useful for cognitive purposes, may often constitute a useful starting-point for *ad hoc* surveys or for the proper layout of sample surveys. In connexion with the latter, it is enough to remember that the census offers a complete list of areal units often adequately small. Moreover, records made for administrative purposes offer an analogous possibility as regards the choice of sample units of different types (voters, taxpayers, schools, factories, etc.) bearing in mind that in surveys of an administrative character the 'population' is often not sufficiently defined, and that it is impossible to rely on the completeness of the relative 'lists'.

As regards the *ad hoc* surveys which may be suggested or thought most advisable after the basic statistics have been studied and analysed, there are a large number of possibilities, e.g., a comparison between the demographic and social structure and development of urbanized and rural zones; the connexion between criminality, school attendance and household structure; the demographic differences among particular areas; the relations between the development of urban zones and that of public services, housing and the like. All these types of analyses are useful for focusing problems and for pin-pointing the zones or sectors on which to carry out further researches.

On a national level it is often sufficient to have a series of censuses at our disposal to be able to pin-point the most obvious maladjustments in the territorial settlement of the population, or to foresee the difficulties which may arise in the more or less immediate future. This latter is important for the planning of policy, so as to eliminate the necessity for adoption of remedies on an emergency basis.

It is often absolutely necessary to have recourse to such remedies, but they almost always turn out to be a useless waste of money when they are not taken as part of a previously prepared comprehensive plan. For instance, a programme for the building of working-class houses cannot properly be laid down or carried out except as part of a whole scheme of town-planning and in the expectation of an approximate equilibrium between the development of economic activities and the growth of the urban population.

Once an urbanization policy has been defined and the objectives of the programmes have been formulated (on a local, regional or national level), the basic data of which we have spoken in this chapter are often indispensable to take the most appropriate action in relation to the characteristics of the single zones or sectors. For example, a programme of educational development with definite aims will have to be carried out in different ways depending on the demographic, social and ethnic structure of the population concerned, and in consideration of its expansion tendencies and of the forms taken by the expected increase (whether by natural growth of population or by immigration, etc.).

Once a programme has been carried out, no matter what field has been chosen for it, its effects, even if not directly measurable, cannot fail to be evident to some degree, in the demographic or social composition of the population concerned.

Such changes measured against the basic data of which we have spoken make it possible to evaluate the success of the programme carried out.

Bibliography

HAYES, S. P., Jr. *Measuring the results of development projects.* Paris, Unesco, 1959. (Monographs in the applied social sciences.)

UNITED NATIONS STATISTICAL COMMISSION. *A brief statement on the uses of sampling.* Lake Success, 1948.

UNITED NATIONS STATISTICAL OFFICE. *Handbook of population census methods.* 3 vols. New York, 1958, 1959.

——. *Handbook of statistical organization.* New York, 1954.

——. *Handbook of vital statistics methods.* New York, 1955.

——. *Industrial censuses and related enquiries.* 2 vols. New York, 1953.

——. *List of statistical series collected by international organizations.* New York, 1955.

——. *Methods of national income estimation.* New York, 1955

——. *Principles for a vital statistics system.* New York, 1953.

——. *Provisional suggestions for national programmes of analyses of population census data as an aid to planning and policy-making.* New York, 1962.

UNITED NATIONS STATISTICAL OFFICE. *Statistical series for the use of less-developed countries in programmes of economic and social development.* New York, 1959.
——. *Survey of social statistics.* New York, 1954.
——. *A system of national accounts and supporting tables.* New York, 1960.
——, jointly with ILO, FAO, UNESCO and WHO. *Compendium of social statistics.* New York, 1963.

3   Field and case studies

P. H. Chombart de Lauwe

Group and individual studies
in urban milieux [1]

Important though they may be, large-scale samplings are not always the
most important part of sociological studies in the urban milieux. Direct
observation of groups and individuals under progressively better controlled
conditions allows a more complete picture to be presented of the life of men
in their social setting and is the only way of interpreting some of the data
from the often more superficial extensive surveys.

Observation as here conceived must be tempered with interpretation,
comparison and experimentation. It is impossible to make valid observations
of facts or groups without taking prior experiences into account, whether
those of the observer himself or derived from other researchers known to
him. At every point the observer is guided by his previous background in
research. True objectivity does not consist in making oneself as neutral as
possible but in knowing and recognizing one's own affiliations and the
personal bias to which they may give rise.

---

1. This chapter relies on many works of which the great bulk appear in the bibliography. Some
    names or titles are quoted in the text as examples but this does not mean that they are more
    important than the others.

The confluence of disciplines and the development of new methods

The observation of social life in an urban milieu is inevitably an inter-disciplinary operation. In some countries such as France there has been repeated stressing of the need for historical, geographical and economic studies as background for specifically sociological surveys. The fact is that it is difficult to understand a population, a group or an individual case without accurately 'placing' them at once in time, in the life of their epoch as its forms have been shaped by the influence of earlier periods, and in a socio-geographic space meticulously described. It is not less important to describe the living conditions and economic system in which the subjects find themselves involved, as well as the evolution of the population structure, to which certain changes in behaviour, certain transformations of social structures and certain attitudes or stereotypes are directly linked.

However the disciplines most directly concerned with the kind of research here described are ethnology, linguistics, sociology and social psychology. Ethnology (and social anthropology) has contributed to research in urban milieux whole series of works of different national schools which will be mentioned later. The ethnological approach enables us to define the civilization and culture forming the framework for the facts and men observed and to show how those facts and men are influenced by cultural patterns and by images deriving from that culture. Again, in this kind of research, linguistics has often been presented as a necessary complement to ethnology: the kind of communication developed between men in a particular culture depends on that culture, speech and its structure and evolution.

Ethnology and social anthropology put the accent on direct observation, qualitative appreciations, the study of the area and the relations between behaviour patterns and the social milieu. Men are studied in the framework of the groups to which they attach themselves within their societies, in which connexion Marcel Mauss has stressed the importance of the 'total social phenomenon' in sociological research. Most countries offer examples of notable case studies which enable us to appreciate all that research in urban settings owes to the pioneers of ethnology, for instance, among many others, the work of Firth in England, Redfield in America, Leenhardt in France, etc.

In sociology, the emphasis, since the nineteenth century, has been on descriptive research whose usefulness was stressed by Spencer himself, in his 'descriptive sociology', and later by Durkheim. The well-known works of Villerme or Buret on the working classes in France, Le Play's research on European working men, and the writings of Engels on sociology, of Engel on economics in Germany, and of Gusti in Rumania can provide source material worth consulting. The social investigations undertaken in England, such as Booth's great survey of London, or Rowntree's study of New York started a whole research tradition which is still bearing fruit today. In France, Halbwachs's studies of the working class and family budgets make it possible to relate the problems of economic evolution more precisely into the study of a basic social milieu.

Holland contributed Steinmetz's 'sociography' whose influence on the creation of empirical sociology is common knowledge. In Poland a whole school of sociology has grown up round Znaniecki's researches undertaken in conjunction with Thomas in America; these have had a decisive influence on the whole trend of sociological research in conjunction with ethnological observations and social psychology.

In psychology itself due weight must be given, for studies of individuals in particular, to the contribution of social psychiatry and the schools of psychology which, though working from very different premises, have stressed the connexion between the environment and alteration of behaviour patterns. Whether working from Freud's teaching on the subconscious or from Pavlov's on conditioning, all the best published research works in social psychology on the individual and the society have demonstrated the instance of connexions between personality, groups and living conditions. Research on the 'socialization of the child' by authorities as varied as Gesell, Piaget or Wallon make it clear that there is no clear-cut boundary between individual and social life. Any suggestion of an antinomy between the individual and the society is based on a misconception.

All these publications have helped to 'organize' both basic empirical research and research on individual cases. The two, incidentally, are closely connected. It is not possible to understand the behaviour patterns and motivations of an individual without sound prior investigation of the social milieu in which that individual lives and for this it is important that all such research should include both the quantitative data obtained in statistical surveys and the qualitative observations made by other methods. Another thing to be avoided is studying a small group or a social milieu out of the context of the society as a whole. The writer's own belief is that behaviour patterns in small groups are explainable from the social, economic and cultural contexts of the country-wide society. It is not, as some have thought, the structures of the small groups which explain the society but the society which explains the small groups.

Studies of groups or case histories should not, either, be carried out exclusively in one milieu or even one culture. Comparative research is becoming progressively more ineluctable. The description of a group 'set-up' or of a case must be completed by comparison with the equivalents in other cultural contexts. Nevertheless such comparisons must be undertaken with great caution for it is necessary, as the ethnologists have frequently pointed out, to allow for the connexion already discussed between each detail of behaviour and the sum of the societal life in a particular culture. Comparisons between country and country require a profound knowledge of their distinctive cultures.

The study of urban groups and milieux

Studies of urban groups and milieux have varied widely in complexion among different researchers and in different countries. Despite this it is possible, taking them as a whole, to extract certain practical rules for the conduct and checking of the observations, training the researchers and developing the results. Let us begin by attempting to exhibit a few broad research sectors corresponding to different fields or subjects.

TYPES OF RESEARCH

The sociological study of towns must take into consideration, first, the observations on smaller local groups such as villages and secondly, those on the conurbations in which the towns are increasingly involved and even on the regions to which they are attached by nature. The studies of West on an American, or Bernot on a French, village are important in this connexion. Studies of small or medium-sized towns such as Lynd's on Middletown, the study by Clément and Xydias of Vienne in France, or Balandier's study of Brazzaville and Mercier's of Dakar have enabled researches to be effected on the combinations of activities of larger communities, as have the work of Rowntree and Ruth Glass and others in England. Among studies of major conurbations, Booth's survey of London, already mentioned, is basic; other case studies of Chicago or Paris, Bordeaux, Liverpool, etc., show that very extensive urban groups can be studied as entities. Studies of city wards or sectors have been extremely successful in a number of countries, for instance White's *Street Corner Society* or Zorbaugh on *The Gold Coast and the Slum*, both from the United States. The writer himself has made a number of studies of *quartiers* of Paris.

As regards sectors other than residential, our present purpose calls for no more than a reminder that many works of industrial sociology have been written on researches into business and industry. It is nevertheless useful, to follow the example, say of Warner in *Yankee City* and study the links which exist between life at work in the factory and social life outside.

Within the limits of the town, case studies of organized groups such as youth movements, women's movements and miscellaneous associations should occupy an important place in the mind of the researcher and study of the general situation as regards associations should be completed with exhaustive studies of selected examples. Political parties and pressure groups can also be most interesting subjects for descriptive observation and analysis. However, the investigation of broad non-organized groups is still more important. We are still under-supplied with case studies of the various social classes and the new social milieux emerging increasingly in urban life. Major occupational sectors such as the motor trades, banking, hotel-keeping, etc., constitute 'linkages' which are not formal social groups but within which we find easier communication between men, similarities of behaviour and common attitudes which cause these sectors to play a capital role in contemporary urban life.

Observations of occurrences can be subjects for snap studies for which special techniques will have to be used. The analysis of a strike or the description of a revolutionary rising may present considerable difficulties for the sociologist who happens to become involved, but these are of incomparable interest both historically and sociologically. Researchers must keep a close watch for exceptional situations in which they can study the reactions of social groups or milieux with which it would be impossible for them to acquaint themselves in ordinary conditions.

Apart from research on extensive social groups and on events, attention must be directed increasingly to the small neighbourhood groups, the small friendship groups and the youth gangs, whose influence has not always been well understood. The personality of the city-dweller is scored by his membership of such groups at various stages in his life and observing them properly is much more than mere description; here, perhaps better than anywhere, the analytical study enables us to time accurately the intimate links between the individual and society as a whole. The small groups play a key role in the individual's satisfactory integration into his society.

OBSERVATION

Such groups can be studied by direct observation which is pursued by more or less active participation in the life of these members and which, particularly at the beginning, can either be 'free ranging' with no explicit hypothesis to verify, or channelled or organized, often using a team of interviewers who must be carefully briefed. Direct observation can take the form of more or less slanted interviews, or of studies of individual personalities, daily scenes, occurences and groups, with attention to discovering the best points of observation and the most alert informants.

With regard to direct observation a capital question which arises is whether to have the observation conducted by a researcher external to the group who brings a fresh eye to bear on it and who puts his questions as an outsider; or to favour another form of observation consisting either in joining the group or in asking one of its members to conduct the study under the researcher's guidance. In the writer's view all three choices—observing from outside, observing from inside, and using a stalking horse—are satisfactory and mutually complementary. Which is used depends on circumstances, temperaments and subjects.

Alternatively, observation can be indirect from documents; these can be either historical papers, records and miscellaneous statistics or, again, newspapers or novels produced by members of the groups observed. All these elements can contribute much towards a knowledge of the society's life. Such knowledge may on occasion be as extensive as that secured by direct observation.

Among the observation techniques which can be used apart from questionnaires or interviews, we must not forget to mention the distribution maps which enable the men and facts observed to be better 'located' in space. Great attention should also be given to comparative studies from photographs and increasingly to motion pictures, not forgetting the use of films even as a means of contact between the researchers and the population through the intermediary of television. In this connexion the writer himself has carried out extremely encouraging experiments in France. After shooting a film about a particular quarter of Paris or a village, the actual persons who had been filmed commented on the film on television, and then the other inhabitants of the same quarter were asked to give their impression of the films and of the commentators after seeing both on television.

Lastly, one of the techniques to which great importance should be attached is group discussions. The latter make it easier to secure reactions which are difficult to get in individual conversations. With discussions more or less kept in line by questions posed by the researchers, the proceedings rapidly become a group exploration of the variety of problems on which the inhabitants of a city ward or the members of an urban group ordinarily have few occasions for pronouncing.

CONTROL OF OBSERVATIONS

Observations, direct or indirect, are always of doubtful reliability as to the extent to which the conduct of the interview or the interpretation of a document may reflect some bias of the researchers and interviewers. The primary basis for verifying the observations is the will to truth and openness. The essential requisite in a researcher conducting observations is not to remain completely dispassionate towards men and facts, which is impossible and far from desirable, but (a) the ability to diagnose his own attitude—to know himself—and (b) that at the earliest possible stage he formulates the hypotheses entertained, to avoid being steered in practice by preconceived ideas.

This personal stock-taking, which enables the researcher to measure the discrepancy between his first reaction to the facts and how things really are, needs to be supplemented by mutual checking by researchers and interviewers. Field observations are a team job, and the convergence or divergence of individual comments may give rise to discussions making further observations necessary. In due course an agreed view is reached which is more reliable than the judgement of a single individual.

Direct qualitative observation needs to be positioned and verified by statistical studies of broad samples, but the statistical studies correspondingly need to be interpreted from the qualitative studies. On occasion the results of a statistical survey are completely erroneous, notwithstanding any technical verifications which may have been made, because the questions were ill conceived, for lack of sufficiently precise qualitative observations, to give a good idea of the personal reactions of the individuals interrogated. Some statistical tables can only be really understood if there are studies of individual cases to show the real significance of the combinations of variables noted.

Finally research results differ widely according as the 'subjects' have been any Tom, Dick, or Harry, or committed members of movements or groups in which they have positions of some importance. Generally speaking, the interviews with active group workers yield more definite results with much sharper contrasts than those with all and sundry. It is therefore important to use each to complement the other—a verification procedure which is not envisaged often enough and which should have an increasingly important place in researches.

TRAINING

Since field observation in urban surroundings calls for team-work, it is necessary for the researchers and interviewers to be given appropriate prior training for this. It has already been emphasized that this kind of research is interdisciplinary and this means trying to assemble a team comprising a range of varied and complementary abilities. At the same time a background of university science studies is far from adequate: it is rare to find the desired standard in a discipline of the human sciences and adequate practical knowledge of the social milieux which are to be observed combined in the same person. We need therefore to marry scientific and practical abilities, and the start of the best pieces of research is the successful formation of a balanced team by enlisting individuals with an exhaustive knowledge of the milieux collectively to be observed.

Whatever their prior training, the researchers and field workers must have long working meetings in which they detail their method of observation and agree upon procedures, preferably in writing. They may refer to them individually in the course of their research whenever they are in doubt about anything. Provision should be made for frequent meetings to review the situation, to guard against divergences and misunderstandings.

DEVELOPMENT OF THE RESULTS—SYNTHESIS

No observations can get very far unless guided throughout by hypotheses evolved as the work progresses. When to start hypothesizing in research is perhaps the most delicate decision in observations in the field. If a hypothesis is formulated too early it colours the conduct of the work and invalidates the observations *ab initio*. Yet if no attempt is made to formulate—or grasp—the hypotheses as soon as possible, they often remain unadmitted and as such are an even greater danger than reasoned-out, even if over-rigid, hypotheses.

The ease of development of the results will be proportionate to how well the hypotheses have been formulated. One of the great difficulties in observations in the field is the accumulation of documents which often ends by bogging down the project. Many researchers without sufficient experience in this kind of work have had to abandon their operations because they were discouraged by the accumulation of data which they could no longer reduce to order.

The further the research progresses, the more the observations must be focused on specific points. Many authorities have stressed the importance of focusing interviews and this applies equally to observations of other types.

In interpreting the results, mutual checking between researchers will be as important as it was in the actual observations. A matter of some delicacy is how to distribute documents and chapters to draft between the various members of the team. For this the points to be considered are the personal abilities of each, the basic work done, and the circumstances in which the observations were made. 'Marrying' the parts of the draft is always a difficult moment in team-work and it sometimes is best to have the whole of the report or book in preparation drafted by a single individual. In that case, however, the benefit of the specialized viewpoints of the individual contributors' particular disciplines is lost.

Case studies of individuals

For years past historians and novelists have afforded sociologists object lessons on the importance of biographical studies or personal histories for the understanding of a society's life. Novelists such as Zola or Balzac are masters whom researchers would be wrong to repudiate. In connexion with recent studies in historical sociology, members of the writer's own group examined the methods of observation used by Zola; in his time he carried out full-blown surveys and built up a corpus of documentation of capital importance in sociology. In history the attention devoted by writers to the study of great men, whose careers they explain from the history of their epoch and vice versa, is a yet clearer lesson.

In human science research in urban surroundings, the use of case studies of individuals has been frequent from Thomas and Znaniecki, already mentioned, down to Warner or Lynd and the work done in African towns or towns of various European countries. Here again as in group studies we can distinguish different types of observation and define methods for conducting the research and interpreting the results.

OBSERVATION IN CASE STUDIES OF INDIVIDUALS

The case history of an individual can be built up from interviews either with the subject alone or, additionally, with persons close to him to supplement what he says. The most important thing is to see the different ways in which the subject's character and career are viewed by different people with their individual readings of his role in society, his qualities and defects, and his action in the community.

Use can be made of material already published on the subject, particularly in the case of someone well known, an activist or someone who has played a part in public life. Similarly letters and, in certain cases personal diaries, and photographs can also be used. A variant is research on members of a single family or small coteries of friends of special importance in their day; this is a 'halfway house' between the case history of an individual and the group study.

A particularly useful and instructive study is tracing an individual's history at various periods of his life by studies in time. Unfortunately this form of research is extremely difficult to conduct and is scarcely possible except when the teams formed are working for years on end in the same sector. In this connexion research on the behaviour of families from marriage to the completion of the grown children's education has yielded interesting results.

The medical dossiers, studied in investigating psycho-pathological

63

individuals, are a good example of collections of documents about an individual which may be significant in a much wider context than that of the individual's personal problems. The systematic consideration of psychiatric cases, of behaviour troubles, has made it possible to place in relief the influence of certain variables of the physical or social milieux, but good research on these lines is impossible unless the systematic statistical study of dossiers is rounded out by deeper investigation of a few well-chosen cases. More broadly, for the analysis of individual situations not necessarily pathological, the social services have attached much importance to the case-work approach in which teams of researchers and social workers interpret the history of an individual in a particular social sector either with a view to helping him psychologically or socially or to affording him material relief.

To sum up, the writer's view is that case studies offer wide scope when it is possible to tie in the statistical research with minute observations of the cases of individuals—i.e., when the researcher contrives to select, from a sample of individuals whom he has studied more or less superficially, certain type cases which will permit him to interpret the whole and to give his research a more psychological direction.

SOCIOLOGICAL STUDY OF THE CASES OF INDIVIDUALS

On the strength of the foregoing observations, the writer has tried to develop by degrees a method of sociological study of the cases of individuals in terms of the social milieu or milieux in which the subject is placed, the social milieu regarded as a combination of variables correlated with the variables of behaviour. The listing, selection and re-grouping of these variables and the choice of those items to be correlated are a series of operations which allow of a sounder interpretation of the data collected.

The social milieu is characterized by the complex of systems of relationship in which the individuals are involved and the degree of communication existing between persons in the same milieu, in which the importance of common group attitudes and common lines of behaviour in the same social milieu have already been pointed out. These considerations can be applied for studying the individual in the context not only of his present social milieu but of all the social milieux through which he has passed in the course of his personal history; this permits of a more scientifically rigorous study of the relations between the individual and of the society, of the groups to which he belongs. It is also possible to make a better evaluation of the parts played respectively by heredity and environment which always represent a mixed factor. The outcome is then the identification of a kind of social heredity whose increasing importance becomes progressively more apparent as more work is done in this field.

SOME REMARKS ON TECHNIQUES AND INTERPRETATION

The study of individual cases calls for a gamut of qualities difficult to assemble. Apart from formal qualifications it is necessary for the researchers to have an innate gift for human relations. Here the handling of free, semi-directed interviews is of capital importance.

A similar position arises over the interpretation of documents, which becomes increasingly delicate in proportion as the study focuses more on psychological features of the case.

The evidence may be handled differently according as the main emphasis is to be on using the individual case for sociological purposes or on reaching a psychological analysis of the troubles or merely the personality of the subject. But either way, valid results are once again dependent on carefully planned team-work with the psychologist, the sociologist, the doctor, the social worker and many others each playing his own specialized part.

The importance of case studies of individuals resides mainly, as several times remarked, in the possibility of arriving, through the personalities, behaviour and attitudes of certain well-selected subjects, at an appreciation of systems of values peculiar to a particular society or a social milieu. This will be discussed further in connexion with the consideration of the basic concepts relied on throughout this class of studies.

Experimental observation

Observations must be considered in a clearly defined field, in social milieux whose history and nature emerge progressively, and they must be under increasingly controlled conditions. Controlled observation of this kind, as the writer has endeavoured to demonstrate in a number of studies, becomes steadily closer to experimentation. In the writer's view there is no clear-cut boundary between qualitative case studies of groups or individuals and the 'experimental situations' as presented by various researchers.

It is suggested that a leading place should be given to comparative experimental studies on small random samples from population strata determined by hypothesis without representativeness being necessarily aimed at. It is in such a sample that the case studies can be compared with control observations for valid interpretation. Dealing with samples of reduced size makes it possible both to produce fairly simple statistical studies with the classical proofs of meaning, and also to identify the types of cases to be studied more exhaustively.

Thus by combining ecological analysis of urban sectors, qualitative observation of the behaviour problems of a group or a social milieu, massive statistical samplings and case studies, we continue to present a reasonably comprehensive picture of social life in urban milieux from which wider generalizations can be worked out leading on to synthesis.

Bound up in the whole of the studies here described are certain basic concepts on which a few words are required to conclude this brief outline. To determine needs and aspirations, the researcher is obliged to refer to the systems of values which orient them. We can take it that he can mainly define these needs, aspirations and values by observations firstly of behaviour patterns and secondly of attitudes and accepted stereotypes. The observation of the cultures and sub-cultures of groups or social milieux consists in defining the types of social relations, and modes of communication and the models which orient them. It is by following the daily lives of groups and individuals and posing questions which invite them to particularize the attitudes they have towards the society, themselves, social roles, etc., that an over-all picture is arrived at.

Two points also must be emphasized. The first is the importance of the concept 'social milieu', mentioned earlier, and used for conglomerations of human beings who do not necessarily constitute a group but yet have bonds in the shape of common attitudes, easier inter-member communication, and certain like forms of behaviour. In the life of great cities the social milieu frequently takes the place of the more structured groups characterizing the life of closed societies. Accordingly the former's influence on individuals is no less great but more difficult to trace in proportion as their forms and structures are less clear cut.

The second point relates to the new aspects of functional research: the study of needs having stolen most of the limelight in this type of research, the concept 'aspiration' has perhaps not been accorded the importance due to it. The writer himself has emphasized the role of such aspirations in the emergence of new needs and in the progression from what he has christened 'aspiration needs' to compulsive needs, which the authorities are compelled to take more and more into consideration. Case studies or studies of social milieux in town life need to give a grasp of this mechanism of need development to assist the conception and preparation of plans better adapted to the desires of the people.

Bibliography

THE CONFLUENCE OF DISCIPLINES AND THE DEVELOPMENT OF NEW METHODS

BECKER, H.; BOSKOFF, A. (eds.). *Modern sociological theory in continuity and change.* New York, 1957.

BOOTH, C. *Life and labour of the people of London.* 17 vols. London, Macmillan & Co., 1889-1903. Continued by the London School of Economics as: Smith, H. L. (ed.), *The new survey of London life and labour.* 9 vols. London, P. S. King, 1930-35.

BURET, E. *La misère des classes laborieuses en France et en Angleterre.* 2 vols. Paris, Paulin, 1840.

Social, economic and technological change: a theoretical approach. Paris, Bureau International de Recherches sur les Implications Sociales du Progrès Technique, Conseil International des Sciences Sociales, 6, rue Franklin, Paris-16ᵉ, 1958.

CHOMBART DE LAUWE, P. H. Esquisse d'un plan de recherches sur la vie sociale en milieu urbain. *La vie urbaine,* new series, no. 4, Oct.-Dec. 1959.

CUVILLIER, A. *Manuel de sociologie.* 2 vols. Paris, Presses Universitaires de France, 1958-60.

DURKHEIM, E. *Les règles de la méthode sociologique.* Paris, Alcan, 1895; Presses Universitaires de France, 1960, XXIV + 150 pp.

ENGEL, E. Das Rechnungsbuch der Hausfrau und seine Bedeutung im Wirtschaftsleben der Nation [The family budget of the housewife and its importance in the national economy]. *Volkswirtschaftliche Zeitfragen,* vol. 24, p. 39. Berlin, 1882.

——. Die Lebenskosten belgischer Arbeiterfamilien früher und jetzt [The cost of living of the Belgian working families, formerly and at present]. *Bulletin de l'Institut international de statistique.* Rome, 1895. IX + 124 pp.

ENGELS, F. *Die Lage der arbeitenden Klasse in England* [The position of the working class in England]. Leipzig, 1845.

EVANS-PRITCHARD, E. E. *Social anthropology.* London, Cohen & West Ltd, 1962. 135 pp.

FIRTH, R. *We, the Tikopia. A sociological study of kinship in primitive Polynesia.* London, 1936.

——. *Social change in Tikopia. Re-study of a Polynesian community after a generation.* London, Allen & Unwin, 1959. 360 pp.

GESELL, A.; ILG, F. L. *Le jeune enfant dans la civilisation moderne.* Paris, Presses Universitaires de France, 1949.

GURVITCH, G. (ed.) *Traité de sociologie.* Paris, Presses Universitaires de France, vol. I, 2nd ed., 1962, 514 pp.; vol. II, 1st ed., 1960, 466 pp. (especially: Sociologie et psychologie, by R. Bastide; Histoire et sociologie, by F. Braudel; Sociologie, ethnologie et ethnographie, by G. Balandier; Sociologie géographique, by P. George; Démographie sociale, by A. Girard; Economie politique et sociologie économique, by J. Lhomme and J. Weiller; Sociologie et psychanalyse, by R. Bastide; Compénétration de méthodes ethnologiques et sociologiques, by P. Mercier).

——; MOORE, W. (eds.). *La sociologie au XXème siècle*. 2 vols. Paris, Presses Universitaires de France, 1947. 762 pp.

GUSTI, D. *La science de la réalité sociale*. Paris, Alcan, 1941.

——. La monographie et l'action monographique en Roumanie. *Etudes de sociologie et d'ethnologie juridiques*. Domat, 1935.

HALBWACHS, M. *La classe ouvrière et les niveaux de vie. Recherches sur la hiérarchie des besoins dans les sociétés industrielles contemporaines*. Paris, Alcan, 1913. 495 pp.

——. *L'évolution des besoins dans les classes ouvrières*. Paris, Alcan, 1933. 163 pp.

HALL, R. B. *Area studies: with special reference to their implications for social research in the social sciences*. New York, Social Science Research Council, 1947, *International social science bulletin*. Vol. IV, no. 4: *Area studies*. Paris, Unesco, 1952.

KARDINER, A.; LINTON, R.; DUBOIS, C.; WEST, J. *The psychological frontiers of society*. New York, Columbia University Press, 1950. XXIV + 475 pp.

KOMAROVSKY, M. *Common frontiers of the social sciences*. Glencoe, Il., 1957.

LEENHARDT, M. *Gens de la Grande-Terre*. New ed. Paris, Gallimard, 1953. 228 pp.

LE PLAY, F. *Les ouvriers européens*. Paris, Imprimerie Impériale, 1855. 301 pp.

MAUSS, M. Fragment d'un plan de sociologie générale descriptive. *Annales sociologiques*. Series A, fasc. 1. Paris, Alcan, 1934. 56 pp.

——. *Sociologie et anthropologie*. Paris, Presses Universitaires de France, 1950. 390 pp.

Notes and queries on anthropology. 6th ed., revised and rewritten. London, Routledge & Kegan Paul, 1951. XII + 403 pp.

PIAGET, J. Problèmes de la psycho-sociologie de l'enfance. In: Gurvitch, G., (ed.). *Traité de sociologie*, vol. II, pp. 229-54. Paris, Presses Universitaires de France, 1960.

REDFIELD, R. *The folk culture of Yucatan*. Chicago, Ill., University of Chicago Press, 1941.

ROWNTREE, B. S. *Poverty. A study of town life*. 2nd ed., rev. London, Macmillan, 1902. XXII + 452 pp.

——. *Poverty and progress. A second social survey of York*. 1st ed. London, Longmans Green, 1940. XX + 440 pp.

——; LAVERS. *Poverty and the welfare state. A third social survey of York*. London, Longmans Green, 1951. VII + 104 pp.

SOROKIN, P. A. *Society, culture and personality*. New York, 1937.

SPENCER, H. *Descriptive sociology, or groups of sociological facts*. 8 vols. London, 1873-81.

STEINMETZ, R. Die Soziographie in der Reihe der Geisteswissenschaften. [Sociography and the liberal arts]. *Archiv fur Rechts- und Wirtschaftsphilosophie*, vol. VI, 1913.

THOMAS, W. I.; ZNANIECKI, F. *The Polish peasant in Europe and America*. 3 vols. New York, 1918-20. Rev. ed., 1927, 2 vols.

VILLERME, L. R. *Tableau de l'état physique et moral des ouvriers employés dans les manufactures de coton, de laine et de soie.* 2 vols. Paris, Renouard, 1840.

WALLON, H. Les milieux, les groupes et la psycho-génèse de l'enfant. *Cahiers internationaux de sociologie,* vol. XVI, 1954, pp. 2-13.

——. Étude psychologique et sociologique de l'enfant. *Cahiers internationaux de sociologie,* vol. III, 1947, pp. 3-22.

THE STUDY OF URBAN GROUPS AND MILIEUX

Types of research

ANGELL, R. C. *The family encounters the depression.* New York, 1936.

BALANDIER, G. *Sociologie des Brazzavilles noires.* Paris, A. Colin, 1955. 274 pp. (Cahiers de la Fondation Nationale des Sciences Politiques, no. 67.)

BERNOT, L.; BLANCARD, R. *Nouville, un village français.* Paris, Institut d'Ethnologie, 1953. VII + 447 pp.

BETTELHEIM, C.; FRERE, S. *Une ville française moyenne: Auxerre en 1950, étude de structure sociale et urbaine.* Paris, A. Colin, 1950. XIV + 270 pp. (Cahiers de la Fondation Nationale des Sciences Politiques, no. 17.)

BOOTH, C. *Life and labour of the people of London.* 17 vols. Macmillan & Co., 1889-1903. (See above.)

CHOMBART DE LAUWE, P. H.; ANTOINE, S.; COUVREUR, L.; GAUTHIER, J. *Paris et l'agglomération parisienne.* 2 vols. Vol. I: *L'espace social dans une grande cité,* 262 pp. Paris, Presses Universitaires de France, 1952.

CLAYTON, H.; DRAKE, St. C. *Black metropolis.* London, 1946. XXIV + 809 pp.

CLEMENT, P.; XYDIAS, N. *Vienne sur le Rhône, la ville et ses habitants, situation et attitudes; sociologie d'une cité française.* Paris, A. Colin, 1955. 230 pp. (Cahiers de la Fondation Nationale des Sciences Politiques, no. 71.)

ECOCHARD, M. *Casablanca, le roman d'une ville.* Paris, Éditions de Paris, 1955. 143 pp.

FIRTH, R. *Two studies of kinship in London.* University of London, 1956.

GADOUREK, I. *A Dutch community: social and cultural structure and process in a bulb-growing region in the Netherlands.* Leiden, H. E. Stenfert Kroese, 1956. XVI + 555 pp. (Sassenheim, Netherlands.)

GERMANI, G. The social effects of urbanization in a worker's district in greater Buenos Aires. Chapter VIII in: Hauser, P. M. (ed.). *Urbanization in Latin America.* Paris, Unesco, 1962. 331 pp. (Technology and society.) Proceedings of a Conference on Urbanization Problems in Latin America, Santiago du Chili, 6-18 July 1959.

GLASS, R. *Newcomers: the West Indians in London.* London, Allen & Unwin, 1960. XII + 278 pp. (Centre for urban studies.)

—— et al. *The social background of a plan: a study of Middlesborough.* London, Routledge & Kegan Paul, 1948. XIV + 268 pp.

HOLLINGSHEAD, A. B. *Elmtown's youth, the impact of social classes on adolescents.* New York, J. Wiley & Son, 1949. 480 pp.

INSTITUT DE SOCIOLOGIE SOLVAY. *Études d'agglomérations: Mont Saint-Guilbert*. Bruxelles, 1955. 2 vols. Vol. I: *Géographie, histoire et démographie*, 145 pp; vol. II: *Le rôle social de la profession*, 422 pp.

JONES, D. C. *et al. The social survey of Merseyside*. 3 vols. Liverpool University Press, 1934. XII + 328 pp., XVI + 413 pp., XVIII + 560 pp.

LYND, R. S.; LYND, H. M. *Middletown*. New York, Harcourt, 1929. x + 550 pp.

——. *Middletown in transition: a study in cultural conflict*. New York, Harcourt, 1937. XVIII + 604 pp.

MERCIER, P. *L'agglomération dakaroise, quelques aspects sociologiques et démographiques*. Saint Louis du Sénégal, Institut Français d'Afrique Noire, 1954. 83 pp. (Études sénégalaises, no. 5.)

OESER, O. A.; HAMMOND, S. B. (eds.) *Social structure and personality in an Australian city*. London, Routledge & Kegan Paul, 1954. XIII + 344 pp.

ORLANS, H. *Stevenage, a sociological study of a new town*. London, Routledge & Kegan Paul, 1952. XV + 313 pp.

PARK, R. E.; BURGESS, E. W.; MACKENZIE, R. D. *The city*. Chicago, Ill., University of Chicago Press, 1925. XI + 239 pp.

PONS, V. G.; XYDIAS, N.; CLEMENT, P. Social effects of urbanization in Stanleyville, Belgian Congo: preliminary report of the field research team of the International African Institute. In: International African Institute, *Social implications of industrialization and urbanization in Africa south of the Sahara*, pp. 229-492. Paris, Unesco, 1956. 743 pp. (Tensions and technology).

——. The changing significance of ethnic affiliation and of Westernization in the African settlement patterns in Stanleyville (Belgian Congo). In: International African Institute. *Social implications of industrialization and urbanization in Africa south of the Sahara*, pp. 638-69, Paris. Unesco, 1956. 743 pp. (Tensions and technology.)

QUOIST, M. *La ville et l'homme. Rouen, étude sociologique d'un secteur prolétarien*. Paris, Les Éditions Ouvrières, 1952. 242 pp.

ROBLIN, M. *Les juifs de Paris. Démographie, économie, culture*. Paris, Picard, 1952. 199 pp.

ROWNTREE, B. S. *Poverty. A study of town life*. 2nd ed., rev. London, Macmillan, 1902. XXII + 452 pp.

——. *Poverty and progress. A second social survey of York*. 1st ed. London, Longmans Green, 1940. xx + 440 pp.

——; LAVERS. *Poverty and the welfare state. A third social survey of York*. London, Longmans Green, 1951. VII + 104 pp.

TARDITS, C. *Porto-Novo. Les nouvelles générations africaines entre leurs traditions et l'Occident*. Paris, La Haye, Mouton & Co., 1958. 128 pp.

THRASHER, F. M. *The gang, a study of 1313 gangs in Chicago*. Chicago, Ill., 1928.

WARNER, W. L. *et al. Yankee City*. New Haven, Conn., Yale University Press. Series of 6 vols. since 1941.

WEST, J. *Plainville, U.S.A.* New York, Colombia University Press, 1945. 238 pp.

WHYTE, W. F. *Street corner society: the social structure of an Italian slum*. 2nd ed. Chicago, Ill., University of Chicago Press, 1955. 366 pp.

ZORBAUGH, H. W. *The Gold Coast and the slum*. Chicago, Ill., University of Chicago Press. XV + 287 pp.

Techniques

BETTELHEIM, C. *Comment se mène une enquête sociologique, préparation d'une enquête sur la ville d'Auxerre*. Paris, Conférence du Centre d'Études Sociologiques, Centre de Documentation Universitaire, 1949.

CHOMBART DE LAUWE, P. H. Le rôle de l'observation en sociologie. *Revue de l'Institut de Sociologie*. Bruxelles, Institut de Sociologie Solvay, Université Libre de Bruxelles, 1960. No. 1, pp. 27-43.

—— et al. *Paris et l'agglomération parisienne*. Vol. II: *Méthodes de recherches pour l'étude d'une grande cité*. Paris, Presses Universitaires de France, 1952. 107 pp.

DAVIE, M. R. The fields and problems of urban sociology. In: Bernard, L. L. (ed.). *The fields and methods of sociology*. New York, Ray Long & Richard Smith, 1934.

DUVERGER, M. *Méthodes des sciences sociales*. Paris, Presses Universitaires de France, 1961. VII + 501 pp.

FESTINGER, L.; KATZ, D. (eds.). *Research methods in the behavioral sciences*. New York, The Dryden Press, 1953. XI + 660 pp. (French translation: Paris, Presses Universitaires de France, 1959. 2 vols.)

GEORGE, P.; AGULHON, M.; LAVANDEYRA, L. A.; ELHAI, H. D.; SCHAEFFER, R. *Études sur la banlieue de Paris—essais méthodologiques*. Paris, A. Colin, 1950. 183 pp.

GIBBS, J. P. *Handbook of urban research methods*. Princeton, N.J., D. Van Nostrand Co., 1961.

GRANAI, G. Techniques de l'enquête sociologique. In: Gurvitch, G. (ed.). *Traité de sociologie*, vol. I, pp. 135-51. Paris, Presses Universitaires de France, 1958.

HAUSER, P. M.; DUNCAN, O. D.; DUNCAN, B. D. *Methods of urban analysis: a summary report*. San Antonio, Tex., Air Force Personnel and Training Research Center, January 1956. IX + 178 pp.

MADGE, J. *The tools of social science*. London, Longmans Green, 1953. X + 308 pp.

MAGET, M. *Guide d'étude directe des comportements culturels*. Paris, Civilisations du Sud, 1953. XXXVI + 260 pp.

STEWARD, J. H. *Area research: theory and practice*. New York, Social Science Research Council, 1950. 164 pp.

YOUNG, Pauline. *Scientific social surveys and research*. 2nd ed. New York, Prentice-Hall, 1950. XXVIII + 621 pp.

CASE STUDIES

ALLPORT, G. W. *The use of personal documents in psychological science*. New York, Social Science Research Council, 1942. XIX + 210 pp.

BLUMER, H. *An appraisal of Thomas and Znaniecki's 'The Polish peasant in Europe and America'*. New York, Social Science Research Council, 1939. XVIII + 210 pp. (Critiques of research in the social sciences, I.)

BURGESS, E. W. The family and the person. *Publications of the American Sociological Society. Papers and proceedings*. Chicago, Ill., Vol. XXII, no. 133, 1928.

CHOMBART DE LAUWE, P. H. Le milieu social et l'étude sociologique des cas individuels. *Informations sociales*, February 1959, no. 2, pp. 41-54.

DAMPIERRE, E. DE. Le sociologue et l'analyse des documents personnels. *Annales*, July-September 1957, no. 3, pp. 442-54.

DOLLARD, J. *Criteria for the life history.* 2nd ed. New York, Smith, 1949. 1st ed., 1935.

GOTTSCHALK, L.; KLUCKHOHN, C.; ANGELL, R. *The use of personal documents in history, anthropology and sociology.* New York, Social Science Research Council, 1945. XIV + 243 pp.

KOMAROVSKY, M. *The unemployed man and his family.* New York, 1940.

LYND, R. S.; LYND, H. M. *Middletown.* New York, Harcourt, 1929. x + 550 pp.

——. *Middletown in transition: a study in cultural conflict.* New York, Harcourt, 1937. XVIII + 604 pp.

MEMMI, A. *Portrait d'un Juif. L'impasse.* Paris, Gallimard, 1962. 309 pp.

SHAW, C. R. Case study method. *Publications of the American Sociological Society. Papers and proceedings.* Chicago, Ill., 1927. Vol. XXI, no. 149.

STOETZEL, J. *Without the chrysanthemum and the sword. A study of the attitudes of youth in post-war Japan.* Paris, Unesco, 1953. 334 pp.

STOUFFER, S. A. An experimental comparison of statistical and case history methods of attitude research. 1930. Ph.D. thesis, University of Chicago.

THOMAS, W. I.; ZNANIECKI, F. *The Polish peasant in Europe and America.* 3 vols. New York, 1918-20.

WARNER, W. L. et al. *Yankee City.* New Haven, Conn., Yale University Press. Series of 6 vols. since 1941.

EXPERIMENTAL OBSERVATION

CHAPIN, F. S. *Experimental designs in sociological research.* Rev. ed. New York, Harper & Brothers, 1955. XII + 297 pp.

CHOMBART DE LAUWE, P. H. L'observation expérimentale en sociologie. *Bulletin de la Société de Statistique de Paris.* Paris, 1963.

——; JENNY, J.; COUVREUR, L.; LABAT, P. et al. *Famille et habitation.* Vol. II: *Un essai d'observation expérimentale.* Part 1. Paris, CNRS, 1960. 364 pp. (Travaux du Groupe d'Ethnologie Sociale.)

COCHRAN, W. G.; COX, G. M. *Experimental designs.* New York, 1950.

GREENWOOD, E. *Experimental sociology, a study in method.* New York, King's Crown, 1945.

LEWIN, K. *Field theory in social science.* London, Tavistock Publ., 1952.

4   Other social research approaches

Judah Matras

In this chapter additional social science approaches to the study of urban areas are surveyed. The six points of view examined briefly are separate but not unrelated to each other. The kinds of investigations considered in the present chapter include historical studies, economic studies, geographic studies, ecological studies, content analysis and experimental studies.

Historical studies

Historical studies of urban areas may be said to have three kinds of objectives. In the first place, the historical study attempts to describe—or reconstruct, if necessary—the evolvement of the urban area studied. Such description includes characterizations of the urban area at various points in time and analysis of the nature, directions and magnitudes of the changes occurring in the various facets of the area's physiographic and socio-economic structure.

Secondly, the historical study endeavours to identify and describe the events, personages, trends and movements playing key roles in the development of the urban area. Such identification and description may take the form of biographies, descriptions of important incidents, or analysis of religious, political, social or technological movements. Probably the great bulk of 'historical writing' is concerned with such tasks of identification and description of events, personalities and movements playing key roles in a country's or an area's development.

Finally, the historical study tries to specify the manner in which the events, personages and movements identified bore upon and influenced the course of the development of the country or urban area investigated. Often such analyses may be carried out on a comparative basis, e.g., comparisons of situations similar except for involvement of a given personage, event or movement; but more often such analyses are carried out by attempting to show causal relationships directly.

Almost any item or object may at some time serve as a datum in historical investigations, but the most common data of historical studies are documents and verbal, graphic or symbolic records. Descriptions and accounts, letters and memoirs, statistical records and records of transactions, photographs and maps are the materials with which historical investigations are carried out. More recently, and especially with the advent of relatively inexpensive and easily learned and accessible machines and techniques for sound and voice recording, interviews and verbal accounts, descriptions and recollections have increasingly entered the realm of historical data. Accordingly, although historical data are found primarily in libraries and archives, often interviews may be collected by the investigator directly from participants in or observers of events and movements being recorded and analysed.

Criticism of historical data is concerned chiefly with evaluation of the accuracy of the data. Two approaches, generally independent of each other, are typically employed in such evaluation. Evidence concerning the veracity and authority of the sources is usually considered to have bearing upon the accuracy of the data. For example, an account given by a convicted embezzler of the growth of, say, the financial activities of the victimized business might be considered of doubtful veracity. The second approach involves evaluation of the consistency of accounts and reports emanating from separate sources.

The writing of history demands, aside from the literary abilities which are desirable in all other fields as well, the ability to sort and evaluate the relative interest, importance and relevance of the many types and items of data. Moreover it demands the ability and readiness to interpret data and employ them to reconstruct sequences of events and, often, to come to conclusions about causal relationships. Historical studies sometimes take into account the problems and theories, and exploit the more specialized data and techniques, of the social sciences. Indeed political, social and economic processes are often the very subjects of historical investigations, and the theoretical and methodological tools of the social sciences as well as the substantive findings of these disciplines may be embodied in the writing of history.

Economic studies

Economic studies of urban areas have as objectives the description of the economic activities carried out in the area, identification of the main demographic and social agents and institutions of economic activities and analysis of their relationship to the area's economy, and analysis of the relationship of the economic activities carried out in the urban area in relation to the larger economic unit of which it is a part—the region or the nation. The factors which may be included in description and analysis of economic activities include land and other resources and income-producing wealth, total and *per capita* gross and net product, labour force participation, volume and structure of employment, distribution of income, and volume and structure of consumption, savings and investment.

In the past the various 'schools' of economic theory and analysis have focused upon one or more combination of the above factors, the rest of the factors being considered within a frame of reference oriented to the chosen one or combination of approaches. More recently economics has dealt with models of 'national economies', including analyses of interrelationships between employment, production, consumption and investment alike, particular interest being attached to questions of 'levels' of *per capita* production and consumption and the manner in which such levels change or may be changed.

Typically, the economic activities carried out in an urban area do not comprise an exact smaller-scaled reproduction of the national economy but, rather, urban areas tend to have certain specialized economic activities, to 'export' certain goods and services to places outside the area and to 'import' other goods and services not locally produced in sufficient quantity for the population's needs. The goods and services produced in an urban area exceeding the needs or consumption of that area's population and 'exported' to other areas comprise that urban area's 'economic base'. In economic studies of urban areas, particular attention is paid to the economic base in all its aspects. For example, some cities are manufacturing centres and sell large amounts of manufactured goods outside the city; others are seaports or transportation centres and typically sell administrative, warehousing and storage, and transfer services to agencies using the waterway or other transport services; other cities may be financial centres selling credit and brokerage services to businesses outside the city, etc. In each case, the goods or services produced in excess of the city's own needs and marketed outside the city comprise part or all of that city's economic base, and the employment, investment, trade, etc., associated with the economic base are often of particular significance.

Data used in economic studies include those concerning each of the types of economic activity and may be of the form periodically reported to and published by public or private data-collection bodies or agencies or of the form collected specifically for a given investigation. For example, in many countries data on employment and unemployment, hours of work, wages and production in a given industry or group of industries may be reported regularly to some governmental statistical agency; on the other hand, data on consumption, family expenditures or family budgets would ordinarily be collected by means of a specially-organized survey rather than on any regular or periodic bases. Not only do national and local government agencies often collect and publish data on production, employment, consumption and investment, but often individual enterprises, groups of industries in some sector, labour unions and organizations, private business service companies, and other non-governmental agencies may collect, retain and sometimes even publish data covering their own and related economic activities.

The types of problems to which economic studies in urban areas are addressed include specification, description and analysis of the economic base, analysis of production of goods and services as related to population and resources of the area, description and analysis of the labour force, employment, income and consumption in the urban area, and analysis of the relationship of the urban area's economy with the broader regional, national or international economies. The first of these, specification and analysis of the economic base, involves measurement of volume of production in the various sectors, of volume of trade, and of value of services on a *per capita* basis and comparing *per capita* production in the various sectors to that of the country as a whole. Those sectors substantially above average in *per capita* volume of production are ordinarily said to comprise the area's economic base. Typically, the proportion of the labour force employed in the sectors comprising the economic base is correspondingly above average relative to the national economy. Usually special interest is focused upon production, employment and productivity of industries in the economic base due to their importance in determining the competitive position of an urban area and the economic health of supporting sectors as well.

Analysis of the labour force ordinarily includes study of differential rates of labour force participation, study of the size and composition of the labour force by age and sex, analysis of the educational levels and occupational distributions of the labour force, analysis of employment, total unemployment and differential unemployment, and analysis of personal or *per capita* income in the different occupation groups. Analysis of consumption usually includes analysis of family expenditures and the structure of consumption of the various income groups, consumption being classified by

type of goods or services and families being classified by structural characteristics as well as by income.

Production, employment, consumption and savings and investment in
the urban area being studied is often compared with that of the entire country or of other urban areas. Similarly, the urban area is often divided into
sub-areas, and the economic relationships between the parts are studied.

Geographic studies

The purpose of geographic studies of urban areas is the description of
physical characteristics and of the spatial relationships obtaining in the
urban area and its surroundings and the analysis of the distribution of
population and of social and economic activities with reference to these
physical characteristics. Geographic investigation of the urban area begins
with accurate description of its area, shape, topographical, geological and
climatic characteristics, and proceeds with classification of sub-areas and
analysis of geographic differentiation in the area in question. The geographic
investigation continues by studying the distribution of the population and
of cultural attributes of the area in relation to the physical, i.e., topographical, geological and climatic, variation characterizing the area.

The data of geographic studies consist primarily of measurements on
earth materials, soils, water, vegetation, land forms and meteorological
phenomena and processes, and the techniques of analysis include carto-
graphy and, more recently, mathematical and statistical representation and
analysis. Data and methods are employed both in description of physical
characteristics and spatial relationships obtaining at any given moment and
in discovery and analysis of physiographic changes.

A central problem of geographic studies of urban areas is that of location
of the urban place itself with reference to the region, and of location of
economic activities and land-use patterns within the urban area. The effect
of access to transportation routes and to resources upon the relative growth
and development of cities within a region or country on the one hand, and
the relationship of spatial distribution of population, activities and institutions to routes of transportation and access to facilities within cities on the
other hand are considered in such studies. In the latter type of investigation
the central business district is typically taken as the focal point of the city's
or urban area's activities, and patterns of growth, land use and extension
of the local transportation network are seen as emanating from the central
business district. Study of the relationship between characteristics of the

location and urban area services and functions is also a central problem. For example, the relationship between topography and water sources on the one hand and types of sanitary and water services on the other hand may be plotted for a given urban area or for the several urban areas of a region or country.

Ecological studies

Ecological studies of urban areas describe and analyse the relationships between population, environment, technology and organization which obtain in the area. Usually, though not always, the variations in social, economic, geographic or 'ecological' organization of the urban area and its population are the direct objects of study and the organization of the urban area is seen as affected and influenced by the other three factors: environment, population and technology. However, ecological studies may also investigate the influence of environment, organization and technology upon patterns of population composition and growth, i.e., focus upon population patterns as the direct objective of the investigation. There have also been recent beginnings of attempts to study the development of technology as affected by environment, population and social and ecological organization, and doubtless such studies will increase in number and interest in the near future.

Ecological studies view the patterns of spatial distribution of population, economic activities and social institutions in the urban area as an important facet of ecological organization in and of itself; and, moreover, patterns of spatial distribution in an urban area are seen as indicators of social and economic organization and relationships obtaining in the area. Thus the growth, development and settlement patterns of urban areas, the concentration and segregation of population groups and of sectors of the area's economy, the location of services and of institutions within the area, the daily movements of population, the structure and spatial distribution of residence and of employment of the labour force, and patterns of succession and population mobility within the area are all examined not only because of their own inherent interest and importance for description and analysis of the physical or material characteristics of the urban area but, also, as reflecting the social and economic organization of the area and its population.

The unit of analysis in ecological studies is the population aggregate in a specified area, and a basic assumption of such investigations is that a population aggregate defined by specified areal bounds has some unit character and attributes, that the aggregate has some properties different from those of individuals in the population. A population lives in an environment and its very survival and mode of existence are determined by the manner in which it adjusts to or exploits the environment. Human populations can, in exploiting or adjusting to their environments, draw upon the experiences of previous human populations, i.e., upon 'culture'. In particular, human populations have technology, sets of techniques employed to gain sustenance and to facilitate the organization of sustenance-producing activity. Moreover, the collective life of human populations tends to be organized in distinctive manners, not independent of the environment and technologies, but rather must be adapted to the population's environment, the technologies available to it, and to the very size and composition of the population itself.

The key concepts employed in ecological studies are concerned with population size, composition and distributions, as related to areal units, physiographic features and time, and include those of concentration and segregation, density, density gradients, access to population or population potential, and concepts of population movements, including natural increase, migration, succession and assimilation. The data of ecological studies consist of population data, data on economic activities, data on urban or areal environment and plant, and data on technologies all having reference, in so far as possible, to primary analytical units. Techniques employed are usually of the form of plotting, analysing and comparing composition and distributions of populations and population sub-groups with respect to different classes and categories of areas, using both numerical representations (e.g., proportions and indexes) of distributions and graphic representations (e.g., graphs and maps) of distributions. For example, residential distributions of ethnic, religious, racial or socio-economic groups which have been studied in ecological investigation typically reflect marked concentration and segregation patterns, but different degrees of concentration and segregation characteristic of the different population groups. Similarly, comparison of distributions by residence and by place of employment of different occupation groups has shown dissimilar patterns of daily travel to work associated with the different occupation groups.

Ecological studies begin with the observation of a population of some given size located or settled in an area of given size and characteristics. The manner in which the population 'adapts' to the environment is related to the social and economic differentiation of the population, the division of labour and technology obtaining and the corresponding division of space in the area and land use differentiation. Classifications of environments, of populations and of adaptative arrangements, and description and analysis of their interrelationships is one major type of problem considered by ecological studies. A second type of problem involves consideration of the dynamic aspects of the same interrelationships: in the absence of institutional or biological barriers, populations grow or increase in size, density increases and the adaptative arrangements are upset. Alternatively, populations can grow or decline or change in composition due to migration, upsetting the previous balance of population and resources. Ecological studies investigate the range and variability of social and economic arrangements made by the human population both to cope with the problems posed by changing size and composition of the population and to try to control its own size and composition.

More specifically ecological studies may focus upon the relationship between patterns of housing, daily and long-term population movements, use of public and private facilities and services, and land-use patterns in relation to compositional characteristics of the population. In addition such studies may seek to classify cities and towns in terms of environmental characteristics, economic base or characteristic technologies, and examine the relationships between these factors, population composition and spatial distributions of population and activities.

Content analysis

Content analysis studies in urban areas may be employed to describe and analyse virtually any type of phenomenon which receives verbal expression in communications and mass media, in publications of books or periodicals, in speeches, church sermons, court records, etc. Content analysis has been defined as 'a research technique for the objective, systematic and quantitative description of the manifest content of communications'. In this definition the term 'systematic' implies that such a study employs an exhaustive set of categories and covers all the material of the body of communications being studied, rather than simply abstracting material supporting a given hypothesis or point of view. The term 'manifest content' implies that such studies are to have reference to that part or aspect of a communication which is similarly understood by the initiator of the communication, by the receiver of the communication and by the investigator, and not to 'latent content', i.e., to 'hidden intentions' of the initiator or to unanticipated reactions of the receiver of the communication.

The broadcasting services, newspapers and periodicals published in an urban area are themselves a subject for investigation in the framework of social research in urban areas. Accordingly the nature and the distribution by types and categories of the materials and communications emanating from these media are of importance both in characterizing the media themselves and as indicative of the categories of information and opinion available to the population through these media. Comparative studies of urban and rural media, of variations among the different types of media within the urban setting, in the same type of media among different types of urban mileux or at different points in time, can be carried out using content analysis.

In so far as the media represent attitudes more or less widely held by the public, or in so far as different segments of the media represent viewpoints and interests held by different segments of the population, changes in outlooks and attitudes over time may be plotted by content analysis of the respective media. Similarly, sermons, speeches, etc., may reflect interest and opinion both of the speakers and of their audiences. For example, comparison of speeches delivered before chambers of commerce and businessmen's associations with those delivered before labour unions would probably reflect differences both in style and in content.

The primary use of content analysis is to describe, as objectively as possible and using some standardized system of classification, the content of communications. Such description of content focuses on two aspects: substance and form. Analysis of the form of the communications content examines the symbols employed in communications, while analysis of the substance of the communications examines the referents of the symbols. Analysis of substance has been used to study trends in communication content, to trace the development of scholarship, to reveal international differences in communication content, to compare media or 'levels' of communication, to audit communication content against objectives, to construct and apply communications standards and to aid in technical research operations. Analyses of the form of communication content has been utilized to expose propaganda techniques, to measure 'readability' of communication materials and to discover stylistic features of communications.

A type of content analysis distinct and somewhat different from that defined above is sometimes called 'qualitative' content analysis, whereas that considered above thus far may be denoted 'quantitative' content analysis. Qualitative content analysis departs from the definition above in that it is less often consciously quantitative in so far as it depends much less upon comparison of frequencies of appearance of communications of different categories. Often qualitative content analysis is based upon the question of presence or absence of some particular content, rather than upon relative frequencies of the different categories of content. Qualitative content analysis is less concerned with manifest content than with latent content, using manifest content to infer the intentions of the communicator or the effects upon the audience. Finally, qualitative content analysis is less concerned with establishing the relationship between the specific materials analysed and some wider universe of communications, i.e., quality content analysis is usually not concerned about problems of sampling. By contrast, quantitative content analysis seeks to base its conclusions upon analysis of relative frequencies of communications exhibiting the various categories of content; quantitative content analysis deals with manifest, rather than with latent, content, and quantitative content analysis seeks to relate the particular communications materials studied to a larger population of communications materials.

The major units of analysis in content analysis are words, themes, characters, items and space-and-time measures. The smallest unit is, of course, the word and it is sometimes called 'symbol' or 'unit symbol' or 'term' in the technical literature. Typically words or terms with contrasting or dissimilar meanings or implications in a given area of interest (e.g., in politics, in history or in literature) are chosen and the relative frequency of their appearance in different types of communications is measured. Similarly, the relative frequency of themes may be measured in different types of communications materials. In the case of themes it is not, of course, possible simply to count themes appearing, but rather it is necessary to interpret phrases, sentences, paragraphs or chapters in order to ascertain whether or not one of the themes relevant to a study does in fact appear and in order to assign a theme its appropriate category. On the other hand, when characters are the units of analysis, it is necessary to ascertain the attributes of the characters surveyed in order to assign them to their respective categories. Thus content analyses using words, themes or characters as units of analysis would typically set up classification systems, and proceed to survey the materials at hand for the purpose of ascertaining the relative frequencies of appearance of the respective categories of units.

The item is the unit most frequently employed in content analysis, and item here refers to the entire 'natural' unit used by the initiators of the communications or producers of the symbol material. Analysis by entire items, e.g., books, articles, speeches, letters, programmes, editorial, etc., as the case may be in the various media, may be employed when the variations within each item are small or relatively unimportant. The entire item is classified, usually according to subject matter, and the item as unit of analysis is especially convenient in analysing trends in time, e.g., trends in distribution by subject matter of newspaper articles, books published, motion pictures, painting and other works of art, etc.

The last type of unit, the space-and-time measures, is employed when it is most convenient to measure frequency of appearance of categories of subject matter in physical terms. Thus, instead of recording the number of items, a content analysis may be carried out in terms of number of pages, lines, column inches, footage or minutes of motion-picture film, etc., devoted to each of the respective subject-matter categories. Obviously the various units of analysis are not independent, and in many instances a given unit may readily be expressed in terms of some alternative unit.

The use and interpretation of content analysis studies depends primarily upon the system of categories devised and upon the extent to which a meaningful set of categories may be formulated in terms of the problem being studied. Two types of categories, the 'what is said' type and the 'how it is said' type of categories, may be distinguished; and these correspond to the distinctions made earlier between content studies focusing upon substance as distinguished from those focusing upon form. 'What is said' categories may be devised to describe the nature of the subject matter, its direction or orientation, the standards or grounds upon which classifications by orientation are made, the values or goals expressed, methods or means of action represented, the traits described, the actors, persons or groups appearing in central positions, the authority or source in whose name the statements are made, origin of the communications, or targets or addresses, or persons or groups to whom the communications are directed. 'How it is said' categories may describe the form or type of communication, the form of statement, the intensity of the communication and the devices employed in communicating.

The essential point is that the categories of substance or form of communications content be derived, in so far as is possible, from the nature of the problem being investigated. When this is the case, interpretation of the distribution of communications content by categories bears directly upon the problem studied. For example, in a study of the attention given by local newspapers to problems of education, the problem may be formulated in terms of change over time in total 'volume' of interest as measured by space, number of articles, etc., or in distribution of articles devoted to separate types of problems, e.g., problems of instruction, staffing, plant and facilities, etc., or in distribution of articles or items by nature of relationship of 'education' to other aspects of the community, e.g., parents and parent-teacher groups, city administration, national administration, business groups, institutions of higher learning, etc. For each instance, entirely different sets of content categories would be devised; but in each case, interpretation of the results of the analysis in terms of the initial problem would follow from the fact that categories are derived from the problem itself.

Experimental studies

Experimental studies in urban areas are addressed to the direct study of causal relationships between variables. The discovery and description of causal relationships obtaining between variables is of central importance in social research no less than in any other scientific research. However, the nature and complexity of the subject matter of social research ordinarily renders the inferences about causal relationships between variables extremely problematic even though variables may be designated 'dependent' and 'independent' as a matter of convenience or to reflect logical or temporal relationships between variables (e.g., in studying correlations between marriage rates and birth rates, marriage rates would ordinarily be denoted the independent and birth rates the dependent variables respectively).

The distinctive feature of the experiment is that it involves manipulation by the investigator of the independent variable and direct observation of the effects of such manipulation upon the dependent variable, i.e., measurements upon the dependent variable are taken before and after manipulation of the independent variable hypothesized to be a causal factor in the former's variations. Conventionally 'before' and 'after' measurements are also taken upon the dependent variable without manipulation of the independent variable (the 'control' instance).

Actually the conventional procedure of an experiment calls for two pairs of measurements upon a dependent variable: 'before' and 'after' measurements in the experimental instance, and 'before' and 'after' measurements in a control instance. In the experimental instance, the investigator manipulates the independent variable after the 'before' measurement is taken; and in the control instance there is no manipulation of the independent variable. This is done in order to ascertain whether the difference in 'before' and 'after' measurements in the first instance (the experimental instance) is in fact due to the manipulation of the independent variable and not simply to passage of time or to carrying out of the two separate measurements. The difference between the 'after' measurements in the experimental and control instances is, then, attributed to the effect of the investigator's manipulation of the independent variable.

Since in social research both dependent and independent variables are human beings, social relations between human beings or conditions affecting human beings, it is ordinarily not feasible to carry out studies under experimental conditions. However, many situations are adapted to experimental studies, and careful research designs permitting use of the experimental method in social research have recently been employed in increasing numbers of social investigations.

Two kinds of experiments in social research may be broadly distinguished, the laboratory experiment and the field experiment. In the laboratory experiment, the investigator is able to control the conditions under which the experiment is carried out; he may manipulate the independent variable and make measurements upon the dependent variable in a situation in which he chooses the subjects, sets up standardized time and procedural conditions, etc. In the field experiment the investigator ordinarily has little or no control over the conditions of the experiment, but he can choose which subjects will comprise the experimental and which the control instances or groups, he may manipulate the independent variable, and may take measurements on the dependent variable. An example of a laboratory experiment in social research might be the study of the effect upon the speed or efficiency of a group's problem-solving of imposing some given seating or communications arrangement upon the group. Two groups would be chosen and, under controlled conditions, the speed or efficiency of solving some problem requiring group co-operation would be measured, both groups being seated in the same manner and both groups having the same communications arrangements. One group would then be chosen and re-seated in some predetermined manner, or its communications arrangements would be altered in some predetermined manner, and this group would constitute the experimental group. Speed or efficiency of problem-solving in both groups, the manipulated and altered (experimental) group and the unaltered (control) group would be measured again to ascertain the effect of the change in seating or in communications arrangements.

An example of a field experiment might be the introduction of a new teaching method in some, but not all, of the classes of a given grade. In this situation the investigator must work with the pupils who happen to be in the grade in question, and he must work within a school situation over which, by and large, he has little or no control. The procedure would be to measure the distributions or averages of, say, reading scores characterizing the different classes, i.e., take 'before' measurements on all the classes of a given grade. In some classes the new teaching method would be introduced, while others would continue with the old methods. At the end of a given period, measurements would again be taken in all classes (i.e., 'after' measurements on both the experimental and control classes) and the extent of changes in reading scores in the experimental and control classes respectively would be compared to assess the effectiveness of the new teaching method.

Field experiments of the latter types have a very large range of possible uses in social research in urban areas. They may be useful in planning and decision-making in housing, traffic, public administration, school, urban renewal and other programmes. Teaching methods, methods of combating delinquency, of traffic control, etc., may be tested and evaluated by use of field experiments. Causes of waste in administration, drop-outs from school, absenteeism from employment, deterioration of housing and other problems of urban areas may be investigated by broad and far-reaching studies employing experimental methods.

Interrelations of social research methods

As indicated at the beginning of the chapter, the approaches and points of view surveyed in the chapter are not unrelated to one another. It seems clear that all approaches to social research in urban areas, regardless of the specific discipline to which they are oriented, might fruitfully employ the techniques of content analysis or might employ experimental designs. That historical studies draw upon the other disciplines both in the very statement of problems and in use of tools and techniques has already been noted. But conversely, studies oriented to or originating with the other disciplines, economics, geography or human ecology, also draw upon historical methods as well as mutually drawing upon one another both in formulating problems and hypotheses and in borrowing and adapting research techniques.

Bibliography

BERELSON, B. *Content analysis communication research.* Glencoe, Ill., The Free Press, 1952.

BOGUE, D. J. *The structure of the metropolitan community.* Ann Arbor, Mich., H. H. Rackham School of Graduate Studies, University of Michigan, 1949.

CHOMBART DE LAUWE, P. H. *et al. Paris et l'agglomération parisienne.* Paris, Presses Universitaires de France, 1952.

DUNCAN, O. D. *et al. Metropolis and region.* Baltimore, Md., Johns Hopkins Press, 1960.

DUVERGER, M. *Méthodes des sciences sociales.* Paris, Presses Universitaires de France, 1961.

FESTINGER, L.; KATZ, D. *Research methods in the behavioral sciences.* New York, Dryden Press, 1953.

GEORGE, P. *Précis de géographie urbaine.* Paris, Presses Universitaires de France, 1961.

GIBBS, Jack P. *Urban research methods.* Princeton, N.J., Toronto, London and New York, D. Van Nostrand Co., 1961.

GOLDHAMMER, H.; MARSHALL, A. *Psychosis and civilization*. Glencoe, Ill., The Free Press, 1949.

GOODE, W. J.; HATT, P. K. *Methods in social research*. New York, McGraw-Hill, 1952.

HANDLIN, O.; BURCHARD, J. *The historian and the city*. Cambridge, Mass., MIT Press and Harvard University Press, 1963.

HANSEN, M. H.; HURWITZ, W. N.; MADOW, W. G. *Sample survey methods and theory*. 2 vols. New York, J. Wiley & Sons, 1953.

HAWLEY, Amos H. *Human ecology*. New York, Ronald Press, 1950.

HOOVER, E. M.; VERNON, R. *Anatomy of a metropolis*. Cambridge, Mass., Harvard University Press, 1959.

HYMAN, H. H. *Survey design and analysis*. Glencoe, Ill., The Free Press, 1955.

INTERNATIONAL LABOUR OFFICE. *Méthodes d'enquête sur des conditions de vie des familles*. Geneva, 1949.

ISARD, W. *Methods of regional analysis*. New York, J. Wiley & Sons, 1960.

JAHODA, M.; DEUTSCH, M.; COOK, S. W. *Research methods in social relations*. 2 vols. New York, Dryden Press, 1951.

LAZARSFELD, P. F.; ROSENBERG, M. (eds.). *The language of social research*. Glencoe, Ill., The Free Press, 1955.

PERLOFF, H. S. *et al. Regions, resources, and economic growth*. Baltimore, Md., Johns Hopkins Press, 1960.

STOUFFER, S. A. *Social research to test ideas*. New York, Free Press of Glencoe, 1962.

—— *et al. The American soldier*. Vol. IV: *Measurement and prediction*. Princeton, N.J., Princeton University Press, 1950.

UNESCO. *Regional seminar on techniques of social research*. Calcutta, 1959.

WARREN, R. L. *Community.* New York, Russell Sage Foundation, 1955.

YOUNG, P. V. *Scientific social surveys and research*. 3rd ed. Englewood Cliffs, N.J., Prentice-Hall, 1956.

Part II   Types of studies

5 Comprehensive urban studies

Philip M. Hauser

The explosive increase in world population and the concentration of population in urban areas are among the most dramatic developments of the modern era. Since 1650, world population has increased sixfold; and within the last century and a half, urban population has increased more than tenfold. World population estimated at about 500 million at the mid-seventeenth century exceeded 3,000 million in 1964. Population living in places of 5,000 or more inhabitants, approximately 3 per cent in 1800, had reached 30 per cent by 1960.

The increase in urban population has been accelerating for the world as a whole for as long as it is possible to trace urban growth, i.e. since 1800. For example, population in cities of 100,000 or more increased by 76 per cent between 1800 and 1850, by 220 per cent between 1850 and 1900, and by 255 per cent between 1900 and 1950. During the nineteenth century most of the impetus to world urbanization was provided by the growth of city populations in the economically-advanced areas—Europe and North America. During the twentieth century, however, the increase in the urban population of the developing areas—Asia, Latin America and Africa—has been the main factor in the increasing rate of world urbanization. That is, the growth of urban populations in Asia, Latin America and Africa is now proceeding at a more rapid rate than in Europe or North America because the latter areas are already so highly urbanized. As of 1950, the degree of urbanization in the major areas as measured by the proportion of the total population living in places of 20,000 or more was as follows: world 21, Oceania 47, North America 42, Europe (excluding U.S.S.R.) 35, U.S.S.R. 31, South America 26, Middle America 21, Asia 13, Africa 9 per cent.

In the economically-advanced nations, rapid urbanization was both a consequence and cause of rapid industrialization and economic development. It was associated with increased division of labour, specialization, technological advance and great increases in productivity. In the developing nations in the post-war world, rapid urbanization is by no means the result of the same factors. Although urbanization in these areas does undoubtedly to some extent result from, and contribute to, increased productivity, it represents more the transfer of under-employment and poverty from the overpopulated rural countryside to the urban setting. The rapid growth of cities in the Far East, for example, according to the conclusions of the United Nations/Unesco seminar held in Bangkok in 1956 was attributed to the following types of factors:

1. The low land population ratio arising from rapid population growth in relation to agricultural resources. People left rural areas, in brief, because there was no way, in the existing social, land tenure and technological conditions of procuring a livelihood on already over-populated land, or by technically obsolescent handicrafts.
2. The disruption and disorganization produced by the last war, and the political changes which followed. Many of the cities of Asia are choked with refugees who have swelled urban population out of proportion to their economic development.
3. The lure of urban existence to which large parts of the peasant population were exposed as the result of military service as well as migratory refugee flows.
4. The actual exhaustion of natural resources in some areas which deprived some localities of their economic base.
5. Seasonality of employment in agriculture which creates migratory flows bringing many people in contact with the attractions of city life.

Rapid urbanization in the developing areas is, therefore, usually accompanied by severe physical, social, economic and governmental problems. Efforts to deal with these problems by means of physical, economic or social planning require research to lay a sound foundation of knowledge as a basis for policy formation and programme administration. Such research may be considered in three categories: general studies of urbanization, comprehensive studies of individual cities, and studies of various categories of urban problems.

General studies

The purpose of general studies of urbanization is to provide a broad understanding of the factors associated with the emergence and evolution of cities on the one hand and the consequences of urbanization on the other—economic, physical, social and political. Such general studies have the great value of providing a framework for the design and conduct of studies of individual urban places or specific urban problems, and they provide a background against which such studies may be compared and evaluated. The general studies of urbanization already in the literature should be consulted and used as models for studies for a given nation, region or locale.

For a general historical overview of the rise of cities and urban culture, writers such as Ralph Turner, V. Gordon Childe and Lewis Mumford should be consulted (see bibliography). They summarize what is known about the origin of cities and provide historical overviews of urban development, with some consideration of the social, economic and political implications of urbanization. Especially useful in providing broad perspectives for general urban studies is the volume *The Pre-Industrial City— Past and Present*, by Gideon Sjoberg. This book contains a summary of what is known about the origin of cities and an analysis of the characteristics of pre-industrial cities. A few hours devoted to one or more of these general studies would provide valuable perspectives with which to approach the study of almost any aspect of the city.

Broad perspectives of another type may be gained by consulting the proceedings of the joint United Nations and Unesco seminars on urbanization in Asia and the Far East and in Latin America, respectively (see bibliography). The chapter titles in the published proceedings of these seminars point to the types of topics to be covered in urban studies and highlight the problems requiring attention and remediation. For example, the subjects covered in the seminar reports include: consideration of urbanization in relation to economic development and social change, the demographic aspects of urbanization, economic development policy in relation to urbanization, problems of manpower and productivity, the effects of urbanization on family life, urbanization and crime and delinquency, changes in the traditional arts and crafts, forms of cultural enjoyment, policies of town- and country-planning, the creation of employment opportunities, migration and urbanization, the social consequences of urbanization, the effect of urbanization on a working-class sector, aspects of adjustment of rural migrants to urban industrial conditions, psychological and mental health problems of urbanization, and the policy implications of urbanization.

Other useful general works include *India's Urban Future*, edited by Roy Turner, and *Industrialization and Society*, edited by Bert F. Hoselitz and Wilbert E. Moore. The former considers demographic, sociological, economic and political aspects of urbanization in India and is oriented to planning and action programmes. The latter volume, the outgrowth of a conference sponsored jointly by Unesco, the United States and Canadian

National Commissions for Unesco and the University of Chicago focuses on industrialization and its impact on society. By reason of the close relationship between industrialization and urbanization, however, it also provides a good list of subjects for general studies on urbanization. Also noteworthy in this volume are the four appendixes concerned with various aspects of social research and the utilization of research findings.

Examples of intensive studies of specific regions or nations may be found in *Social Implications of Industrialization and Urbanization in Africa South of the Sahara*, also published by Unesco. In this volume, summaries are presented of surveys or other studies in Africa. The volume provides a choice of approaches and prototypes for determining study objectives and designs. The volume also contains a valuable bibliography, questionnaires and other protocols for the conduct of research.

Useful prototype studies may also be found in *The Social Implications of Industrialization and Urbanization*, also published by Unesco. Although these studies are more narrow and more specific than the African studies, they afford useful examples of types of research which may be incorporated into general studies.

The references cited above which are directly concerned with urban areas in Asia, Latin America and Africa touch on the types of problems and conditions common to all the developing countries and contain suggestions of special usefulness for research in such areas.

Studies of individual cities

Studies of individual cities may be undertaken through a variety of approaches (see Chapters 3 and 4). Many examples of comprehensive studies of individual cities are to be found in the literature. Most of them focus on cities in the economically-advanced areas, but an increasing number of studies are becoming available for cities in the developing regions.

Classical studies of individual cities in the economically-advanced areas include the pioneer works of the Lynds on *Middletown* and Warner's *Yankee City* series. Warner's work has recently become available in a single volume which may be used as an excellent prototype for the study of a city. Lynd and Warner and their associates employed sociological-anthropological methods in their research. The approach is well exemplified in the table of contents of the single-volume edition of *Yankee City* which is reproduced below:

PART III. TRANSITION: THE MOVEMENT OF ETHNIC GROUPS INTO
THE LIFE OF THE COMMUNITY

Another good example of a study, restricted to a single ward in a city, is that by Dore, *City Life in Japan*. He also employs a sociological-anthropological approach and his outline may also serve as a model for research.

In the developing areas, India is especially rich in studies of individual cities. Rapid urbanization in India since 1941, with its attendant problems, has stimulated a number of surveys and research efforts. The surveys of cities begun during the war and pursued in the post-war period by the Gokhale Institute at Poona set the pattern for many of the subsequent studies. The study of Poona is the most comprehensive of these investigations and is available in two parts, the first published in 1945 and the second in 1952.

In 1952, Unesco initiated a series of studies leading to the publication, *The Social Implications of Industrialization and Urbanization*. The Planning Commission of India, through its Research Programmes Committee, sponsored a number of studies on the social and economic conditions in about twenty cities in India, described by Hoselitz in the 'Survey of the Literature' in *India's Urban Future*.

The Planning Commission's series of studies, when all are published, will constitute the largest collection of materials on individual cities in any developing area. Among them, the study of Calcutta by Sen is especially interesting and its outline reproduced below may serve as another useful model for the sociological study of an individual city:

Other city studies have originated at universities in various disciplines. Among these the study of Banaras by Singh (*Banaras—A Study in Urban Geography*) provides a fine example of the geographic approach in contrast to the sociological approach. It contains many items of greater usefulness for physical city planning purposes than the sociological studies. This is indicated in the outline of its contents below:

Chapter   I   *Historical development*
Nomenclature. Ancient period. Muslim period. The revival of Banaras.

Chapter II   *Physical setting of the city*
Site and situation. Early physiography. Present topography. Climate and weather: Cold weather season; Hot weather season; Season of general rains; Season of retreating monsoon; Variability of rainfall.

Chapter III   *Evolution of cultural landscape in general*
Ancient sites. Controversy regarding the shifting of the site. Evolution of the city in early nineteenth century. Evolution of the city during 1830-1880. The existing pattern of the urban habitat: Geographical zones and municipal wards; River-side aspect; Present condition of the Ghats; The inner zone; The middle zone; The outer zone; Civil lines; Cantonment; Malviyanagar; Suburban zone.

Chapter IV   *Demographic features*
Early census. The trend of population movement since 1881. Comparison with other cities. Distribution and movement of population within the city limits. Centrifugal trends during last decade. Distribution of population by community. Sex composition. Occupational structure of population. Mortality and diseases. Mortality by wards.

Chapter   V   *Functional zones*
Business areas. Industries and the industrial landscape: Cotton textile industry; The oil industry; Iron and steel industry; General engineering; Hosiery industry; Ice factory; Chemical industry; Aluminium industry; Silk and brocade-work; Brass ware industry; Tobacco industry; Toy industry. Industrial zones and the nature of the industrial landscape. Residential areas.

Chapter   VI   *Social and public institutions*
Educational institutions. Religious institutions. Parks, playgrounds and public meeting places. Health services.

Chapter VII   *Public utility services*
A. Transport and communication: Street plan; Width and nature of roads; Nature of traffic flow; Bus services; Railways; Water transport; Air transport service. B. Water supply. C. Drainage and sewage disposal: Early drainage works; Modern drainage arrangements. D. Conservancy. E. Light and telephone.

Chapter VIII   *Umland of Banaras*
Meaning and use of Umland. Boundary of Umland. Vegetable zone. The milk supply zone. The zone of supply of grain and other agricultural products. Bus service zone. Newspaper circulation zone. Administrative zones. Some negative influences. Position and extent. Regional centre or regional capital.

Chapter   IX   *Geographic personality of the Umland of Banaras in general*
A. Physical setting: Relief and geology; Drainage; Climate, vegetation and soils: Natural regions. B. Cultural setting: Demographic features; Agriculture; Industry; Means of transport and communication; Literacy and language; Rural settlement; Urban settlements.

Chapter   X   *Planning and improvement of Banaras*
Housing and general accomodation schemes. Park schemes. Road widening schemes. Possibility of the growth of satellites. Some other proposals for the improvement of the city.

Other studies illustrative of relatively comprehensive investigations of individual cities and worthy of note include Venkatarayappa's work, *Bangalore—A Socio-ecological Study*, and Bopegamage's *Delhi—A Study in Urban Sociology*.

As examples of much more comprehensive studies of individual cities and metropolitan areas the investigations of the New York and Pittsburgh regions may be consulted. The New York studies were conducted under the aegis of the Regional Plan Association. Their purpose was to promote the co-ordination and development of the twenty-two counties making up the New York region. The studies are considered as a preliminary to planning studies which will more specifically aim at recommendations and planning proposals. The *New York Metropolitan Region Study* is published in nine volumes (see bibliography) and focuses primarily on the economic problems of the region with special emphasis on its implication for the future.

The Pittsburgh study is to be reported in four volumes (together with some supplementary monographs) three of which are published at present (see bibliography). It is essentially a comprehensive study of the economy of the Pittsburgh area, concerned with its past, present and future. The study was conducted under the aegis of the Pittsburgh Regional Planning Association and provides a basis for long-range physical planning.

Study of urban problems

The purpose of social research in urban areas to which this handbook is addressed is, primarily, to provide a basis for dealing with problems arising from urbanism as a way of life. Urban problems may be classified in a number of ways. The classification employed here is: economic, physical, social, governmental and administrative.

ECONOMIC

The city may be studied as an economic mechanism. It owes its origin to economic developments in the Neolithic period—that is, to the domestication of plants and animals and the proliferation of the crafts. The rise of cities has developed and greatly transformed the way in which man makes his living, making possible a greater division of labour and specialization, resulting in great increases in productivity. City life has greatly altered such key economic concepts as 'work', 'property', 'poverty', 'power', and 'luxury'. It has transformed the relationships among workers and produced new economic relationships such as those between workers and employers. It has led to the organization of both workers and employers and to problems of 'industrial relations'.

Increased division of labour and specialization in the economically-advanced areas provided stimulus to technological advance and the utilization of non-human energy. This, in turn, gave rise to industrialization and the 'factory system'. Increased productivity led to increased levels of living, to broader markets, to mass production and to new forms of economic organization. The corporate enterprise emerged, leading to the separation of management from ownership. The urban setting supported the market mechanism, on the one hand, and, on the other, led to the re-definition of the role of government and to increased intervention by government in the economy.

Many of the developing countries are acutely aware of present and impending urban problems in relation to their programmes for economic development. Urbanization imposes a heavy requirement for capital for-mation—for urban infrastructure including public utilities and housing—an especially difficult burden when urbanization is outpacing economic development and productivity. Some developing countries are seeking to decelerate the rate of urbanization or even to induce swelled urban popu-lations to return to rural areas by efforts to increase agricultural produc-tivity and to make village life more attractive and through efforts to decen-tralize new industrial development. Because of rapid population growth and inability to provide essential facilities and services, many cities in developing areas have experienced serious dis-economies in production (power and transport shortages, etc.).

In most of the smaller developing countries, especially in South-East Asia, urban population distribution differs from that in the more developed nations in being characterized by the presence of a 'primate' or great city many times, sometimes five to ten times, the size of the second city. These cities are not so much the result of indigenous economic development as the product of economic development oriented essentially to one or more foreign countries. For many cities this external orientation emerged during the colonial period during which the great city developed as a link between the colony and the mother country. In a number of cases the great city still preserves this external orientation in serving as a link between the local *élite* and the outside world rather than an economic outgrowth of the indi-genous national economy. Moreover, the great city tends to be more of an external than indigenous economic development in still another sense. This has been stated as follows:[1]

... in certain ECAFE countries, the proportion of the total population living in such cities undoubtedly exaggerates the extent to which urbanization has proceeded. For example, in Malaya, Indonesia, Thailand, Burma and Indochina, recent or earlier records show that substantial proportions of the inhabitants of large cities are aliens.

Moreover, many of these cities tend to be economically 'alien' to the countries in which they are located, since their activities and commerce tend to be transacted more with alien people and on world markets rather than with the indigenous people.

1. 'Aspects of Urbanization in ECAFE Countries', *Economic Bulletin for Asia and the Far East*, Vol. IV, No. 1, May 1953, p. 4. Published in Bangkok by the United Nations Economic Commission for Asia and the Far East.

The relationship between industrialization and urbanization in developing countries is complicated by the presence of the 'primate' city. The fact that the great cities are already there creates a tendency for further centralization of industrial, commercial and service development. Moreover, the great city may also have a paralytic effect on the development of other urban places. Thus, the city in developing countries unlike its counterpart in the more developed areas of the world may be a barrier to, rather than a product of, economic development; it calls for further national economic development to provide it with a sound economic base rather than being a product of such economic development.

Historically the growth and economic characteristics of urban areas in developing countries can be treated in three well-defined phases or stages—namely the pre-industrial, the commercial and industrial. In the pre-industrial phase, subsistence agriculture predominates and means of transportation are fairly primitive. In consequence, the number and size of urban areas in the interior are limited. A large number of urban places in this phase are primarily administrative, military or religious centres with little economic base beyond the performance of these functions. However, even in this stage of economic development there are probably a few large towns especially at the confluence of rivers which, besides being marketing and distribution centres for the tributary area, contain considerable specialized but traditional handicraft manufacture.

With the development of international trade, cities begin to grow on the sea coast. Sea-coast cities develop a significant economic base in performing the functions of collection, storage, handling and distribution of exports and imports. In time, processing of raw materials received from the hinterland become an added function. During this same period, the improvement of means of transportation widen commercial potentialities among interior urban places. City development during this period is based primarily on commercial activity and in many of the developing countries this commercial phase of urbanization is related to the colonial period.

It is only in recent years that active industrial development has begun in most developing countries. New industrial and mining towns and other specialized single function towns and cities are slowly making their appearance even while industrial development tends, in the main, to be concentrated in the relatively few great cities. The emphasis placed upon industrialization in most plans for economic development contains potentialities for changing the whole character of urbanization in the coming years. At the present time, by reason of the heterogeneous and unintegrated character of underdeveloped economies, many cities are characterized by the coexistence of all three phases of urbanization—pre-industrial, commercial and industrial.

Among the difficult problems posed by continued and accelerated rates of urbanization in developing countries is that relating to locational patterns. Small commercial towns serving agricultural areas tend to be widely distributed largely in accordance with the location of agricultural activity and the density of agricultural population. Larger-size towns are superimposed on the widespread distributional pattern of the smaller commercial centres usually at transport nodal points—river and road junctions and more recently railway junctions. These centres, as well as the seaports are the 'break of bulk' points and serve essentially the function of trans-shipment and distribution of goods between land and water and within the interior. These centres have increasingly become convenient points of location for processing and light manufacturing industry. In most developing countries the development of towns and cities, in respect of economic function, has gone little beyond this point.

With the adoption of Western technology and industrial enterprise new patterns of location of cities are emerging and strategic policy decisions are required. The new locational factors centre around raw material and power sources, the availability of labour and the location of consumer markets; and national policies with respect to centralization and decentralization of industry, regional development and the relation between industrial development and general national economic development.

Increased industrialization necessarily implies a change in the occupational structure of the working force toward non-agricultural activities and specialization in economic function. This means increased population agglomeration and, therefore, increased rates of urbanization because of the difference in the spatial distribution requirements of agricultural and non-agricultural activities. To achieve the gains from the economies of specialization and localization, developing countries are, in the short run, confronted with the need for providing urban economic and social infrastructure or urban overhead investment.

In the earlier stages of economic development in which most developing nations find themselves, the demand for such infrastructure investment is outrunning the pace of economic development in general, and constitutes a serious burden on scarce capital resources. Developing nations in the early crucial stages of industrialization are confronted, therefore, with serious problems of allocating scarce capital resources among infrastructure projects on the one hand, and more immediately productive projects on the other. This question obviously has a bearing on whether new industrial and economic development projects should be located in existing urban centres or in new localities, and vitally affects policy in respect of centralization or decentralization and regional development. The fact that existing urban centres in developing countries are already short of infrastructure facilities makes the problem all the more acute.

Within this framework developing countries are further confronted with two special problems of major import. One is that relating to the choice to be made in the allocation of scarce resources to 'social' as contrasted with 'productive' investment. This is merely a special aspect of the infrastructure problem but, more specifically, concerns the extent to which resources are utilized for such 'social' objectives as better housing, environmental sanitation, health projects and education versus the production of general consumer goods. Such 'social' investments are, of course, also 'productive' investments in the longer run, but compete with more immediate productive enterprises in the short run.

The second problem, is that concerning the creation of employment opportunities without retarding technological progress. Emphasis on labour-intensive techniques is frequently necessary but, if carried too far, may adversely affect the growth of the nation's net aggregate product by retarding labour-saving technological development. In general, policy determination presumably aims at obtaining balance in industrial development as between employment opportunities and technology to assure maximum product per head.

Policy makers in developing nations are faced with quite crucial decisions on the problems indicated. Moreover, it may be noted that risks involved in respect of these decisions are much more centralized than were decisions in Western economically-developed countries where risks were widely dispersed in the play of the market mechanism.

Urbanism produces alterations in consumption patterns. Such fragmentary data as are available show that the proportion of consumer expenditures for food in towns and cities decreases appreciably below the village level. Clothing accounts for approximately the same proportion of expenditures in villages, towns and cities. On the other hand, expenditures on amusements, education, transport, services, footwear, rent and taxes tend to rise as do also expenditures on selected food items such as milk and milk products, meat, eggs and fish, fruits and refreshments.[1]

There is also evidence that consumption in urban centres relies more heavily on imported commodities which, of course, increases the drain on foreign exchange. Urban consumption tends also to be more modern than rural including increased use of running water, electricity and some durable consumer goods such as sewing machines and electric irons. Once the modern habits are acquired the population seems to grow dependent upon them. City consumption also increases what are regarded by some as 'wasteful' habits such as increased expenditures for smoking, theatre, cinema, tea drinking, etc.

1. Government of India, Ministry of Finance, *National Sample Survey Fund*, No. 3, August-November 1951.

Although it is difficult in view of low national productivity and poverty to analyse the effect of urbanization on saving propensities, the evidence seems to indicate that the propensity to save is reduced in the city as compared with rural areas in developing nations. Studies in Bombay City, Ceylon, Taiwan and Singapore indicate that urban consumer expenditures tend to outrun income and that the worker's family is often in debt. It should be mentioned, however, in respect of the propensity to save that the shift from the rural to urban economy involves the shift from a subsistence to a monetary economy in which mobilization of savings can be facilitated.

Finally, to conclude consideration of some of the more important economic aspects of urbanization in developing nations, it should be observed that the concentration of purchasing power in cities serves as a stimulant to developing industry. The broadening of consumption patterns and ready markets stimulates production on the one hand; the economies of localization derived, for example, from the availability of public utility services, distributive and organizational channels and labour supply, also greatly benefit industrial and commercial enterprise. Moreover, in the urban environment, cultural and social changes, which will be further discussed below, tend to bring about highly significant changes in economic motivation more conducive to increased productivity than that embedded in the rigid socio-economic structure in village communities.

This discussion of the economic aspects of urbanization in developing areas points to the types of problems which may confront economic planners and, therefore, to the types of studies needed to help them in determining policy and programme. Economic studies require high levels of technical competence and training and, in general, should be undertaken only with the participation, or at least with the advice, of economists.

PHYSICAL

The city may also be studied as a physical construction. This is the way the city is viewed by the physical planner who is concerned primarily with its physical problems. The emergence and growth of the city have greatly transformed the physical aspects of man's life. Land-use patterns have become greatly modified and housing has assumed new dimensions and proportions in the urban setting. Aggregative living has also created the need for new types of amenities including water supply, sewerage and drainage, and transport for both persons and goods; and has created problems of congestion, and air and water pollution. Urban living has been accompanied by great increases in the use of non-human energy—the use of power. Finally, urban living also requires the attention of the physical planner to aesthetic recreational and cultural facilities.

The physical problems of the city are dealt with in greater detail, and the procedures for conducting research in respect to these problems are contained in Chapter 10.

SOCIAL

The city represents not only a changed physical environment and new forms of economic organization but it also profoundly affects culture, the social order and man's conduct and thought. Urbanization produces not only the city as a physical and economic structure but also 'urbanism as a way of life'. The abstract aspects of a city—such as size, density and heterogeneity of population—influence the nature, frequency and intensity of social contact and therefore the process of socialization and human nature itself.

In relatively small, sparsely-settled areas the potential of human contact and interaction is much below that in large cities. In a small community, contacts are not only fewer but quite different in character than in a large community. They tend to be face-to-face contacts, intimate, and to involve people in all spheres of their respective lives. In contrast, in large cities contacts may become not only much more numerous, but change in character. They may become segmental, that is, involve only one facet of the person's experience. Under such circumstances relationships become utilitarian rather than sentimental, that is, people tend to use one another at those points where they interact.

In a large, dense population, people are more apt to be of different cultural and social backgrounds. Exposure to variations in thought and behaviour tends to undermine the values and norms of each group. In consequence, behaviour tends to become rational as opposed to traditional, that is, the person is increasingly forced to make decisions about what constitutes right or wrong or desirable or undesirable behaviour. Urbanization in the Western world, for example, has resulted in persons making decisions about many things which in the past were determined largely at birth, by his culture and tradition. Such new areas of decision include the amount and type of education, occupation or profession, residential location, choice of spouse, size of family, political affiliation and religiosity.

Urbanization, especially when accompanied by heterogeneity—differences in background—tends to break down traditional behaviour and produce many problems of personal disorganization. It has precipitated such problems as juvenile delinquency, crime, prostitution, alcoholism, drug addiction, suicide, mental disease, social unrest and political instability. Many of these problems are especially manifest among in-migrant populations who must make the adjustment from rural to urban patterns of living.

Adjustment of in-migrants

Insight into the nature of social and personal changes in cities of Asia is afforded by a series of five studies prepared for Unesco on the problems of the in-migrant to cities. These studies in Bangkok, Bombay, Dacca, Delhi and Djakarta reveal a recognizable and common pattern in the adjustment of the newcomer to life in the urban setting. They show how the in-migrant, typically from a relatively small and homogeneous place of origin, is confronted in the city with a bewildering and almost incomprehensible vastness and heterogeneity. The newcomer, where possible, lives for some time with his fellow-villagers or relatives and only gradually becomes accommodated to city life. Among the more important new situations to which he must adapt are new and unfamiliar ways of making a living, a money economy, regular working hours, the absence of warm family living, a large number of impersonal contacts with other human beings, new forms of recreation, and a quite different physical setting often involving new forms of housing, sanitation, traffic congestion and noise. The greatest problem of adjustment seems to centre around the shift from a subsistence to a monetary economy and the necessity to have a job for subsistence.

Although the above describes a discernible general pattern, there is also considerable variation evident in the adjustment of newcomers to cities. For example, there are great differences, as between Delhi and Bangkok, in the extent to which religious practices continue to be observed and religious attitudes are modified. There is variability also, as for example between Delhi and Bangkok, in the extent to which the traditional social controls break down and personal disorganization becomes manifest. The observed differences seem largely to depend on the extent to which the in-migrant joins and becomes a part of a relatively homogeneous grouping of relatives or fellow-villagers who manage to maintain many of the elements of a folk society within the urban environment. The situation in Djakarta, which seems more to resemble an agglomerationn of villages than a metropolis in the Western sense, affords quite different opportunity for adjustment to the in-migrant than some of the relatively impersonal, heterogeneous and disorganized areas as, for example in Delhi, described in the Unesco studies. Especially difficult are the adjustment problems of footloose refugee populations and 'floating migrants' who have lost all ties to stable and integrated home bases.

Gino Germani in Chapter 8 presents a conceptual framework and considers the types of analytical problems involved in the study of migration and acculturation.

The family

The family in developing areas as in the West is also being subjected to changes in the city. The structure and organization of the family has been and continues to be diverse among the various nations in Asia, Latin America and Africa. In China and India the family is an extended or joint one—inclusive of a number of generations and subject to the control of a patriarchal head. In other countries, however—Indonesia and Thailand, for example—the small conjugal family (parents and unmarried children) are prevalent; and in still other countries, as in Japan and the Philippines, intermediate types, including married children and other relatives, may be found.

A major point of origin of change in the nature of family in the urban environment may be traced to the disruption of the family as a producing economic unit. This is generally occasioned by the out-migration of its members—sometimes unmarried males, sometimes the married bread-winner, and sometimes entire conjugal units. It is accelerated also by the increasing need in the city to adapt to a monetary as distinguished from a subsistence economy.

The nature of family problems and the character of changes in the family vary considerably with the patterns of internal migration. The problems created by out-migration of unmarried male villagers, both in the place of his origin and his destination, vary considerably from those posed by the out-migration of the husband or father, or of an entire conjugal unit. In many of the cities in developing areas out-migrant males, especially the married ones, maintain contacts with the family in their villages through a constant stream of movement between the city and their home villages. Such shuttling between city and village poses many problems because of its disruptive influence on family life and, also, of urban employment.

Especially in the family which migrates as a group to the city are changes in the traditional family possible. In the urban environment not only is the economic function of the family often drastically altered but the nature of inter-personal relations among its members and the roles of parents, children and siblings may also be modified. Particularly evident may be the tendency for patriarchal authority to diminish, the rights of women to be stressed, the prestige of elders to wane, and increased individualism to characterize all members.

The disruption of traditional family life often has adverse effects on all members of the family and particularly on children, especially when they become victims of child labour practices. The breakdown of traditional family ties is evidenced by increased separation and divorce in the city, by the breakdown of informal social controls manifest in the problems of personal maladjustment and disorganization, and by the acute nature of problems with which the changing family is often unable to cope in the urban setting such as illness, unemployment, orphanhood, old age and widowhood.

These changes are creating increasing pressures among developing nations for legal and institutional changes to meet the problems of the family as a whole and of its members. Protective legislation as represented by child and female labour laws, social security measures and provisions for medical care, and the development of institutions such as schools, orphanages, homes for the aged and hospitals are in large measure designed to meet problems created by the changed situation in the city and the breakdown of traditional family controls.

Although broad changes in the family in developing areas can be described, the data are, on the whole, inadequate and fragmentary as a basis for sound generalization and conclusion. Further information and research on the family in the city in developing areas are badly needed.

Social disorganization

In developing areas, as in Western cities, social disorganization is often a symptom of cultural and social change in the urban environment. Personal disorganization, including crime and delinquency, is a reflection of social disorganization. The breakdown of informal social controls of the folk society is increasingly evident in cities and is manifest partly in the changes in the traditional family discussed above. Problems of personal disorganization in the city include, in addition to delinquency and crime, alcoholism, neurosis, suicide and prostitution. As a special case, prostitution, a fairly widespread social problem in many cities in developing areas, is a product of the predominantly masculine character of in-migration and the economic difficulties experienced by many women in the transition from a subsistence to a monetary economy.

Increased industrialization and urbanization may increase social and personal disorganization, including crime and delinquency. In many cities in developing areas, large elements of the population have not yet become exposed to the urban way of life, have retained many elements of their folk culture and have remained more or less impervious to the disorganizing factors of urban life. With increased industrialization and urbanization the situation is expected to change. It is possible that developing countries may avoid the levels of social disorganization, including crime and delinquency, which occurred in some Western countries under comparable conditions because of the following characteristics of many developing nations: (a) the great general devotion to religion which is an important binding force and a form of social control; (b) the stabilizing effect of the high degree of nationalism prevalent in many developing countries; and (c) the general orientation of the governments toward the concept of the welfare state, in which government is intimately concerned with the well-being of each individual as well as general social progress and social protection. Moreover, the experience of Western countries is available to help developing countries as urbanization progresses.

Labour problems

In most developing countries, towns have expanded faster, and the exodus from rural areas to the towns has been greater, than warranted by the growth of economic opportunities. A large proportion of the workers who migrate from rural areas find jobs only in casual employment in cities— that is, in service occupations and trades, such as pedlars, trishaw operators, domestic servants, common labourers, etc. 'Tertiary' employment, i.e., service occupations, in many cities in developing areas are an index not of economic progress but of under-employment.

Workers who do become absorbed in expanding industry are faced with difficult adaptations both technical and psychological. Workers abruptly transplanted from rural to urban areas, especially if the shift involves transition from a subsistence to a monetary economy, lack stability, have no training or experience for industrial work, and in consequence have very low productivity. The problem of the in-migrant worker is further aggravated by the fact that he is often separated from his family for long periods, a factor which contributes to his instability and to his return from time to time to his native village. When he is joined by his family, they contribute to the problem of adjustment in the urban environment and often tend to become themselves sources of additional labour problems in the form of female and child labour, frequently under exploitative conditions.

Developing nations are facing a difficult problem in their efforts to protect the in-migrant worker and his family from abuses, to develop training and needed skills in the labour force and to increase productivity.

Arts and crafts

Among the social changes set in motion by the city in the developing areas are changes in the arts and crafts and forms of cultural enjoyment. Traditional art was usually utilitarian rather than art *per se*. In the city the traditional products of handicrafts are coming into competition with modern methods of manufacture and in many fields are unable to survive such competition. Some governments are making efforts to preserve the traditional arts and, at the same time, to support the use of the articles produced through handicrafts. Such efforts cannot be expected to be successful, however, unless the products can, in fact, successfully compete with machine products, either in utility or artistry or both. It must be anticipated that increasing industrialization and urbanization are likely to contribute to the breakdown of many of the traditional forms of art and handicraft.

The city also creates significant changes in forms of recreation and mass participation in cultural activities. Museums and libraries are becoming available in cities in developing areas, although only on a modest scale far below either present or potential demand. A significant change in recreational habits of city-dwellers is visible in the impact of the cinema. Practically all developing countries report an increase in popularity of the motion picture and many question the content and cultural impact of the film. Reports indicate increases in spectator and commercial, as contrasted with participant, forms of recreation. Among the more popular spectator sports, football (soccer) has received a prominent place. It may be expected that the developing countries will experience increases in commercialized recreation and that many of the urban forms of recreation will be diffused to the rural population of the country.

Education

Educational facilities in the cities in developing nations, as in fact for the nations as a whole, are inadequate both for children and adults. Mass illiteracy, reflecting low levels of living, tends to augment many types of urban problems. Although developing nations are striving to increase educational facilities in urban areas, the need for food, clothing and shelter —particularly for incoming migrants—often claims a higher priority. Provision of more and better educational facilities in the cities of developing countries remains a major problem.

Population

In addition to the other types of problems, urbanization has produced new forms of population problems, that is, problems relating to fertility, mortality, internal migration and composition of the population. In the early history of cities, in general, and in many cities today, death rates are much higher than in rural areas. In contrast, in the urban setting, birth rates tend to be lower than in rural areas in many parts of the world, although not uniformly so.

Since the death rate may be considered a general measurement of all the conditions of life, social, economic and political, that permit the retention of life itself, it deserves careful study for the urban area as a whole, and for specific sub-groupings of the population. In general, however, since the end of the Second World War, the developing areas have been characterized by rapidly declining death rates. Because of continued high birth rates, unprecedented rates of population increase are occurring throughout the nation in urban as well as in rural areas.

The high rates of population growth tend to obstruct efforts to raise levels of living and, in consequence, a number of countries including India, Pakistan, Mainland China, Korea, Egypt and Tunisia have adopted national policies to dampen rates of population increase. In these and other areas, research is needed to provide a basis for planning and administering pro-grammes of family limitation. Information is needed on knowledge about restriction of, and attitudes towards, family size. It goes without saying that such studies should in every instance be consistent with prevalent religious or other value systems. Whether studies focusing on fertility be-haviour should be conducted is a matter, of course, for each community to decide for itself in accordance with prevailing norms and policy.

Studies of internal migration and its consequences are often of special importance in developing areas. Large migratory streams from overpopu-lated rural to urban areas create many problems of adjustment for the in-migrants and for the communities to which they come. Studies of in-migration and problems of adjustment and acculturation are a prerequisite to dealing with the many problems generated by internal migratory flows.

Finally, it may be noted that there is need for study of various aspects of population composition. Especially important in such studies is the study of variation in respect to such characteristics as sex, age, ethnicity and race, education, occupational and industrial skills and the like.

Greater elaboration of demographic types of research may be found in Chapter 6.

GOVERNMENT AND ADMINISTRATION

As has been indicated above, the urban complex and urban living requires mechanisms for integrating and co-ordinating activity. This is evident in the new problems created for local or city government and in the problems requiring re-definition of relationships between local government and state or provincial and national government.

Complex urban problems require increasing numbers of specialists, as well as persons trained in general administration. The urban setting raises many questions relating to the selection, training and recruiting of govern-mental officials, and the creation of 'civil service' systems. It involves ques-tions of adequate conditions of public service so as to attract able and honest officials. It involves the devising and installing of effective and efficient administrative procedures.

The emergence of the city has posed new problems in the relation of city government to regional or national governments. These problems include consideration of the centralization or decentralization of various functions; the allocation of resources for tax purposes between the national, regional, or municipal government; and broad problems of intergovernmental powers and relationships.

At the local level, many administrative problems arise from the fact that local government boundaries frequently do not coincide with the economic, demographic or geographic or ecological reality referred to as the 'metropolitan area'. In consequence, local governments are often incapable of dealing with the problems of the entire metropolitan area. Finally, it may be noted that it is not clear what governmental levels should be primarily concerned with 'urban problems'. Such difficulties are to be found throughout the world in the economically-advanced as well as in the developing areas. Problems of government in the urban setting require research and attention.

Concluding observations

Economic development objectives and programmes in developing areas are likely to result in increased industrialization and therefore increased urbanization. The already rapid pace of urbanization is creating many problems—economic and social. In dealing with the problems of urbanization, countries in the developing areas may be helped by the experience of the West. There is increasing evidence, however, that the experience in the urbanization of the West is not completely applicable to the problems of developing nations.

Although this chapter is primarily concerned with urban problems, it must be emphasized that the total impact of the city is far from a negative one. After all, it is the city which has paved the way for the great achievements of Western civilization in technology, in productivity and in levels of living on the one hand; and, also, in the growth of universities, the development of science, the creation of new art forms and, in general, in the great intellectual, scientific and aesthetic aspects of Western civilization. Needless to say, the city may be expected to play a similar role in the further development of culture in the developing areas. It is not to be expected that this development will necessarily take the same forms as in the West. What may be anticipated, in addition to technological and scientific developments, will be further development of the basic elements in present indigenous intellectual, philosophical and aesthetic cultural traits. The positive as well as the negative consequences of urbanization also require co-ordination and study.

Some of the topics discussed in this chapter are elaborated in subsequent chapters, as more specific types of urban research are considered.

Bibliography

GENERAL STUDIES

CHILDE, V. G. *Man makes himself.* London, Watts, 1941.

DUNCAN, O. D.; REISS, A. J. *Social characteristics of urban and rural communities: 1950.* New York, J. Wiley & Sons, 1950.

HANDLIN, O.; BURCHARD, J. *The historian and the city.* Cambridge, Mass., MIT Press and Harvard University Press, 1963.

HATT, P. K.; REISS, A. J. *Cities and society.* Glencoe, Ill., The Free Press, 1951.

HAUSER, P. M. (ed.). *Urbanization in Latin America.* Paris, Unesco, 1961. (Technology and society.)

——. *Urbanization in Asia and the Far East.* Calcutta, Unesco, 1947. (Tensions and technology.)

HOSELITZ, B. F.; MOORE, W. E. *Industrialization and society.* Paris, Unesco, 1963.

INTERNATIONAL AFRICAN INSTITUTE. *Social implications of industrialization and urbanization in Africa south of the Sahara.* Paris, Unesco, 1956.

MUMFORD, L. *The city in history.* New York, Harcourt, Brace & World, 1961.

SJOBERG, G. *The pre-industrial city—past and present.* Glencoe, Ill., The Free Press, 1960.

TEXTOR, R. B. *et al. The social implications of industrialization and urbanization. Five studies of urban populations . . . of southern Asia.* Calcutta, Unesco, 1956.

TURNER, R. *The great cultural traditions.* Vol. I: *The ancient cities.* New York and London, McGraw-Hill, 1941.

TURNER, R. *India's urban future.* Berkeley and Los Angeles, University of California Press, 1962.

STUDIES OF INDIVIDUAL CITIES

BETTELHEIM, Ch.; FRERE, S. *Une ville française moyenne: Auxerre en 1950. Étude de structure sociale et urbaine.* Paris, A. Colin, 1950.

BOPEGAMAGE, A. *Delhi—a study in urban sociology.* Bombay, University of Bombay, 1957.

CHOMBART DE LAUWE, P. H.; ANTOINE, S.; COUVREUR, L.; GAUTHIER, J. *Paris et l'agglomération parisienne*. 2 vols. Paris, Presses Universitaires de France, 1952.

CLEMENT, P.; XYDIAS, N. *Vienne sur le Rhône, la ville et ses habitants, situation et attitudes. Sociologie d'une cité française*. Paris, A. Colin, 1955.

DENNIS, J. *Le phénomène urbain en Afrique Centrale*. Vol. XIX, fasc. 1: *Mémoires*. Bruxelles, Ac. Roy. des Sc. Colon., 1958.

DORE, R. P. *City life in Japan — a study of Tokyo ward*. Berkeley and Los Angeles, Calif., University of California Press, 1958.

ECOCHARD, M. *Casablanca, le roman d'une ville*. Paris, Éditions de Paris, 1955.

LYND, R. S.; LYND, H. M. *Middletown*. New York, Harcourt, 1959.

MAJUMDAR, D. N. *Social contours of an industrial city—social survey of Kanpur*. Bombay, London and New York, Asia Publishing House.

New York metropolitan region study. 1: *Anatomy of a metropolis*; 2: *Made in New York*; 3: *The newcomers*; 4: *Wages in the metropolis*; 5: *Money metropolis*; 6: *Freight and the metropolis*; 7: *One-tenth of a nation*; 8: *1400 governments*; 9: *Metropolis 1985*; Technical supplement: *Projection of a metropolis*. Cambridge, Mass., Harvard University Press, 1963.

PITTSBURGH REGIONAL PLANNING ASSOCIATION. *Economic study of the Pittsburgh region*. Vol. 1: *Region in transition*; Vol. 2: *Portrait of a region*; Vol. 3: *Region with a future*; Vol. 4: *Summary* (in press). Pittsburgh, Pa., University of Pittsburgh Press, 1963.

SEN, S. N. *The city of Calcutta, a socio-economic survey 1954-55 to 1957-58*. Calcutta, Bookland Private Limited, 1960.

SINGH, R. L. *Banaras—a study in urban geography*. Banaras, Nand Kishore & Bros., 1955.

VENKATARAYAPPA, K. N. *Bangalore — a socio-ecological study*. Bombay, University of Bombay, 1957.

WARNER, W. L. (ed.). *Yankee City*. 1 vol., abridged edition. New Haven, Conn., Yale University Press, 1963.

URBAN PROBLEMS

AITKEN, H. G. *The State and economic growth*. New York, Social Science Research Council, 1959.

ARON, R. *Le développement de la société industrielle et la stratification sociale*. Paris, CDU, 1956-57.

BALANDIER, G. *Conséquences sociales de l'industrialisation et problèmes urbains en Afrique*. Paris, 1954.

CHELINI, J. *La ville et l'Église, premier bilan des enquêtes de sociologie religieuse urbaine*. Paris, Les Éditions du Cerf, 1958.

CHOMBART DE LAUWE, P. H. *La vie quotidienne des familles ouvrières*. Paris, CNRS, 1956.

—— *et al. Famille et habitation*. 2 vols. Paris, CNRS, 1960.

GIRARD, A.; STOETZEL, J. *Français et immigrés: l'attitude française et l'adaptation des Algériens, des Italiens et des Polonais*. 2 vols. Paris, Presses Universitaires de France, 1953, 1954. (INED travaux et documents, no. 19 and 20.)

Hoselitz, B. F. *The progress of underdeveloped countries*. Chicago, Ill., University of Chicago Press, 1952.

Kuznets, S.; Moore, W. E.; Spengler, J. *Economic growth: Brazil, India, Japan*. Durham, N.C., Duke University Press, 1955.

Lebret, J. et al. *Economie et civilisation*. Paris, Les Éditions Ouvrières, 1956.

Lewis, W. A. *The theory of economic growth*. Homewood, Ill., Richard D. Inwin, 1955.

Meister, A. *Coopération d'habitation et sociologie du voisinage*. Paris, Éditions de Minuit, 1957.

Michel, A. *Famille, industrialisation, logement*. Paris, CNRS, 1959.

Moore, W. E. *Industrialization and labor*. New York, 1951.

Quoist, M. *La ville et l'homme. Rouen, étude sociologique d'un secteur prolétarien*. Paris, Les Éditions Ouvrières, 1952.

Robson, W. A. (ed.). *Great cities of the world: their government, politics and planning*. New York, Macmillan, 1957.

Rostow, W. W. *The process of economic growth*. New York, 1952.

Staley, E. *The future of underdeveloped countries*. New York, Harper & Brothers, 1954.

Szabo, D. *Crimes et villes*. Paris, Ed. Cuzas, 1960.

United Nations. *Measures for the economic development of underdeveloped countries*. New York, 1951.

——. *Les aspects sociaux de l'habitat*. Paris, Sèvres, 1957.

——. *Processes and problems of industrialization in underdeveloped countries*. New York, 1955.

Vexliard, A. *Introduction à la sociologie de vagabondage*. Paris, Librairie M. Rivière, 1956. 244 p.

Wirth, L. *Community life and social policy*. Chicago, Ill., University of Chicago Press, 1956.

GENERAL BIBLIOGRAPHY

Centre d'Études des Groupes Sociaux. *Notes bibliographiques de sociologie urbaine*. Fasc. I: *Analyses d'ouvrages, et étude*; fasc. II: *Bibliographie signalétique*. 1, rue du 11 Novembre, Montrouge (Seine).

Gibbs, J. P. *Urban research methods*. Princeton, N.J. Toronto, New York and London, D. Van Nostrand Co., 1961.

6 Demographic trends in urban areas

Judah Matras

Studies of demographic trends in urban areas are typically addressed to one or a combination of four types of problems: the extent of urbanization in a country, region, or given area; the nature of urban population growth, i.e., of natural increase and migratory movements: the composition and territorial distribution of urban populations; and the consequences of patterns of heterogeneity and differentiation of urban social relationships and economic activities for the components of population growth. These four categories of problems are, to be sure, closely interrelated, but the distinctions between them are useful in so far as the different problems and purposes of studies of demographic trends ordinarily call for distinct approaches, emphases, and sometimes for different research techniques.

From the demographic point of view, urbanization may be considered a process of population concentration which occurs by increase in the number of points of concentration or agglomeration and by increase in the size of individual population concentrations or agglomerations. Assessment of the extent of urbanization implies, then, the study of the number of urban places and their respective sizes, the absolute total number of persons living in urban places and the proportion of the total population in urban places. Such studies may be restricted in scope to a given area and a given point in time, or their scope may extend over time, over a plurality of areas, or over both. Obviously for a given country or other area the relative importance, and the pace of the development and spread of the social, economic and political consequences of urbanization (the study of which is considered in the various chapters of this volume) is in large measure dependent upon the extent of urbanization in that country or area. Conversely, in so far as urbanization itself takes place as a result of social, political, economic and technological processes, the extent of urbanization may be viewed as a major index of changes and developments occurring in the country or area in question.

116

Growth of the urban population occurs as a result of natural increase and of migratory movements. Increase in the number of persons in urban places may occur as a consequence of natural increase alone and, when urban rates of natural increase are higher than the corresponding rural rates, the excess of births over deaths may by itself give rise to an increase in the proportion urban of the total population. More frequently, however, increases in the proportion urban occur in large degree as a result of rural-urban migration, a process which, on the one hand, reflects the operation of social, economic and technological forces attracting migrants to urban places of residence and occupation or generating pressures to leave rural residences and occupations, and, on the other hand, itself operates to alter significantly the structure and composition of the urban population. Thus the study of the nature of absolute and relative urban population growth focuses upon measurement and analysis of rural-urban differences in rates of natural increase and, especially, upon measurement and analysis of migratory movements.

Although demographic studies have as their scientific purpose the statement and verification of generalizations concerning human populations, their size, territorial distributions, composition and changes and components of changes therein, any given demographic study has reference to some specific population or set of populations and to some attribute or set of attributes of the population in question. Very generally, we may distinguish between demographic studies which are comprehensive and those which are focused with respect to the range of the populations and with respect to the range of attributes considered.

In principle, the scope of a demographic study is determined by the purposes of the investigation, and data covering the range of populations and attributes treated are sought or generated for the problem at hand. In practice, however, the scope of a study may very often be limited by availability of data or feasibility of collection of new data. In any case, explicit statement of the scope of a given study serves to guide all subsequent steps of data collection, analysis and interpretation; and a pitfall to be avoided is that of ambiguity of scope and of discontinuities and inconsistencies between data collection, analysis and interpretation of results.

Sources of data

The usual sources of data for studies of demographic trends are censuses, sample surveys, and vital registration systems (see Chapter 2). In addition a number of countries maintain a continuous population register for various

legal and administrative purposes, and in those countries the population register has been an important source of data. Finally the records of various public or private agencies, e.g., school systems, social security administrations, hospitals, insurance companies and the like may often serve as important sources of data for demographic studies.

A population census is primarily a count of the number of inhabitants of a given area, and usually the numbers of inhabitants in different population categories are obtained. Thus most modern population censuses enumerate not only the total population, but the population of each sex and age and marital status, the populations of individual places of residence and of administrative areas, the population economically active, etc. A population census yields data on the size of the total population at the time of the census, on the composition of the population by major biological, ethnic, social or economic characteristics, on the territorial distribution of the population, and on the distribution of the population with respect to categories of key social or economic attributes. In principle there is no limit to the variety and detail of the information concerning characteristics of the population obtainable in a census. In practice considerations of cost and difficulties in the development of valid and reliable measurement instruments always limit the scope of a population census.

A sample survey is used ordinarily to estimate compositional and distributional characteristics of a population on the basis of enumeration of only a part of the population in question; recently, however, sample surveys have also been designed to estimate the number of inhabitants of a given area. Because of advantages in terms of decreased costs due to enumeration of a fraction of the total population, shorter time required to process the data, and better quality of data made possible by feasibility of increased expenditure per person enumerated, sample surveys have become increasingly important in data collection. Indeed, recent use of sampling in conjunction with population censuses has permitted great savings in costs of enumeration and processing and advantages in quality of data through reduction of the number of questions asked in the complete enumeration, many of the detailed questions being asked in the sample survey only.

In areas in which it is carried out at all, the registration of births, deaths, marriages, divorces and related vital events has ordinarily some legal or administrative purpose. However, information based upon vital records, when used in conjunction with population data obtained from a census or sample survey, provides the basic data on components of population change, fertility and mortality, and on components of family formation, marriage and divorce. Since it requires the organization of a permanent and comprehensive system of local registration offices and elaborate procedures to assure co-operation of government officials, medical and other persons

concerned with vital events, and the population as a whole, the nation-wide registration of vital events is carried out only in those countries able to allocate the not inconsiderable personnel and economic resources required. Even in such countries completeness of registration is not always satisfactory. Nonetheless, data based upon vital records, even if incomplete in some respects, are often adequate enough for research purposes and represent the most direct information obtainable regarding components of population change.

The critical aspects of data collection systems are the coverage, comparability and quality of the data produced. Coverage refers to the completeness with which the population or events being studied are in fact enumerated and the range of information obtained about the unit of observation. In addition the time referent of the observation, i.e., whether they have reference to an instant or to an interval in time, may be considered under this heading as well. Studies and analyses drawing upon data collected in different places, at different times or utilizing different data collection systems are beset by questions of comparability. Lack of comparability occurs most often as a result of dissimilarities of definitions, but may arise from dissimilarity of coverage, differential accuracy and differential reliability and validity of the data-collecting instruments. Quality refers primarily to the accuracy of the data, the extent to which the recorded observation corresponds to the characteristic or attribute of the unit observed, but also to the validity and reliability of recording or data-collecting instrument or technique. Validity is the extent to which the data-collecting instrument records a datum referring to the attribute or characteristic being studied rather than to some alternative, perhaps closely related, attribute or characteristic of the unit of observation. Reliability is the extent to which the particular datum obtained for the unit of observation is independent of the person or agency obtaining it.

Techniques of measurement of the extent of coverage of a census or of a vital registration system are still in a developmental stage and those existing and in use are fairly complicated and cannot be treated here. As a rule, censuses and vital registration systems are subject to under-enumeration and under-registration respectively rather than to over-enumeration or over-registration, and the enumerating or registration agencies are often able to estimate the proportion of the total number of persons or events studied which has in fact been enumerated or registered. Correction of results to account for under-enumeration or under-registration ordinarily involves multiplication of the uncorrected results by the reciprocal of the proportion enumerated or registered. Thus, for example, the estimated size of the school-age (say, aged 6 to 14) population at the time of a census would be:

$$\begin{pmatrix} \text{Corrected} \\ \text{school-age} \\ \text{population} \end{pmatrix} = \begin{pmatrix} \text{Enumerated} \\ \text{population} \\ \text{aged 6-14} \end{pmatrix} \times \left(\cfrac{1}{\begin{array}{c}\text{Proportion enumerated} \\ \text{among population aged 6-14}\end{array}} \right)$$

and similarly, the estimated number of births to women in urban places would be

$$\begin{pmatrix} \text{Corrected number} \\ \text{of births, urban} \\ \text{mothers} \end{pmatrix} = \begin{pmatrix} \text{Number of regis-} \\ \text{tered births,} \\ \text{urban mothers} \end{pmatrix} \times \left(\cfrac{1}{\begin{array}{c}\text{Proportion registered} \\ \text{of total births,} \\ \text{urban mothers}\end{array}} \right)$$

Agencies concerned with production of population data on a recurring basis, e.g., decennial censuses, annual surveys, etc., are faced with a chronic conflict between the desire to assure comparability of data over time and the need to change definitions and procedures in accordance with changing requirements for current data. This conflict is never fully resolved: any change, however minute, in definitions and procedures affects comparability over time. Moreover, procedures and definitions can never be changed instantaneously and simultaneously with each changing current requirement and with each new idea for improving the data. The most effective compromise is that involving tabulation of data according to both old and new procedures and definitions at least at the time of the changeover. However, even this type of compromise is ordinarily too costly to be applied to all the data produced by a census or survey, and usually such double presentations of data in terms of both old and new procedures and definitions are limited to some part of the total data presented.

It is not possible fully to discuss measurement of the accuracy, validity and reliability of data. In the present context we may note only that data referring to population growth and its components has an internal consistency embodied in the relationship

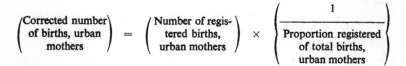

$$\begin{pmatrix} \text{Population} \\ \text{size at end} \\ \text{of period} \end{pmatrix} = \begin{pmatrix} \text{Population} \\ \text{size at} \\ \text{beginning of} \\ \text{period} \end{pmatrix} + \begin{pmatrix} \text{No. of} \\ \text{births} \\ \text{in} \\ \text{period} \end{pmatrix} - \begin{pmatrix} \text{No. of} \\ \text{deaths} \\ \text{in} \\ \text{period} \end{pmatrix} + \begin{pmatrix} \text{No. of in-} \\ \text{migrants} \\ \text{in period} \end{pmatrix} - \begin{pmatrix} \text{No. of out-} \\ \text{migrants} \\ \text{in period} \end{pmatrix}$$

A common procedure for evaluating the accuracy of data referring to population size or to one or more of the components of growth involves checking the consistency of the data in question relative to the other components of this relationship.

Finally, certain kinds of errors are known to recur in population data, and demographers have developed techniques for 'correcting' data to take account of such errors. For example, there is a common tendency to mis-report ages, giving a number divisible by five (e.g., reporting age 40 or 45 instead of 42 or 43), and mathematical techniques of 'smoothing' are often employed to adjust age-distribution data to eliminate the 'heaping' at ages ending in the digits zero or five.

Growth of total population in the area studied

A key element of demographic studies generally, and of studies of demo-graphic trends in urban areas particularly, is the measurement of population growth in the area or areas in question. The first consideration in the study of growth of the urban population is definition of what constitutes the urban population or the population of an urban place. A common problem in comparative international studies of urbanization is the dissimilarity of definition of urban places and of total urban population. The first step in a study of the demography of an urban area, then, is to adapt a definition of the area regarded as 'urban'. The considerations involved to accomplish this are discussed in Chapter 1.

The growth of a population is measured always with reference to the size of that population at some initial point in time. The basic relationship is of the form

$$\begin{pmatrix} \text{Size of population} \\ \text{at terminal point} \end{pmatrix} = \begin{pmatrix} \text{Size of population} \\ \text{at initial point} \end{pmatrix} + \begin{pmatrix} \text{Growth in the} \\ \text{interval of time} \end{pmatrix}$$

and two measures of population growth are conventionally employed. The first measure, the percentage change in the size of the population during the interval, is obtained by calculating the ratio of the growth in the interval of time to the initial population size and multiplying by 100:

$$\text{Percentage change} = \frac{\text{Growth in the interval}}{\text{Initial population size}} \times 100.$$

The second measure, the average annual rate of change in the size of the population during the interval, is obtained by calculating the ratio of the growth in the interval to the initial population size and dividing that ratio by the number of years in the interval:

121

$$\text{Average annual rate of change} = \frac{\text{(Growth in the interval)/(Initial population size)}}{\text{Number of years in the interval}}$$

Other, somewhat more elaborate, measures of population growth are sometimes employed. References to these are given in the bibliography at the end of the chapter.

Components of population growth

The growth of a population during a given interval of time may be divided into four major components, as follows:

$$\begin{pmatrix}\text{Growth in}\\\text{the interval}\end{pmatrix} = \begin{pmatrix}\text{Births in}\\\text{the interval}\end{pmatrix} - \begin{pmatrix}\text{Deaths in}\\\text{the interval}\end{pmatrix} + \begin{pmatrix}\text{No. of}\\\text{in-migrants}\end{pmatrix} - \begin{pmatrix}\text{No. of}\\\text{out-migrants}\end{pmatrix}$$

Combining the birth and death components yields

$$\begin{pmatrix}\text{Growth due to}\\\text{natural increase}\end{pmatrix} = \begin{pmatrix}\text{Number of births}\\\text{in the interval}\end{pmatrix} - \begin{pmatrix}\text{Number of deaths}\\\text{in the interval}\end{pmatrix}$$

and combining the in-migration and out-migration components yields

$$\begin{pmatrix}\text{Growth due to}\\\text{net migration}\end{pmatrix} = \begin{pmatrix}\text{Number of in-migrants}\\\text{in the interval}\end{pmatrix} - \begin{pmatrix}\text{Number of out-migrants}\\\text{in the interval}\end{pmatrix}$$

Measurement of population growth due to natural increase and of growth due to net migration is effected analogously to measurement of total population growth:

Percentage change due to natural increase

$$= \frac{\text{Growth due to natural increase}}{\text{Initial population size}} \times 100,$$

Average annual rate of growth due to national increase

$$= \frac{\text{(Growth due to natural increase)/(Initial population)}}{\text{Number of years in the interval}},$$

and similarly:

Percentage change due to net migration

$$= \frac{\text{Growth due to net migration}}{\text{Initial population size}} \times 100,$$

Average annual rate of growth due to net migration

$$= \frac{(\text{Growth due to net migration})/(\text{Initial population})}{\text{Number of years in the interval}}$$

It is very often the case that data indicating total population growth and natural increase components are available for a given urban or other areally delineated population, but no data relating to the net migration component are available. The volume of net migration to (or from) the area in question may be inferred by subtracting the increment due to natural increase from total population growth:

$$\left(\begin{array}{c} \text{Growth due to} \\ \text{net migration} \end{array} \right) = \left(\begin{array}{c} \text{Total population} \\ \text{growth} \end{array} \right) - \left(\begin{array}{c} \text{Growth due to} \\ \text{natural increase} \end{array} \right)$$

which follows from the relationships outlined above.

MORTALITY ANALYSIS

Analysis of mortality requires a measure of the frequency of deaths relative to the number of persons in the population exposed to the risk of mortality. In a given interval of time, the number of persons exposed to the risk of mortality includes (a) those persons initially in the population and remaining in the population throughout the interval; (b) persons initially in the population but leaving (through death or out-migration) the population during the interval; and (c) persons initially not in the population but entering (through birth or in-migration) the population during the interval. Only persons in the first category are exposed to the risks obtaining for the population being studied throughout the entire interval; those in the second and third categories are exposed through only part of the time interval.

Similarly, the actual number of deaths in a population in a given time interval includes deaths to persons in all three of the above categories. The simplest measure of the frequency of deaths in a population is the crude death rate, which is 1,000 times the ratio of the number of deaths in the population during the interval to the average population exposed to risk of mortality throughout the interval; and it is conventionally computed with reference to single-year intervals.

$$\text{Crude death rate} = \frac{\text{Deaths in the population during the year}}{\text{Average population size during the year}} \times 1{,}000$$

or alternatively

$$\text{Crude death rate} = \frac{\text{Deaths in the population during the year}}{\text{Mid-year population size}} \times 1{,}000.$$

The alternative is generally used because the 'mid-year population', which is easier to obtain than the 'average population', is taken as a good enough approximation of the 'average population'. Thus the crude death rate measures the number of deaths in a year per 1,000 persons in the population being studied.

It is obvious that crude death rates may be quite different in different populations or in the same population in different years. But just as the rate of incidence of death may differ among populations, rates of incidence of death may vary among different sub-groups or categories within a single population. We can always compute category-specific death rates analogous to the crude death rate, using the ratio of the number of deaths to persons in the category in question to the average number of person in that population category during the year:

Category-specific death rate

$$= \frac{\text{Deaths of persons in the given category}}{\text{Average or mid-year population in the given category}} \times 1{,}000.$$

Age-specific death rates are almost always computed for males and for females separately. The set of age-specific death rates, i.e., the male and female age-specific death rates for ages 0, 1, 2 . . . etc., observed for a population for a given year is called the schedule of age-specific death rates or the mortality schedule, and it is the most common detailed representation of mortality conditions obtaining in a population in the year in question.

A special age-specific death rate is the infant mortality rate, which commands particular interest both because of its magnitude relative to other age-specific death rates and because of its great sensitivity to socio-economic conditions obtaining in the community. Since the risk of death to infants tends to be highly concentrated subsequent to the event of birth, the denominator of the infant mortality rate is conventionally taken as the number of births during the year. The numerator is as in other age-specific death rates, but restricted to the first year of life

Infant mortality rate

$$= \frac{\text{Number of deaths of infants under 1 year of age in the year}}{\text{Number of births in the year}} \times 1,000.$$

Standardization

It is very often desirable to compare mortality conditions in two different communities or populations, or in the same community or population at two different times. If the schedule of age-specific death rates is known for each of the communities, it is possible to compare these by comparing the age-specific death rates for each age-sex category in the two communities. But comparison of complete mortality schedules tends to be very detailed and often awkward, and it is preferable to be able to use and compare some summary measure of mortality conditions obtaining in each of the two communities.

Now, the crude death rate is an over-all, summary measure of mortality in a community, and comparison of crude death rates for two communities does enable some inferences about comparative mortality conditions obtaining in the respective communities. However careful analysis of the relationship between the schedule of age-specific death rates and the crude death rate indicates that the crude death rate is, in fact, an average of the various age-specific death rates but with each age-specific death rate weighted by the proportion of the total population in that age-sex category. Thus the crude death rate measures the joint effects of the age distribution of the population and of the mortality schedule upon the over-all rate of incidence of death in the community. As a consequence, the difference between the crude death rates for two communities may be due either to differences in the schedules of age-specific death rates or to differences in the age composition of the two populations or to both kinds of differences.

This problem of confounding the effects of age, sex or other category composition of a population with those of the mortality schedule may in large measure be overcome by the use of a procedure called 'standardization' and employed quite extensively in demographic studies. Standardization controls the effects of composition by applying a schedule of specific rates to a corresponding schedule of compositional categories of a population

125

that has been adopted as a standard for a particular comparison. For example, application of the mortality schedules for the United States urban and rural populations respectively to the age distribution of the total population of the United States (the latter adopted as standard population) would yield standardized death rates for the urban and rural populations respectively. Detailed standardization procedures are given in the handbooks and manuals cited.

Life expectancy

Using a mathematical model called a life table (sometimes called a mortality table) it can be shown that with every schedule of age-specific death rates there are associated an average number of years of future life remaining to persons born, and similar average numbers of years of future life remaining to persons at each subsequent age, in a population subject indefinitely to the observed age-specific death rates. The average number of future years of life remaining to persons born into a population is conventionally called the 'expectation of life at birth', or 'life expectancy at birth'.

The expectation of life at birth is dependent upon the entire schedule of age-specific death rates, but is entirely independent of the age structure of the population in which these death rates are observed. Hence expectation of life at birth is frequently employed as a summary measure of mortality conditions prevailing in a community, and comparison of two such measures, say the expectations of life at birth in two separate communities, is very often used to compare mortality conditions in the two communities.

In addition, the life expectancy or expectation of life is a measure of average longevity at birth and at subsequent ages implied by a given schedule of age-specific death rates. As such, it is widely used by insurance companies, social security administrations and other agencies concerned with longevity and its measurement. Computation of life expectancy is by means of the life table whose computation is described in detail in the manuals and handbooks cited.

FERTILITY ANALYSIS

As in the case of measurement of mortality, the chief focus in the study of fertility is measurement of the frequency of incidence of a vital event—in this case births—relative to the population exposed to the risk of the event. Certain analogies to measurement of mortality will be immediately evident in the measurement of fertility. The simplest measure of fertility is the crude birth rate which is, indeed, the exact analogue of the crude death rate, and is defined

$$\text{Crude birth rate} = \frac{\text{Number of births during the year}}{\text{Average or mid-year population}} \times 1,000.$$

The difference between the crude birth rate and the crude death rate, is called the crude rate of natural increase, and is a widely used measure of population growth.

Now it is obvious that the entire population is not, in fact, exposed to the 'risk' of births; e.g., a population composed entirely of males, or entirely of very young girls and very old women, is exposed to no risk at all; a population including a large proportion of women in childbearing ages is exposed to substantially greater 'risk' than is a population including a smaller proportion of women in the reproductive ages, etc. Considerable refinement of the measure is hence achieved by limiting the denominator to the population more directly 'exposed to risk', namely, the female population in the reproductive ages. A second simple rate, the general fertility rate, is defined

$$\text{General fertility rate} = \frac{\text{Number of births during the year}}{\begin{array}{c}\text{Mid-year or average number of women in}\\\text{reproductive ages (usually 15-44 or 15-49)}\end{array}} \times 1,000.$$

Category-specific birth rates are ordinarily defined only with reference to women in the categories in question, i.e., have denominators indicating the number of women in the category, although there has in recent years been a certain amount of interest in male fertility rates. In particular, age-specific birth rates are defined

Age-specific birth rate for women aged, say, 20-24

$$= \frac{\text{Births during the year to women aged 20-24}}{\begin{array}{c}\text{Average or mid-year number of women}\\\text{aged 20-24 in the population}\end{array}} \times 1,000.$$

A second common category-specific birth rate is the duration-of-marriage-specific birth rate, defined analogously, but with reference to women married for specified periods of time. Finally, a category-specific birth rate receiving increased attention in recent years is the parity-specific birth rate. Parity denotes the birth order of a woman's last birth, i.e., her total number of births, including the present one. Ordinarily duration-of-marriage- and parity-specific birth rates may be computed only in connexion with a census enumeration, as estimates of the female population by duration of marriage and by parity (the denominators of the two rates) are extremely difficult to obtain except in years of census enumerations or in surveys specifically designed to yield such estimates. Thus age-specific birth rates are the most common detailed measures of fertility regularly computed in countries maintaining a vital registration system.

Comparison of fertility conditions obtaining in two communities presents the same kinds of problems encountered in comparison of mortality conditions. In particular comparison of crude birth rates presents the danger of confounding the effects of age-sex distribution with those of the schedule of age-specific birth rates similar to the pitfall inherent in comparison of crude death rates. In a manner entirely analogous to the procedure described for age-standardized death rates, age-standardized birth rates may be computed and compared for two populations.

Two commonly employed summary measures of fertility are the gross reproduction rate and the net reproduction rate. The gross reproduction rate is often interpreted as the ratio of mothers-to-daughters implied by the observed schedule of age-specific birth rates; while the net reproduction rate is likewise interpreted as the ratio of mothers-to-daughters implied by the observed schedule of age-specific birth rates, but with account taken of mortality conditions to which females in the population are subject up to and through their reproductive ages. Procedures for deriving these and other refined measures of fertility are given in the texts and manuals cited.

The measures of fertility described so far are without exception based upon the numbers of registered births and cannot be used where births are not registered. There is, however, an important set of measures of fertility which may be derived from census or population survey data alone and do not presuppose an effective system of birth registration. Of these, the simplest and most widely employed is the effective fertility rate, a measure requiring only a detailed enumeration or estimate of the population by age and sex, and defined

Effective fertility rate

$$= \frac{\text{Number of children under 5 years old in the population}}{\substack{\text{Number of women in reproductive ages (usually} \\ \text{15-44 or 15-49) in the population}}} \times 1{,}000.$$

This is the measure used in the United Nations Population Branch, Davis, and Duncan & Reiss studies cited, and for the historical comparisons of urban and rural fertility in the United States in the Grabill, Kiser and Whelpton study.

When census or survey data are available giving relationships of persons enumerated to heads of households, a relationship between children of household heads and wives of household heads (or female heads of households) may ordinarily be correctly inferred so that the fertility ratio, the ratio of the number of 'own children' under 5 years old to women of childbearing age, may be computed. Age-specific fertility ratios, restricting the numerators to 'own children' of women of a specified age and the denominators to the number of women that age, may similarly be computed,

Fertility ratio for women, say, aged 20-24

$$= \frac{\text{Number of 'own children' of women aged 20-24}}{\text{Total women in the population aged 20-24}} \times 1{,}000.$$

Finally, when census or survey data giving numbers of children ever born to women enumerated are available, distributions of women by number of children ever born and derivative measures, e.g., proportion childless, mean and median numbers of children ever born, etc., may be analysed both for women with completed fertility and for women with incomplete fertility (usually by age).

All the measures and indexes of fertility have been discussed with reference to cross-sectional studies of women in a population at a given instant or interval in time. The various age-specific birth rates ordinarily have reference to different age groups of women all present in the population during the period in question. However, most of the measures and indexes may be applied to the study of real cohorts of women, say, born in the same year or marrying in the same year. In cohort fertility analysis, the fertility of cohorts of women is measured at successive ages or durations-of-marriage of each cohort, and the resulting analysis compares fertility histories of women entering the 'fertile population' at different times.

Population composition

As indicated at the beginning of this chapter, analysis of composition of the population may be viewed as an inventory of a society's human resources. Age and sex are, in all societies, key differentiating attributes with respect to social roles and statuses and the rights, perquisites and prescriptions associated with them; and the composition of a population by age and sex implies in each society both minimum requirements for and limits upon the range of social and economic institutions and activities. Similarly other attributes—fixed, changing in the course of the life cycle and changeable without reference to the life cycle—have far-reaching implications for individual and social behaviour, and the composition of the population by key attributes represents the basic outlines of the social structure. Examples of studies of interrelationships between population composition and components of population growth have been cited in this chapter and studies of interrelationships between population composition and other social and economic processes are discussed in other chapters.

The variables most commonly studied in the analysis of population composition include sex, age, marital status, sub-cultural groups such as racial, religious or ethnic groups, literacy and educational attainment and economic activity. The conventional measure of sex composition of a population is the number of males per 100 females in the population, called the sex ratio:

$$\text{Sex ratio} = \frac{\text{Number of males in population}}{\text{Number of females in population}} \times 100.$$

The sex ratio may be computed for the entire population or for sub-groups or categories of the population, and it is very often computed by age. Typically the sex ratio is highest at lowest ages, diminishes at successively higher ages due to higher mortality among males, and is lowest at oldest ages. However patterns of in-migration often operate to alter this pattern very substantially for cities and immigration may affect the sex ratio for the nation as a whole.

The age distribution of a population is ordinarily measured in terms of percentage distribution over a set of age intervals. Summary measures of age distribution include the mean age, the median age and the dependency ratio. The dependency ratio is of particular interest with reference to the relationship between age composition of the population and economic activity, as it measures the ratio of the number of persons in normally non-economically active ages (say, in childhood, from age 0 to 14, and in old age, over age 65) to the number of persons in the economically-active ages (say, 15 to 64), i.e.,

$$\text{Dependency ratio} = \frac{(\text{Population aged 0-14}) + (\text{Population 65 +})}{(\text{Population aged 15-64})}.$$

The specific age limits (e.g., 0-14 or 0-19, etc.) may vary from country to country in accordance with compulsory school attendance or minimum age of employment laws, usual age at retirement, etc.

Percentage distributions are also used to describe the composition of a population and of population sub-groups and age categories by marital status. The usual marital status categories are single, married, widowed and divorced; for certain purposes these may be combined into two categories, single and ever-married, or married and not-married, or expanded into more than four categories (e.g., married, spouse-present and married, spouse absent). Percentages single, married, widowed and divorced vary sharply by age and also by sex. For populations considered at all ages, percentages single, married, widowed or divorced are ordinarily computed with reference to the part of the population older than some minimum age:

Percentage married of population aged 14 or over

$$= \frac{\text{Number of married persons}}{\text{Total population aged 14 and over}} \times 100.$$

The percentage distributions of a population with respect to the two literacy categories, literate and non-literate, and with respect to two economic activity categories, economically active or not economically active (or 'in the labour force' and 'not in the labour force') serve to describe the composition of a population with respect to these two attributes. Very often the percentage of a population illiterate is called the 'illiteracy rate'. Similarly, the percentage of a population economically active or 'in the labour force' is often called the 'economically-active rate' or 'labour force participation rate'.

Ethnic, religious and racial characteristics of a population are often of very great importance in that they differentiate a population by demographic, social and economic characteristics as well. Thus in addition to the composition of the population by ethnic, religious and racial characteristics, usually described by percentage distributions, differential mortality, fertility and natural increase and differences in socio-economic characteristics of the sub-groups defined by ethnic, religious and racial characteristics are often studied. In addition, and especially in connexion with studies of urban areas, the various sub-groups may be characterized by differences in rates of migratory movement, the latter having far-reaching implications for the ethnic, religious or racial composition of the urban population.

FAMILIES AND FAMILY COMPOSITION

Throughout time and space, the family has been recognized as the basic social unit with living arrangements, consumption and economic welfare, socialization of children, social and economic status all very closely associated with family units. Family studies deal with family formation, family composition, social and economic characteristics of families and family dissolution. Closely related to family studies are studies of households, usually defined in terms of living arrangements rather than kinship relationships but overlapping family units to a considerable extent.

The definition of 'family' may vary from country to country, but always the nucleus of the family is the married couple, and the event of marriage represents formation of a new family. Dissolution of a marriage through death or divorce (or sometimes through separation) may represent the dissolution of a family, but often parent-child, sibling or other kinship household units may be considered as 'families' even in the absence of a married couple.

In areas where marriages and divorces are recorded as part of a vital events registration system, it is possible to measure frequencies of marriage and divorce in a manner corresponding to measurement of mortality and of fertility. Thus crude marriage rates and crude divorce rates per 1,000 average or mid-year population are defined

$$\text{Crude marriage rate} = \frac{\text{Number of marriages}}{\text{Average or mid-year population}} \times 1{,}000;$$

$$\text{Crude divorce rate} = \frac{\text{Number of divorces}}{\text{Average or mid-year population}} \times 1{,}000.$$

Considerable refinement in the measurement of marriage and divorce is obtained when rates are computed, when possible, with reference to the population single in the case of marriages, and with reference to the population married in the case of divorces. Divorce rates are also often computed with reference to the number of marriages in the same year.

Censuses or sample surveys in which households or families are the primary units of observation provide direct data on size, composition and characteristics of family units. Families may be classified by age, sex, colour, employment characteristics, income, etc., of the head of the family, and size and composition of families typically varies among these classes delineated by characteristics of the family head.

Population distribution within an urban area

As has been indicated in Chapter 1, the geographic boundaries of a muni-
cipality or other incorporated urban centre do not necessarily circumscribe
exactly the limits of the urban agglomeration, and concepts such as metropolitan area, urbanized area, urban fringe and suburbia have been employed
to indicate extension of urban residence or of activities related to the central
urban agglomeration beyond the boundaries of the central city. But the
extension of urban residence and activities beyond the boundaries of the
central city does not imply random or even distribution of population
categories or of urban activities within the extended urban area. On the
contrary, various sub-groups of the population and types of urban activities
both tend to be unevenly distributed within the extended urban area and,
indeed, within the central city itself.

Description and analysis of population distribution within the extended
urban area, say the metropolitan area, focuses firstly upon absolute and
relative numbers of persons in the various parts of the metropolitan area,
e.g., in the central city, in the various incorporated places outside the city,
in unincorporated places in the area. The distribution by place of residence
of the population of an extended urban area may change in time in either or
all of three ways: the rates of natural increase may differ among individual
or types of places of residence within the area; rates of net in-migration
from outside the area may differ among places of residence; and persons
may move from one place of residence to another within the extended urban
area. Measurement of these movements follows procedures for measurement
of fertility and mortality outlined above.

More detailed analysis of population distribution with the extended
urban area follows two general approaches. The first approach considers
sub-groups in the population of the extended urban area as a whole, e.g.,
children, adolescents, young adults, middle-aged and older adults in the
extended urban area and compares the distributions of the respective
sub-groups by places of residence, measuring relative segregation or concentration in one or some combination of places of residence within the
extended urban area. The second approach considers the populations of
the various individual or types of places of residence and compares their
respective compositions by demographic, social and economic characteristics. In both types of analysis, the techniques of description and comparison
of percentage distributions discussed above are applicable.

Within cities, and especially within very large cities, uneven distribution
of various population categories in the various sections or communities of
the city is the rule rather than the exception, and patterns of residential

distribution are typically associated with patterns of land use, intra-city transportation and communication, economic organization and activity, and social organization and activities. Techniques of description and analysis of population distribution within communities and sub-areas of a city parallel very closely the techniques applicable for description and analysis of population distribution and composition generally, particularly frequent use being made of techniques for comparison of distributions and measurement of concentration and segregation, and these have already been discussed in the present and in previous chapters.

Problems of analysis

In studies of demographic trends in urban areas, particular interest is centred upon the analysis of the impact of urbanism and its concomitant density and heterogeneity characteristics upon the components of population growth. The risks of mortality to persons at various ages differ in rural and in urban communities and, within an urban community, mortality rates differ among the sub-areas. Moreover, the composition of mortality by cause of death differs evidently between rural and urban communities and among the sub-areas and socio-economic sub-groups within the urban community. In particular, there are, even in countries of the lowest over-all mortality, sharp variations in the infant mortality rate among the different sub-groups of the population. Because of the very heterogeneity of sub-groups in the urban community, detailed analysis of mortality in urban areas offers opportunities for studying the relationships between social and economic conditions and patterns of mortality.

Differences between fertility in rural and in urban communities have received the attention of demographers for many decades. Typically there has been found an inverse relationship between size of cities and levels of fertility, and there are variations within urban communities by socio-economic status. In part the differences in fertility levels may be imputed to differences in age at marriage of women in urban and in rural areas and it has been hypothesized also that sub-fecund women tend to migrate to cities to a greater extent than is the case for normally fecund women. However, a major hypothesis concerning rural-urban fertility differentials has been that of differentials in the extent and degree of success in the practice of family planning, and a similar hypothesis is often advanced to account for fertility differentials within urban areas. Considerable support for this hypothesis is found in the results of direct investigations of practice of family planning carried out in Europe and North America.

Different cities and urban areas attract different numbers and different types of in-migrants, and the same city or urban area may attract different numbers of in-migrants at different times or under different conditions. Description and analysis of differential migration focuses upon this important component of population change and is considered in some detail in Chapter 9.

Measurement of change

In the foregoing discussion, mention of change in population size, territorial distribution and composition has been mostly incidental to consideration of description of population attributes and analysis of their interrelationships and relationships with social and economic variables at some moment in time. We may now consider the problem of change and its measurement more explicitly.

It has been noted in the previous sections of this chapter that population size, territorial distribution and composition may change in time as a consequence of vital events (births, deaths, marriages, divorces and related events), migratory movements (in-migration and out-migration) and changes in socio-economic characteristics (occupational, or social mobility). The size, territorial distribution and composition of a population characterized by stable or fixed rates of incidence of vital events, migratory movements and changes in social or economic characteristics will change in a stable, usually determinable manner. Thus, for example, if the average annual rate of change in the population size is measured and the actual population size at some initial point in time is known, the size of the population for any future date may be calculated if it is assumed that the average annual rate of change remains fixed over the entire interval. Similarly, if it is assumed that the observed mortality and fertility schedules remain fixed, and that age-specific rates of net migration remain fixed, the size and age composition of the population may be computed for any future date. Such computations of future population size and composition are called population projections and these have many practical and theoretical uses.

Although rates of incidence of vital events, migratory movements and changes in social or economic characteristics do in fact exhibit a certain stability over relatively short intervals of time, these rates may change very substantially over longer intervals of time. Thus the study of change in population size and characteristics is concerned not only with implications of rates of vital events, etc. observed at a given time but with the factors and consequences of changes in the rates of vital events, and in the rates of migratory and socio-economic movements.

In general the study of change requires comparison of distributions and of changes in distributions in successive time intervals and the comparison of rates of vital events and migratory and socio-economic movements in successive time intervals. The measurement techniques discussed in connexion with ordinary comparisons of distributions, e.g., measures of central tendency such as means and medians and indexes of differences between distributions may be applied for the study of changes over successive time intervals in a given population. Similarly, growth rates such as the average annual rate of change, rates of vital events such as crude and standardized death and birth rates, and rates of migratory movements may be used to study changes in successive time intervals.

The 'cohort analysis' technique mentioned in connexion with fertility analysis has wide applications in the study of changes in place of residence and in socio-economic characteristics. Cohorts may be distinguished by date of entry into the particular population being studied, e.g., by birth, date of marriage, date of entry into the labour force, date of migration to an urban area, date of completion of education, etc. To the extent that the same cohort may be identified in successive censuses or surveys, (e.g., persons aged, say, 20-24 in a given census are identifiable as the persons aged 30-34 in the census of ten years later), intra-cohort changes and factors associated with such changes may be studied. Alternatively, in a single inquiry data on past and present characteristics of different cohorts may be obtained and amount and directions of change occurring for the separate cohorts may be studied and compared.

Examples of studies

One of the very earliest of demographic investigations was John Graunt's study of demographic trends in London, in which Graunt attempted to estimate urban and rural rates of natural increase and the contribution of net in-migration to the growth of the population of London. More recently, L. Chevalier has studied the population of Paris in the nineteenth century presenting two kinds of data—population composition by duration of residence in Paris and comparisons of total intercensal change in size of population with intercensal net natural increase—to show that the greater part of the growth of that population is attributable to in-migration. Similarly, I. B. Taeuber has studied the growth of cities in Japan, and especially of the city of Tokyo; and K. Davis has compared the growth of the cities of India, paying special attention to the relationship between occupational and industrial structure and the growth of Indian cities.

Mortality levels have, in general, been found to be higher in urban areas than in rural. Studies in the United States indicate that differentials in life expectancy still favour rural populations, as they did at the turn of the present century; however, mortality conditions for infants, children and young adults are now somewhat more favourable in cities. In Japan it was found that urban mortality exceeds rural mortality but that, in recent years, substantial declines have occurred in infant mortality in urban places.

Within cities, notable differences between levels of mortality have been evident for the different socio-economic sub-groups. In a study carried out in Chicago, it was found that life expectancy is substantially higher in high-rent areas than in low-rent areas of that city, and that life expectancy for whites is notably higher than for non-whites regardless of socio-economic level. In Paris, mortality—and especially infant mortality—has been and evidently still is quite substantially higher in the poorer *arrondissements* than in the more affluent ones, according to studies reported by Sauvy. In a similar study for Amsterdam, the inverse relationship between socio-economic status and mortality is found to be diminishing, the newer workers' sections in that city being characterized by mortality levels about the same as those of the middle-class areas.

Differences between rural and urban levels of fertility have been one of the most stable findings of demographic research. Recent studies have indicated that rural-urban fertility differentials exist in Asian and Latin American countries as well as in European and North American countries, where similar relationships have been documented over a longer period of time. Duncan and Reiss have shown that, among cities in the United States, the level of fertility varies inversely with size of city; a similar conclusion regarding fertility in Indian cities was reached by Davis, although more recently this conclusion has been questioned. Within individual cities, fertility levels have been shown to vary by socio-economic characteristics, by race and by religion. In a study in Chicago, fertility levels are seen to vary by race; for both whites and non-whites fertility is highest in areas of that city characterized by lowest median rentals. In a study in Indianapolis, fertility is shown to vary by religion as well as by socio-economic status, and extent and success of efforts to plan and control number and spacing of children vary sharply by socio-economic status. In Tel Aviv, fertility and extent of practice of family planning were found to vary for the different immigrant groups by geo-cultural area of birth and by duration of residence in Israel; for women in Tel Aviv who were born in Asian and African countries, but not for those born in Israel or in European countries, fertility varies inversely with socio-economic status and extent of practice of family planning varies directly with socio-economic status. In both the Indianapolis and Tel Aviv studies cited, very religious couples had higher fertility and were found to practise family planning to a lesser extent than non-religious couples, but somewhat religious couples did not differ substantially from the non-religious couples.

Further examples are to be found in the bibliography below.

Bibliography

BACHI, R.; MATRAS, J. Contraception and induced abortion among Jewish maternity cases in Israel. *Milbank Memorial Fund Quarterly*, vol. 40, no. 2, April 1962.

BARCLAY, G. W. *Techniques of population analysis.* New York, J. Wiley & Sons, 1958.

BOGUE, D. J.; KITAGAWA, E. M. *Techniques of demographic research.* (In press.)

CHEVALIER, L. *La formation de la population parisienne au XIXe siècle,* Paris, Presses Universitaires de France, 1950.

COX, P. R. *Demography.* Cambridge, Cambridge University Press, 1957.

DAVIS, K. *The population of India and Pakistan.* Princeton, N.J., Princeton University Press, 1951.

DUBLIN, L. I.; LOTKA, A. J.; SPIEGELMAN, M. *Length of life: a study of the life table.* Rev. ed. New York, Ronald Press Co., 1949.

DUNCAN, O. D.; REISS, A. J., Jr. *Social characteristics of urban and rural communities, 1950.* New York, J. Wiley & Sons, 1956.

ELDRIDGE, H. T. The process of urbanization, In: Spengler, J.J. and Duncan, O.D. (eds.). *Demographic analysis.* Glencoe, Ill., The Free Press, 1956.

GLASS, D. V.; GREBENIK, E. *The trend and pattern of fertility in Great Britain.* 2 vols. London, HMSO, 1954.

GRABILL, W. H.; KISER, C. V.; WHELPTON, P. K. *The fertility of American women.* New York, J. Wiley & Sons, 1958.

GRAUNT, J. *Natural and political observations . . . made upon the bills of mortality.* First published 1662. American ed., Baltimore, Md., Johns Hopkins Press, 1939.

HAUSER, P. M.; DUNCAN, O. D. (eds.). *The study of population.* Chicago, Ill., University of Chicago Press, 1959.

JAFFE, A. J. *Handbook of statistical methods for demographers: selected problems in the analysis of census data.* Washington, D.C., Government Printing Office, 1951.

KITAGAWA, E. M. Differential fertility in Chicago, 1920-40. *American journal of sociology,* vol. 58, 1953.

KUCZYNSKI, R. R. *The balance of births and deaths.* 2 vols. New York, Macmillan Co., 1928, 1931.

——. *The measurement of population growth.* London, Sidgwick & Jackson, 1935.

LANDRY, A. *et al. Traité de démographie*. Paris, Payot, 1945.

MAYER, A. J.; HAUSER, P. M. Class differentials in expectation of life at birth. *Revue de l'Institut International de Statistique,* vol. 18, 1950.

PRESSAT, R. *L'analyse démographique*. Paris, Presses Universitaires de France, 1961.

ROYAL COMMISSION ON POPULATION. *Papers of the Royal Commission on Population*. Vol. II. London, HMSO, 1949.

SAUVY, A. *Théorie générale de la population*. 2 vols. Paris, Presses Universitaires de France, 1952, 1954.

SPIEGELMAN, M. *Introduction to demography*. Chicago, Ill., Society of Actuaries, 1956.

TAEUBER, C.; TAEUBER, I. B. *The changing population of the United States*. New York, J. Wiley & Sons, 1958.

TAEUBER, I. B. *The population of Japan*. Princeton, N.J., Princeton University Press, 1958.

UNITED NATIONS POPULATION BRANCH, DEPARTMENT OF SOCIAL AFFAIRS. Demographic aspects of urbanisation in the ECAFE region. In: Hauser, P. M. (ed.). *Urbanization in Asia and the Far East*. Calcutta, Unesco, 1957.

———. Demographic aspects of urbanization in Latin America. In: Hauser, P. M. (ed.). *Urbanization in Latin America*. Paris, Unesco, 1961.

———. *Provisional suggestions for national programmes for analysis of population census data as an aid to planning and policy-making*. New York, 1962.

WHELPTON, P. K.; KISER, C. V. *Social and psychological factors affecting fertility*. 5 vols. New York, Milbank Memorial Fund, 1946-60.

7 Social organization in an urban milieu

P. H. Chombart de Lauwe

A distinction must be drawn, when studying the evolution of an urban society, between the social structures which gradually emerge, disintegrate and re-emerge in a given cultural context and institutions established in response to specific needs which can be ascertained through observation of behaviour patterns and the motives underlying them [1, 2].[1] Social planning implies setting up institutions and organizations adapted to the needs of the population assessed in reference to its evolution.

It is clear from the main studies of urban sociology made in the nineteenth and early twentieth centuries that there are, in the evolution of industrial societies, certain features which are common to them all [1, 3]. If we take, for instance, the comments of Spencer or Durkheim on the importance of growing volume, density and heterogeneity; the same theme taken up again by other writers, such as Louis Wirth [6]; Weber's theories on the emergence of a new type of man [5]; and on the increasing independence of geographical conditions; or again, Sombart's study of the evolution of the towns in the Middle Ages [4]; a growing similarity of conception will be perceived.

In the case of research on countries in the throes of industrialization, the scene shifts at such a speed that new methods of observation have to be devised. Changes which formerly took half a century now occur under our eyes within a few years or even months. As an aid to observing these changes, let us describe briefly the methods used for study of social structures and institutions, behaviour patterns, social relations and personality, voluntary organization and, lastly, planning.

---

1. Figures in brackets refer to the bibliography at the end of this chapter.

Social structures and institutions

These social changes which are taking place in various countries affect all social groups and the main institutions which exist in urban environments. But is is becoming increasingly difficult to enumerate these changes, since the size and the nature of these groups shift with increasing rapidity, and urban environments in the twentieth century are characterized by the emergence of groups of people which, whilst being less homogeneous than those existing in earlier times, are becoming more and more important. We call these groups 'social milieux' [10, 27]. At the same time, industrial societies are becoming progressively more fluid in their social structure.

THE EVOLUTION OF SOCIAL GROUPS

It is virtually impossible at the present juncture to make a detailed survey covering all the social groups of a large centre of population or even a small town. They are so numerous, so diverse, so intricately intertwined that an exhaustive scientific analysis is simply not feasible. Research must concentrate on picking out certain units of special importance in the structure of society as a whole, such as for instance the family, the factory and certain local groups and associations.

Studies of the family in urban environments have been made by numerous authors. We have, for instance, various early monographs such as that of Le Play on European workers [21]; more recent ones, like Lynd's survey of Middletown, or West's of Plainville [22, 23, 31]; and—to bring the list right up to date—Young and Willmott's survey of East London [32]. All these works, without exception, devote considerable attention to family and kinship; and research carried out in France, in recent years, provides further confirmation of the importance still attaching to family relations in urban milieux. On the one hand, the marital couple tends to become increasingly detached from the larger family group of former times and to assume growing importance in individuals' day-to-day life. Indeed, it has sometimes been said [26], though this is only partly true, that the open family unit living in a closed village community has now given place to a closed family unit living in the open society of the large town. On the other hand, as various recent surveys have demonstrated, the importance of the part played by the larger kinship groups has not declined so completely as some sociologists have maintained.

In the developing countries, ties of kinship maintained or re-established in the urban centres are particularly important in that they keep the individual in touch with his traditional milieu, so helping him to conserve his stability in new and alien surroundings. At the same time, they have the disadvantage of preventing the individual from throwing off traditional family pressures and saddling him with the burden of maintaining and assisting less fortunate relatives [14].

The factory also, like the family at a certain stage, constitutes both a social group and an institution. The form it assumes depends both on technical and economic needs and on the legal and cultural structure of each particular civilization. The factory provides material for observation of the type of the social relations existing between administrators and executives, rich and poor, manual and intellectual workers; and is of interest for the study not only of labour relations but also of the nature of urban society (see, for example, the volume edited by Warner, in the *Yankee City* series). The establishment of new industrial enterprises in countries in the process of economic transformation causes radical changes in ways of life and social relations. This is, there can be no doubt, one of the most urgent points to be studied of the subjects to be covered in any survey of the problems of planning in newly industrialized countries. A great deal of research on the sociology of labour indicates that this is so [15], although not enough work has yet been done on countries in the throes of economic change.

Smaller units also, such as the *commune* or small urban district, constitute a form of social structure no longer adapted to the new conditions resulting from technological change. Thus, in some large centres of population we find *communes* with over a million inhabitants, or else split up, like Paris is, into districts (*arrondissements*) having no real social character. The small village, so important as the basic unit of rural life (within which the characteristic relations of a civilization develop), seems to have no counterpart in urban milieux; although we are not alone in pointing out that the local districts (*petits quartiers*) of large towns still have a life of their own, to which people, more especially the working class people [11, 25], are very much attached. These districts, which may have two, three or four thousand inhabitants, have their own tradespeople and professional corps, as well as certain clearly marked features, differing sharply from one civilization to another.

The very fact that local groups such as these emerge indicates the need for new institutions corresponding to changing requirements. This is a point to which we shall return. Within these local groups, in the town as a whole, more and more associations of all kinds are constantly being formed: sports and cultural clubs, trade unions to look after the rights of workers, tenants and so on, family associations, political groups, etc. Even the number and nature of these associations throw interesting light on the structure of the social relations which exist in an urban milieu. Monographs on some of the associations, examined in their general context, will give a clearer idea of their purpose as reflected in their aims and statutes; though it is important to inquire, as well, into the other less obvious functions which these associations also fulfil.

NEW SOCIAL MILIEUX, SOCIAL CLASSES, ETHNIC GROUPS AND URBAN TRENDS

The classes, corporations and other clearly distinctive groups which used to exist in traditional urban milieux have now been replaced, in many instances, by large new groups neither the size nor the precise nature of which it is easy to define, but which nevertheless exercise a profound influence on the entire pattern of the social life of large towns.

In urban societies, the age groups, or 'age classes' which, as we know from the works of numerous anthropologists, played so important a part in pre-machine societies, no longer stand out so clearly; although a study of the relations between different generations, which are tied up with all kinds of demographic factors, shows that a number of age and sex categories, whose importance we shall have to take into account if we wish to make a just assessment of social relations, do still exist [13]. The part played by 'the young generation' regarded as a social factor has not been properly defined in the majority of industrial societies, or countries in the throes of economic transformations [28]; an omission which has led to many difficulties and many mistakes in social planning. A sociological study of small, independent groups of young people and of mass youth movements would throw interesting light on the mechanism of the evolution of an urban society [20].

The observation and analysis of ethnic groups also present difficult problems. In some countries, the tensions existing between inhabitants of different ethnic origins constitute one of the key elements in the shifting pattern of social relations and of the evolution of the structure of society as a whole. Factual research can be done on the juxtaposition of the different groups and their respective positions in the social hierarchy; in each civilization the special features of each type of social structure will have to be taken into consideration [16].

Another feature even more characteristic of new urban societies is the division by social and professional categories and standards of living, which forms the basis of the new social strata and social classes. Certain American authors, alive to the fact that every civilization has a different prestige scale based on its own particular system of values, hold that societies are divided into 'social classes' superimposed one on top of the other [30]. The degree of social mobility as between the different classes is measured in terms of facilities for rising from the bottom towards the apex.

It should be noted, however, that even the term 'social classes' has a different meaning, according to whether it is used by American or by European sociologists. European researchers or theoreticians lay greater stress on the class basis of social groups and the notion of class consciousness [18].

Marxist theory [18] has shown the importance of the connexion between economic transformation and the evolution of the social classes, stressing also social conflicts and dominance factors, which play a key role in the evolution of social structure. But many other authors, working on a different theoretical basis, have pointed out that the social obstacles barring the transition from one class to another have led to the division of a society into two or three sections, reflecting the specific economic and political features of that particular society [9, 17]. However, the gap between these two opposing views narrows slightly subsequently, for some American authors limit the number of social classes to only three or four, whilst European sociologists tend to modify their original theories on class structure [7, 8]. In any case, the mixture of populations of different origins often leads, in countries in the process of social change, to the creation of large groups of people living in extremely difficult conditions and the emergence of small minority ruling groups which inevitably occupy a privileged position. How can these countries be shown how to avoid the mistakes made by certain industrial societies where social barriers have assumed such proportions?

TRADE UNION, POLITICAL, CULTURAL AND RELIGIOUS ACTIVITIES AND GROUPS

The traditional corporations and other groups of former times are gradually being replaced in large industrial population centres and developing towns by groups of a new type. These groups are not formed automatically, on the basis of the *status quo* but, on the contrary, represent certain trends of opinion and are set up deliberately for the purpose of voicing specific aspirations or pressing certain claims. The trade unions dealing with labour conditions and also, more recently, with housing are one of the most striking examples of this type of group. What role do they play in an urban society at the present stage? How far are they connected with more fundamental movements such as the 'working-class movement' in nineteenth-century Europe? [12, 19] What will their future be, and what part do they play on the professional and political plane? All these questions will have to be gone into in order to obtain a correct idea of the social changes now taking place.

Similarly, political parties—with which trade unions are often connected,

either officially or unofficially—comprise groups opposed to one another
by holding different conceptions of how to direct the evolution of their
society. On the strength of the programmes they issue, the man-in-the-street
is induced to vote for one candidate rather than another, at local or national
elections. A study of how people vote constitutes the first step in the analysis
of political behaviour; but the attitudes and ideas underlying their voting
present sociologists with a more difficult and also more interesting problem.
Another important subject for research is the evolution of religious societies,
churches, sects and messianic groups which emerge and change more quickly
in the present-day world than ever before.

Other groups concerned with cultural or leisure activities may also play
an important part in social change. Sports and travel associations and organizations dealing with recreational activities of all kinds have become so
important simply because people living in towns feel the need to get away
from their everyday surroundings and live for a while in entirely different
conditions. Then again, groups formed for the pursuit of philosophy or
ideological research but, unlike certain leagues, having no direct political
affiliations, have their own part to play, less obvious, but no less important.

Social relations, communication, personality

How, in the highly complex world of the multiple social groups which inter-
mingle in urban conditions, are social relations established? How can
communication between people be facilitated or prevented? How can
personality develop?

SOCIAL RELATIONS

Social relations may be of various types: relations at work and in leisure
pursuits, between neighbours, in family and kinship groups; in groups of
friends. Relations of various types are established amongst neighbours,
within the family and amongst friends; and the nature and extent of each
person's communication with his fellows will depend on the relative importance he attaches to each type of relations and, above all, on the opportunities he has. A study of the relations established by one particular
family or person amongst the various circles with which he comes in touch,
supplemented by more general surveys of large samples, should provide
useful data on this subject. The need for social relations of all kinds is always
there, though it may not be consciously felt; but this is a factor which has

seldom been taken into consideration in town-planning. It is, therefore, of urgent importance to carry out research on this subject, and so decide what measures could be taken. [33, 34, 40, 41, 42].

COMMUNICATION, ISOLATION

Little by little, channels of communication appear. Our job is to see how they develop and expand or, on the contrary, shrink. The question of the evolution of channels of communication and of the facilities of various sorts for making contacts with one's fellows is one to which sociologists must devote increasing attention.

Contrary to what has sometimes been assumed, the development of communication media and the concentration of people in towns do not necessarily eliminate social isolation, but sometimes actually intensify it. That opportunities for social contacts are numerous and readily accessible does not mean that they go very deep; they may often be extremely superficial, in which case people find themselves alone in the midst of a crowd unable either to understand their fellow-man or, what is more, to meet with understanding in others [43].

In developing countries, sudden changes of cultural environment accompanying, for instance, the transition from rural to urban life, or from a traditional milieu to a society rent by industrial and social change, intensify the problems of self-expression and understanding.

Loneliness of this kind may sometimes lead to psychic disturbances, the development and origins of which have not yet been sufficiently widely investigated, though there have been a few important surveys on the subject [35, 36, 37, 45]. On the other hand, it would be a mistake to overestimate the seriousness of these phenomena: in this, as in other respects, towns offer exceptional opportunities; and since, in any case, they have come to stay, for better or for worse, the problem is how to adapt this new mode of life so as to make the best use of the new technical facilities whilst mitigating the stresses of the struggle for existence so often described as one of the drawbacks of big town life [44].

PERSONALITY, FREEDOM AND EDUCATION

The process of socialization of the individual is harder, in certain ways, in new urban milieux than in closed traditional milieux. A study of the development of personality, carried out on the basis of cases carefully selected from different social milieux, demonstrates how new cultural elements and the leading images implanted in a person's mind transform his personality and the extent of the freedom he enjoys [38]. Whilst the concept of freedom is one which it is difficult to define and one on which representatives of different ideologies would doubtless disagree, man's desire to free himself from the material and moral pressures to which he is at present subjected does appear to be general [34, 39]. Social life should therefore be so organized as to make contacts both easier and freer. In this respect, education is every bit as important as material progress.

Voluntary organization and planning in response to new needs

Whatever the field concerned—be it education, social relations, communication or the expression of aspirations and demands—the problem of how to meet new needs is assuming ever-growing proportions in the work of the planners. The notion of expanding production with a view to providing growing quantities of material goods is being progressively superseded by social planning for satisfaction of needs classified in order of importance.

The evolution of needs has been the subject of surveys by various authors, including that made by Halbwachs [48] besides more recent ones [2, 9]. Research on this subject must take account both of the influence of living conditions and also of the new cultural models and images which transform people's aspirations.

Whatever their purpose—to enumerate needs or trace their evolution— surveys of urban sociology should provide material for deciding on means for establishing new institutions, or modifying existing ones, in order to cater for these needs. At the same time, any such planned institutions must fit in with the natural line of development of the social structures in each instance.

THE GOVERNMENT AND THE ORGANS OF POWER

The institutions through which the government administers and regulates the life of a country are the municipal and regional authorities and the local machinery of all kinds. Special attention should be paid to the position occupied, in towns, by the institutions representing the various categories of power: legislative, judiciary, executive. The history of institutions in recent periods, and the transformations they have undergone as a result of changes of political constitution, revolutions, wars of liberation, and so on, should occupy a very important place in sociological analyses. No good monographs have yet been produced on most of these changes.

INTERMEDIARIES BETWEEN THE GOVERNMENT AND THE PEOPLE

When studying the various organs of power mentioned above, it is essential not to underrate the importance of other institutions, set up for the purpose of representing certain groups wishing to voice their own particular needs and defend their rights. Trade unions and associations of various different types exist to fulfil this purpose, and act as intermediaries between the people and the government. Institutions such as the labour exchange and the chamber of commerce are very widespread in industrialized countries; but there are also other kinds of institutions, in the socialist countries, for instance.

Our purpose here is not to explain how these institutions function, but to describe the practical methods whereby individuals and organizations express their opinions and organize group action, and the means they have for defending their rights. This involves investigating the machinery set up for arranging meetings and discussions and preparing reports and group resolutions as well as going into the policies adopted by the research departments of the various organizations.

SOCIAL AND CULTURAL ORGANIZATIONS

In order to keep pace with requirements, increasing numbers of organizations are being set up. Social security centres, hospitals, centres providing care of various kinds, are examples. At the local level, there may be composite centres assembling all the social services under one roof for greater efficiency. The organization of crèches and day-nurseries, games and occupations for adolescents raises a whole series of problems which will be discussed elsewhere. Before organizing cultural centres and youth clubs, a study will first have to be made of the needs of these sections of the population [33, 46, 47, 49].

Whatever the type of institution—political or legal, social or cultural—it is clear that they present sociologists with an enormous task; for an analysis of behaviour patterns, social relations and the needs of populations indicates the scale of the difficulties which will be encountered in applying new reforms. These are precisely the problems which the surveys now being proposed set out to solve.

Questions of how to reconcile these different types of institutions at the municipal or district level in societies in the process of transformation may also come within the domain of specialists in the humanistic sciences. The type of the local institutions established will depend upon the political philosophy held, and totally divergent solutions may be adopted, according to whether the interests of the community are placed above those of the private individual, and to the attitude adopted on the subject of authority or social control. It will be necessary to ascertain which of the different existing trends have succeeded in finding means of expression and achieving practical results. Hence, sociological surveys will have to include a study of the press and of the publications issued by the various different groups. The press has sometimes been called 'the fourth estate'. How important a part does it play in the urban milieux investigated? What different forms does it take? What influence does it have at the local or national level? All these questions will have to be examined.

Examples of research carried out

It is virtually impossible to describe in a few lines all the research which has been carried out on the functions of these institutions in different parts of the world. In order to give any real idea of them, we should have to follow the work of researchers right through from the planning stage and include an assessment of the results they obtain—which simply cannot be done within so short a space. All we can do, therefore, is to quote a few examples of research done. This in no way implies that we regard them as the only useful ones, or even the best: our point is to indicate certain areas of research, the difficulties most commonly encountered and the projects planned for the future.

For those countries which have been industrialized longest, very many monographs exist. We shall quote four of them referring to towns of varying sizes. Firstly, the six-volume survey by Lloyd Warner, in the *Yankee City* series, covering private life, enterprises, social classes, cultural activities, etc., and also containing statistics and ethnographical data [82]. Then there is Ruth Glass's survey on newcomers to the towns and the integration of ethnic groups in an industrial city, which contains extremely useful information on the problems of migration and contacts between different civilizations in the new social milieu of large centres of population [60]. Again, the survey carried out by P. Clement and N. Xydias on the town of Vienne (France) in co-operation with Unesco [55] gives an idea of the various aspects of social life in a Western European city; and O. A. Oeser and S. B. Hammond's parallel study of Melbourne [68] made as part of the same Unesco programme which also treats the subject from two points of view, sociological and psychological.

Research surveys such as those by Thomas and Znaniecki [80] on the transplantation of Polish peasants into the industrial cities of America were the first of a whole series of studies on the psychosociology of migration which still remain valid. Little has been written, on the other hand, about social structures in large centres of population; although the University of Chicago has published several volumes, including one by Park and Burgess on 'the city' [3] which is among the earliest and also the most useful. A collective work in German *Daseinsformen der Grosstadt* [56] suggests other lines of research relating to the work of the pioneers of German urban sociology; whilst a French survey made by the Groupe d'Ethnologie Sociale on 'Paris and the Paris area' constitutes an experiment, only the first results of which have so far been published [11]. The subject of the contacts established for this purpose, between the planning services and the sociological research bodies, is one to be discussed when the time comes for setting up joint research teams to ensure better co-ordination between town-planners, social planners and representatives of the humanistic sciences. The major surveys now being initiated in the Eastern European countries, such as Poland [65, 70, 71, 73, 74], Czechoslovakia [64, 67], and the U.S.S.R. [50, 76, 78] will provide useful data for comparison with other European countries, including in particular the Scandinavian countries, where a great deal of work on housing problems has been done [53, 62].

In Asia, South America and Africa, research is only just beginning, but there are immense domains waiting to be explored. The recent survey organized by G. Germani on a working-class district of Buenos Aires deals, for instance, with migrations, family organization, attitudes to work, participation in social life and recreational activities, problems of social adaptation and disruption, etc. [58].

Surveys not yet published, such as those carried out by Robirosa at Rosarie, and also in Brazil, Chile and many other regions of South America will provide data for making a rapid assessment of the new types of social structure now taking shape in the large centres of population in this part of the world [54, 57].

Then again, studies made by sociologists and anthropologists of towns in Oceania [52, 66]; articles by writers such as N. S. Ginsberg [59] or A. B. Wadia [81] on large towns and urban families in South Asia and surveys by Japanese sociologists, etc. [63, 69] provide further useful information; whilst the volumes published by Unesco on urbanization in Asia and the Far East give an idea of what this phenomenon involves [61, 79].

As to Africa, the collective volume on social implications of industrialization, edited by D. Forde [14] contains several serious sociological studies of urban social structures, including that by G. Balandier who is also the author of the well-known monograph on negroes in Brazzaville [51], the one by P. Mercier, Y. Mersadier's on living standards, A. Hauser's survey on the mechanization of cultures, those of A. W. Sonthalt, C. Sofer, and so on. The most exhaustive of the surveys contained in this volume is the one carried out at Stanleyville by a team composed of an ethnologist, a psychologist and a sociologist. P. Clément deals with the forms and values of social life in towns, (including marriage, neighbourhood relations, social classes, etc.), N. Xydias with labour problems, and V. G. Pons with the social and demographic structure of the town [72].

Methods

Other chapters in this volume deal with the methods used in research. We shall confine ourselves, here, to mentioning some of the factors which have to be considered when planning research surveys.

A distinction will have to be drawn between four main sectors of observation each of which calls for the application of its own specific research methods and techniques:

Ecology. Urban ecology which deals with the analysis of environment of variables may be extremely useful in the initial stages of surveys of social organization. Data on the distribution of social and professional categories and social classes, on migration waves and living conditions amongst the various categories of the population, and on segregation and population changes in various districts are all essential for any survey.

Study of social structures, with a view to their evolution. The data mentioned in the foregoing paragraph are of little value unless interpreted with reference to changes occurring. Studies of selected groups whose evolution is particularly indicative of the character of the society concerned should be made on the same pattern as ordinary monographs.

Psycho-sociological studies of behaviour. These may be made either by tests on large samples of population or—and this is a point we wish to emphasize—by the method of experimental observation, which consists in taking small samples and carrying out observations under conditions of increasingly strict control, so that relations can be established between variables which may be isolated and re-grouped in various combinations.

Study of collective representations, images, cultural models, symbols and scales of values. This entails co-ordinating field surveys and documentary research with analysis of contents.

In carrying out the above-listed series of studies, the first step will be to draw up an over-all plan. A list must be made of existing documents and sources of information whilst, at the same time, field observation work is begun. The latter consists of interviews (directional or non-directional) and ethnographic observations designed to yield information on everyday living conditions in the society concerned [83, 84, 85, 86].

It is not possible either to give a detailed description of all the stages involved in the process of elaborating working hypotheses and methods or to go into the problems of observing rapid changes. It should be noted, however, that whenever possible there should be observers stationed in the various different milieux, over a considerable period, to note the changes occurring around them month by month or even day by day.

In all research on social organization, the evolution of social structures, the creation of new institutions or the transformation of old ones in response to changing needs, it is important to be able to make comparisons between conditions in widely different countries. Yet, as already said, it is, in our opinion, not possible even for an international team to issue any very precise directives or outline a uniform research plan applicable to different civilizations. Each country must be allowed to draft its own plan, with the assistance of such experts as it wishes to enlist, after which steps will be taken to bring the various plans increasingly into line for purposes of comparing results. But this must be done in stages. In research on social organization and the evolution of social structures and behaviour patterns, teams working in different cultural contexts should not be constrained by over-many directives: the only sure means of eventually attaining greater understanding of the situation is to see that the initial impetus is given.

Bibliography

1. BOOTH, C. *Life and labour of the people of London.* 17 vols. London, Macmillan & Co., 1889-1903. Continued by the London School of Economics as: Smith, H. L. (ed.). *The new survey of London life and labour.* 9 vols. London, P. S. King, 1930-35.
2. CHOMBART DE LAUWE, P. H.; CHOMBART DE LAUWE, M. J. L'évolution des besoins et la conception dynamique de la famille. *Revue française de sociologie,* vol. I, no. 4, 1960, pp. 403-25.
3. PARK, R. E.; BURGESS, E. W.; MACKENZIE, R. D. *The city.* Chicago, Ill., University of Chicago Press, 1925. xi + 239 pp.
4. SOMBART, W. *Der moderne Kapitalismus.* 5th ed. 2 parts (4 vols). Munich and Leipzig, Düncker & Humblot, 1922. Vol. 1, 462 pp.; vol. 2, 919 pp.; vol. 3, 585 pp.; vol. 4, 1,229 pp. (See part I, vol. 1, chap. IX, pp. 130 et seq.)
5. WEBER, M. Die Stadt [The city]. In: *Wirtschaft and Gesellschaft.* 3rd ed. 2 vols. Tubingen, J. C. B. Mohr, 1947. Vol. II, pp. 514-601. (English ed.: *The city.* London, Heinemann, 1960. 242 pp.)

6. WIRTH, L. Urbanism as a way of life. In: *Community life and social policy.* Chicago, Ill., University of Chicago Press, 1956. pp. 110-32. Selected papers edited by E. Wirth Marwick and A. J. Reiss, Jr.

SOCIAL STRUCTURES AND INSTITUTIONS

7. BENDIX, R.; LIPSET, S. M. *Class, status and power: a reader in social stratification.* Glencoe, Ill., The Free Press, 1953. 725 pp.
8. CENTERS, R. *The psychology of social classes. A study of class consciousness.* New York, Princeton University Press, 1949.
9. CHOMBART DE LAUWE, P. H. *La vie quotidienne des familles ouvrières.* Paris, CNRS, 1956. 309 pp.
10. ——. Le milieu social et l'étude sociologique des cas individuels. *Informations sociales,* no. 2, February 1959, pp. 41-54.
11. ——; ANTOINE, S.; COUVREUR, L.; GAUTHIER, J. *Paris et l'agglomération parisienne.* Vol. I: *L'espace social dans une grande cité,* 262 pp. 2 vols. Paris, Presses Universitaires de France, 1952.
12. DUVEAU, G. *La vie ouvrière en France sous le Second Empire.* Paris, Gallimard, 1946. 593 pp. (La suite des temps, no. 14.)
13. EISENSTADT, S. N. *From generation to generation. Age groups and social structure.* London, Routledge & Kegan Paul, 1956. 373 pp.
14. FORDE, D. Social aspects of urbanization and industrialization in Africa: a general review. In: International African Institute. *Social implications of industrialization and urbanization in Africa south of the Sahara,* pp. 11-50. Paris, Unesco, 743 pp. (Tensions and technology.)
15. FRIEDMANN, G.; NAVILLE, P. et al. *Traité de sociologie du travail.* 2 vols. Paris, A. Colin, 1961-62. 468 pp., 440 pp.
16. GIRARD, A.; STOETZEL, J. *Français et immigrés: l'attitude française et l'adaptation des Algériens, des Italiens et des Polonais.* 2 vols. Paris, Presses Universitaires de France, 1953, 532 pp., 1954, 296 pp. (INED, travaux et documents, no. 19 and 20.)
17. GOBLOT, E. *La barrière et le niveau, étude sociologique sur la bourgeoisie française moderne.* Paris, 1925.
18. GURWITCH, G. *Le concept de classes sociales de Marx à nos jours.* Paris, CDU, 1954. (Cours ronéotypé.)
19. *Histoire générale du travail.* 4 vols. Paris, Nouvelle Librairie de France, 1959.
20. HOLLINGSHEAD, A. B. *Elmtown's youth, the impact of social classes on adolescents.* New York, J. Wiley & Sons, 1949. 480 pp.
21. LE PLAY. *Les ouvriers européens.* Paris, Imprimerie Impériale, 1855. 301 pp.
22. LYND, R. S.; LYND, H. M. *Middletown.* New York, Harcourt, 1929. x + 550 pp.
23. ——. *Middletown in transition: a study in cultural conflict.* New York, Harcourt, 1937, XVIII + 604 pp.
24. MARX, K. *Le 18-Brumaire de Louis Bonaparte. 1852.* Paris, Éditions Sociales, 1956. 122 pp.
25. QUOIST, M. *La ville et l'homme. Rouen, étude sociologique d'un secteur prolétarien.* Paris, Les Éditions Ouvrières, 1952. 242 pp.

26. *Recherches sur la famille. Séminaire international de recherche sur la famille et de l'institut de l'Unesco des sciences sociales à Cologne, 1954.* 3 vols. Tübingen, J. C. B. Mohr, 1956.
27. RETEL, J. *Les gens de l'hotellerie.* Paris, 1963.
28. TARDITS, C. *Porto-Novo. Les nouvelles générations africaines entre leurs traditions et l'occident.* Paris, La Haye, Mouton & Co, 1958. 128 pp. (Collection le monde d'outre-mer passé et présent.)
29. WARNER, W. L.; LOW, J. O. *The social system of the modern factory. The strike: a social analysis.* New Haven, Conn., Yale University Press, 1947. (Yankee City series, vol. 4.)
30. ——; LUNT, P. S. *The social life of a modern community.* New Haven, Conn., Yale University Press, 1941. xx + 460 pp. (Yankee City series, vol. 1.)
31. WEST, J. *Plainville, U.S.A.* New York, Columbia University Press, 1945. 238 pp.
32. YOUNG, M.; WILLMOTT, P. *Family and kinship in East London.* London, Routledge & Kegan Paul, 1957. xix + 232 pp.

SOCIAL RELATIONS. COMMUNICATION, PERSONALITY

33. CENTRE D'ÉTUDES DES GROUPES SOCIAUX. *L'intégration du citadin à sa ville et à son quartier.* 1, rue de 11 Novembre, Montrouge (Seine). Fasc. 1: *Les équipements,* 1961, 167 pp.; fasc. 2: *Les relations sociales et les catégories socio-professionnelles. Le quartier et la ville,* 1961, 181 pp.; fasc. 3: *La pyramide des âges. La dimension du quartier,* 1962, 118 pp.; by M. Huguet, B. Lamy, P. Rendu, and J. Retel. Fasc. 4: *La représentation de la ville,* 1962, 58 pp., under the direction of P. H. Chombart de Lauwe with the collaboration of B. Lamy, P. Rendu, J. Retel and G. Mercadel. *Les citadins et la ville,* 1961, 58 pp., by P. H. Chombart de Lauwe.
34. CHOMBART DE LAUWE, P. H. *et al. Famille et habitation.* 2 vols. Paris, CNRS, Vol. I: *Sciences humaines et conception de l'habitation,* 1959, 220 pp.; vol. II: *Un essai d'observation expérimentale,* 1960, 374 pp.
35. *Études de socio-psychiatrie.* Paris, Institut National d'Hygiène, 1955. 125 pp. (Monographie no. 7.)
36. FARIS, R. E. L.; DUNHAM, H. W. *Mental disorders in urban areas. An ecological study of schizophrenia and other psychoses.* Chicago, Ill., University of Chicago Press; Cambridge, Cambridge University Press, 1939. xxxviii + 270 pp.
37. HARE, E. H. The ecology of mental disease. A dissertation on the influence of environmental factors in the distribution, development and variation of mental disease. *Journal of mental science,* vol. XCVIII, no. 413, October 1952, p. 579-94.
38. KARDINER, A. *The psychological frontiers of society.* New York, 1945.
39. MALINOWSKI, B. *Freedom and civilization.* Bloomington, Ind., Indiana University Press, 1960. xiv + 338 pp.
40. MEISTER, A. *Coopération d'habitation et sociologie du voisinage.* Paris, Les Éditions de Minuit, 1957. 176 pp.

41. MERTON, R. K. The social psychology of housing. In: Dennis, W. *et al.* *Current trends in social psychology.* Pittsburgh, Pa., University of Pittsburgh Press, 1948. pp. 153-217.

42. MOGEY, V. M. *Family and the neighbourhood, two studies in Oxford.* London, Oxford University Press, 1956. 156 pp.

43. RIESMAN, D. *et al. The lonely crowd: a study of the changing American character.* New Haven, Conn., Yale University Press, 1950.

44. SHAW, C. R.; McKAY, H. D. *Juvenile delinquency and urban areas.* Chicago, Ill., University of Chicago Press, 1942.

45. WORLD FEDERATION FOR MENTAL HEALTH. *Mental health aspects of urbanization.* London, 1957. 45 pp. Report of a panel discussion conducted in the Economic and Social Council Chamber, United Nations, New York, 11 March 1957, by the World Federation for Mental Health.

VOLUNTARY ORGANIZATION AND PLANNING
IN RESPONSE TO NEW NEEDS

46. DUMAZEDIER, J. *Loisir et développement socio-culturel d'une agglomération industrielle (Annecy).* CNRS. (In press.)

47. FERGUSON, R.; CUNNISON, J. *In their early twenties: a study of Glasgow youth.* Oxford University Press, 1951. 110 pp.

48. HALBWACHS, M. *L'évolution des besoins dans les classes ouvrières.* Paris, Alcan, 1933. 163 pp.

49. JENNY, J. *Les équipements socio-culturels pour les jeunes dans les nouveaux groupes d'habitation (problèmes psycho-sociologiques).* Paris, Éducation et Vie Sociale, 1961. 88 pp.

EXAMPLES OF RESEARCH

50. ARCHANGIELSKAJA, Z.; BOBDANOW, N. Organizacja sieti pried prijatij byrowowo obsluziwanja [The organization of the equipment network]. *Architektura SSSR,* no. 10, 1959.

51. BALANDIER, G. *Sociologie des Brazzavilles noires.* Paris, A. Colin, 1955. 274 pp. (Cahiers de la Fondation Nationale des Sciences Politiques, no. 67.)

52. BELSHAW, C. S. *The great village. The economic and social welfare of Hanuabada, an urban community in Papua.* London, Routledge & Kegan Paul, 1957. XVIII + 302 pp.

53. BROCHMANN, O. *Livsform og boligform* [Ways of life and housing]. Oslo Byes vel's boligunders ø kelser. Oslo, Johan Grundt Tanum Forlag, 1952. 278 pp.

54. CAPLOW, T. *The modern Latin American city.* Chicago, Ill., University of Chicago Press, 1952.

55. CLEMENT, P.; XYDIAS, N. *Vienne sur le Rhône, la ville et ses habitants, situation et attitudes: sociologie d'une cité française.* Paris, A. Colin, 1955. 230 pp. (Cahiers de la Fondation Nationale des Sciences Politiques, no. 71.)

56. *Daseinsformen der Grosstadt, typische Formen sozialer Existenz in Stadtmitte, Vorstadt und Gürtel der industriellen Grosstadt* [Morphology of the large city, typical patterns of life in the central districts, in the suburbs and in the surrounding urban districts of a large industrial town]. Compiled and edited by R. Mackensen, J. C. Papalekas, E. Pfeil, W. Schutte, L. Burckhardt, Tübingen, J. C. B. Mohr, 1959. XIII + 375 pp.

57. DORSELAER, J.; GREGORY, A. *La Urbanización en America Latina* ..., 2 vols. Friburgo, Suiza, Bogotà, Colombie, Centro International de Investigaciones Sociales de Feres; Bruxelles, Centro de Investigaciones Socio-religiosas (CRSR) 1962. (Estudios sociologicos latino-americanos, 2-3.)

58. GERMANI, G. The social effects of urbanization in a worker's district in greater Buenos Aires. Chapter VIII in: Hauser P. M. (ed.). *Urbanization in Latin America*. Paris, Unesco, 1962. 331 pp. (Technology and society.) Proceedings of a Conference on Urbanization Problems in Latin America, Santiago du Chili, 6-18 July 1959.

59. GINSBERG, N. S. The great city in Southeast Asia. *American journal of sociology*, vol. IX, no. 5, March 1955.

60. GLASS, R. *Newcomers: the West Indians in London*. London, Allen & Unwin, 1960. XIII + 278 pp. (Centre for urban studies.)

61. HAUSER, P. M. *Urbanization in Asia and the Far East*. Calcutta, Unesco Research Centre on the Social Implications of Industrialization in Southern Asia, 1957. 628 pp. (Tensions and technology.) Proceedings of the joint United Nations/Unesco seminar ... Bangkok, 8-18 August, 1956.

62. HOLM, L. *Familj och bostad* [Family and housing]. Stockholm, Hemmens Forskningsinstitut, 1955. 216 pp.

63. ISOMURA, E. (ed.). *Tokyo*. Tokyo, Yûhikaku, 1961. V + 206 pp.

64. KLOFAC, J.; LIBROVA, E. La construction de logements en Tchécoslovaquie. In: *L'homme et la ville*, pp. 166-95. Paris, Ed. de la Nouvelle Critique, 1961. 268 pp. (Recherches internationales à la lumière du marxisme, no. 20-21.)

65. MATEJKO, A. Socjologiczne aspekty budownictwa miesz kaniowego [Social aspects of the construction of houses]. *Przelad Socjologiczny*, no. 12, 1958, pp. 72-120.

66. METGE, A. J. *Continuity in change—Urbanization and modern Maori society*. London, 1958. University of London Ph.D. thesis. Unpublished MS. (Turnbull Library.)

67. MUSIL, J. Evolution de la structure démographique de la ville de Prague. *Démographie. Revue pour l'étude de l'évolution démographique*, no. 3, 1960, pp. 234-49.

68. OESER, O. A.; HAMMOND, S. B. (eds.). *Social structure and personality in an Australian city*. London, Routledge & Kegan Paul, 1954. XIII + 344 pp.

69. OOHASHI, K. *Toshi no Kasô Shakai* [The social life of the lower class people in the urban community]. Tokyo, Seiskin Shobô, 1962. 393 pp.

70. OSSOWSKI, St. Urbanistyka i socjologia [Urbanism and sociology]. *Problemy*, no. 1, 1945.

71. PIORO, Z. *Ekologia spoteczna in urbanistyce* [Human ecology and urbanization]. Warsaw, Arkady, 1962.

72. PONS, V. G.; XYDIAS, N.; CLEMENT, P. Social effects of urbanization in Stanleyville, Belgian Congo: preliminary report of the field research team of the International African Institute. In: International African Institute. *Social implications of industrialization and urbanization in Africa south of the Sahara*, pp. 229-492. Paris, Unesco, 1956. 743 pp. (Tensions and technology.)
73. —. The changing significance of ethnic affiliation and of Westernization in the African settlement patterns in Stanleyville (Belgian Congo). In: International African Institute. *Social implications of industrialization and urbanization in Africa south of the Sahara*, pp. 638-69. Paris, Unesco, 1956. 743 pp. (Tensions and technology.)
73. The changing significance of ethnic affiliation and of Westernization in the African settlement patterns in Stanleyville (Belgian Congo). In: International African Institute. *Social implications of industrialization and urbanization in Africa south of the Sahara*, pp. 638-69. Paris, Unesco, 1956. 743 pp. (Tensions and technology.)
74. RYBICKI, P. Problematyka srodowiska miejskiego [Urban problems]. *Przeglad Socjologiczny*, vol. XIV, no. 1, 1960, pp. 7-40.
75. RYCHLINSKI, St. Miasto wspólczesne jako srodowisko rozprzezenia spolecznego [The modern city as a factor of social disintegration]. *Droga*, 1933.
76. SOSNOVY, T. The housing situation today. *Soviet studies*, vol. XI, no. 1, 1959.
77. SUZUKI, E. *Toshishakaigaku Genri* [Principles of urban sociology]. Tokyo, Yûhikaku, 1957. VI + 463 pp.
78. SVETLICHNY, B. Les villes de l'avenir. In: *L'homme et la ville*, pp. 208-29. Paris, Ed. de la Nouvelle Critique, 1961. 268 pp. (Recherches internationales à la lumière du marxisme, no. 20-21.)
79. TEXTOR, R. B. et al. The social implications of industrialization and urbanization. Five studies of urban populations . . . of southern Asia. Calcutta, Unesco, 1956. 268 pp.
80. THOMAS, W. I.; ZNANIECKI, F. *The Polish peasant in Europe and America*. 3 vols. New York, 1918-20. ev. Red. 1927, 2 vols.
81. WADIA, A. B. Some aspects of family welfare in India. *Marriage and family living*, vol. XVII, no. 3, August 1955.
82. WARNER, W. L. et al. *Yankee City*. 6 vols. since 1941. New Haven, Conn., Yale University Press.

METHODS

83. CHOMBART DE LAUWE, P. H. et al. *Paris et l'agglomération parisienne*. Vol. 2: *Méthodes de recherches pour l'étude d'une grande cité*. Paris, Presses Universitaires de France, 1952. 107 pp., figs.
84. DUVERGER, M. *Méthodes des sciences sociales*. Paris, Presses Universitaires de France, 1961. VII + 501 pp.
85. GIBBS, J. P. *Handbook of urban research methods*. Introduction by Kingsley Davis. Princeton, N.J., D. Van Nostrand & Co., 1961.
86. HAUSER, P. M.; DUNCAN, O. D.; DUNCAN, B. D. *Methods of urban analysis: a summary report*. San Antonio, Texas, Air Force Personnel and Training Research Center, January, 1956. IX + 178 pp.

The following important studies in urban sociology are not mentioned in the text.

AHLMANN, H. W.-son; EKSTEDT, I.; JONSSON, G.; WILLIAM-OLSSON, W. *Stockholms inre differentiering* [The internal structural patterns of Stockholm]. Stockholm, 1934.

BERGEL, E. *Urban sociology*. New York, McGraw-Hill, 1955. 588 pp. (McGraw-Hill series in sociology and anthropology.)

DIENA, L. *Gli uomi e le masse* [Men and the crowd]. Torino, Einaudi, 1960. 246 pp.

FRIEDMANN, G. (ed.). *Villes et campagnes—civilisation urbaine et civilisation rurale en France*. Paris, A. Colin, 1953. XXIV + 480 pp.

GIST, N. P.; HALBERT, L. A. *Urban society*. 4th ed. New York, Thomas Crowell, 1956. XIV + 513 pp. 1st ed. 1933.

HATT, P. K.; REISS A., Jr. *et al. Cities and society: the revised reader in urban sociology*. Glencoe, Ill., The Free Press, 1957. 852 pp. First published in 1951 under the title: *Reader in urban sociology*.

HELLPACH, W. *Mensch und Volk der Grosstadt* [Man and people in the large city]. Stuttgart, Ferdinand Enke Verlag, 1952. X + 153 pp.

KUPER, L. *et al. Living in towns. Selected papers in urban sociology*. London, The Cresset Press, 1953. XI + 370 pp.

√ MUMFORD, L. *The culture of cities*. New York, Harcourt & Brace; London, Secker & Warburg, 1938. XII + 586 pp.

PAGANI, A. *Classi e dimanica sociale* [Classes and social dynamics]. Congresso Internazionale di Studio sul Progresso Tecnologico e la Societa Italiana, Milano, 28 giugno-3 luglio 1960.

PIZZORNO, A. Développement économique et urbanisation. *Actes du Cinquième congrès mondial de sociologie, Washington D.C. 2-8 septembre 1962*. Vol. II: *La sociologie du développement*, pp. 91-115. Louvain, International Sociological Association, 1962.

PFEIL, E. *Grosstadtforschung* [Research on large cities]. Bremen, Horn, W. Dorn, 1950. 272 pp.

SZABO, D. L'étude de la société urbaine: synthèse de recherches. *Bulletin de l'Institut de recherches économiques et sociales de Louvain*, no. 7, November 1953, pp. 599-669.

8   Migration and acculturation

Gino Germani

While urbanization is a complex process including many and different aspects, there is no doubt that internal and international migration constitute the most important elements in urban dynamics. Most of urban demographic growth is caused by population movements, and, moreover, migration itself, as a social process, is an expression of those basic changes which are transforming the world from a planet of villages and deserts into a planet of cities and metropolises.

We may distinguish in the analysis of migration, at least three main processes: the decision to emigrate, the actual transfer, and the acculturation into the urban society.[1] While most studies are concerned chiefly with the latter, we will include in our discussion all the three stages.

In any case, the study of assimilation would require a knowledge and an understanding of the whole process of migration, including the process which occurs in the place of origin, the outcome of which is the decision to emigrate and the actual physical transfer to the city.

Three levels in the analysis of migration

It is usual to analyse rural-urban migration in terms of push-pull factors. Migration is then considered to be the outcome of the inter-play and balance of expulsive forces existing in the countryside and of attractive forces operating in the city. Different combinations of such forces may result sometimes in population movements having the same direction. Thus, it

---

1. S. N. Eisenstadt, *The Absorption of Immigrants*, London, Routledge & Kegan Paul, 1954, Chapter 1.

has been frequently observed that, while rural-urban migration in developed countries is related mainly to increases in the labour demand created by urban industrial growth, in many developing nations mass movements towards the cities take place even when such new and better employment opportunities are extremely low or even completely lacking. In this case we have a different combination of forces in which the weight of the push factors in the countryside is much stronger than the pull factors in the urban areas.[1] In other instances we may even find situations in which rural conditions, although actually improving, are still insufficient to countervail overwhelming incentives irradiating from the cities.[2] Analogous mechanisms may be used of course to describe not only the existence and degree of rural-urban migration, but also the lack of it.

While this approach may be quite useful in certain respects, it must be recognized that it has the risk of over-simplifying the process, reducing it to a kind of mechanical balance of external impersonal forces. At the same time it seems to put an excessive emphasis on 'rational' or instrumental motivations, not taking into account the possible complexity of the psychological process which results in a decision to move or to stay. For purposes of macroscopic analysis using mainly aggregate data this model may be adequate. But where the research is aiming at a study of migration differentials, a description of the adjustment, participation and acculturation of migrants in urban areas, and a causal analysis of the major factors associated with these processes, the model to be used must take into account not only push and pull factors but, also, the other social, cultural and subjective conditions under which such factors operate both at the place of residence and at the place of destination.

In fact, we suggest the convenience of distinguishing three levels of analysis: an objective level, a normative level and a psycho-social level.[3]

1. Chapter II in P. Hauser (ed.), *Urbanization in Asia and the Far East*. Proceedings of the joint United Nations/Unesco Seminar ... Bangkok, 8-18 August, 1956. Calcutta, Unesco Research Centre on the Social Implications of Industrialization in Southern Asia, 1957, 286 pp. (Tensions and technology); P. Hauser, 'The Social, Economic and Technological Problems of Rapid Urbanization', in: W. E. Moore and B. F. Hoselitz (eds.), *Industrialization and Society*, Paris, Unesco, Mouton & Co., 1963; P. Hauser (ed.), *Urbanization in Latin America*, Paris, Unesco, 1961. (Technology and society), Chapters I and II; K. Davis and H. H. Golden, 'Urbanization and the Development of Pre-industrial Areas', *Economic Development and Cultural Change*, Vol. III, 1954, pp. 6-26.
2. This seems to be the case in certain rural sectors in Italy and elsewhere in Europe, specially for the younger generation. See G. Beijer, *Rural Migrants in Urban Setting*, The Hague, M. N. Nijoff, 1963, p. 281; F. Alberoni, 'Caratteristiche e tendenze delle migrazioni interne in Italia', (Trends and characteristics of internal migration in Italy), *Studi de Sociologia*, Vol. I, 1963, pp. 23-50.
3. G. Germani, 'Social Change and Intergroup Conflict', in: L. I. Horowitz (ed.), *The New Sociology*, New York, Oxford University Press, 1964.

OBJECTIVE LEVEL

Under this heading we will include two main categories: on one side the push and pull factors, and on the other the nature and conditions of communications, accessibility and contact between rural and urban areas, or, in more general terms, between place of origin and place of destination.

Push and pull factors are well known and there is no need to describe them here.[1] It is necessary, however, to indicate that we should not limit ourselves to the contrasts between rural and urban conditions if we want to cover all kinds of urban migrations. In many countries (either developing or advanced ones) migration may and does occur between urban places, generally between cities of different size and characteristics, and in such urban centres attractive and repulsive forces operate and influence the flow of in- or out-migration.

Communications and accessibility between place of origin and place of destination are another set of objective factors which condition migration (formal and informal contacts, mass media, transportation system, distance, costs and so forth).

NORMATIVE LEVEL

Objective conditions do not operate in a vacuum: they operate in a normative and a socio-psychological context. Not only criteria of what must be considered bad or good conditions, attractions or repulsions are to be found in the norms, beliefs and values of the society of origin, but also attitudes and behaviour patterns which in this society regulate migration. That is: at the normative level[2] institutionalized roles, expectations and behaviour patterns will provide the framework within which the persons will perceive and evaluate them. It is well known that one frequent trait of many rural areas, and in general of more traditional societies (with such exceptions as nomad peoples and the like), is the emphasis on stability, isolation and fixation of the people to the native soil. In industrial and more fully modernized societies, ecological mobility is just another possible

1. In a very short summary form we could enumerate such factors thus : (a) favourable or unfavourable economic conditions in the countryside (state of natural resources, their deterioration or improvement, rate of demographic growth, population and ratio, tenure system, degree of concentration of land property, inefficient or backward techniques and low productivity in agriculture or, conversely, modernization and reduction of demand of rural labour); (b) lack—or existence—of alternate opportunities in rural setting; (c) favourable or unfavourable economic conditions in the cities : job opportunities, wage level, and so forth; (d) other non-economic rural-urban differentials, such as educational and sanitary ones, recreational facilities, political conditions of personal security (such as guerilla warfare and banditry).
2. Ideal norms may be defined by contrast to real norms : the latter refer to the empirical behaviour of individuals, while the former indicates the behaviour prescribed by the society.

answer (among many) to certain situations. While in the former it is no' normally expected, and even, in some cases, it is considered 'deviantt behaviour and negatively sanctioned, in the latter ecological mobility is at least permitted, if not actually facilitated and emphasized.

The normative pattern may also facilitate the migration of certain categories of persons, while making difficult the migration of others, as for instance is the case in the migration of women which may depend on their status within the society. In any case, norms and values must be considered as intervening variables in the analysis of the impact of push and pull factors. What to an outside observer would appear as exceptionally bad economic conditions, will not operate as a push factor at all if they correspond to a traditional pattern which not only is institutionalized in the norms, values and beliefs of the society but, also, continues to operate as an internalized expectation in the mind of the people. This last observation indicates, however, that the knowledge of ideal norms and values alone is not enough for the study of migration; here arises the need of a third level of analysis.

PSYCHO-SOCIAL LEVEL

At the psycho-social level the attitudes and expectations of concrete individuals must be taken into account. In a perfectly integrated society with no deviants from the ideal pattern, the normative framework would be accurately reflected in the internalized attitudes and expectations of the people. Another basic condition for the maintenance of such integration would be that objective conditions do correspond to the expectations, attitudes and actual behaviour. Such a situation of perfect or quasi perfect correspondence between the three levels (objective conditions, normative framework and internalized attitudes) will be in fact extremely rare to find, and it must be remembered that a certain proportion of deviance must be considered normal in every society. In present developing nations, the opposite situation will be much more frequent, if not universal. Lack of correspondence may occur in a variety of manners: changes in the objective conditions (such as over-population, low wages, war, etc.) may make it impossible to carry on the social actions as expected by the institutionalized framework and the internalized roles and attitudes; or changes in the expectations may have been brought about by cultural contacts, mass communication, etc.; or perhaps, as is more likely, different causes of change may operate simultaneously. In any case, either directly or indirectly, the psychological level will be involved, and the way in which individual attitudes are affected conditions precisely, not only the decision to emigrate, but also the character of the migration, and the subsequent behaviour of the migrant in the receiving society.

Let us emphasize that we are not reducing the causes of migration solely to a psychological process; what we are trying to point out is the need to use a psychological and a normative context in order to understand the working of the objective factors. Furthermore it must be remembered that this or an equivalent conceptual scheme must be used in analysing all the stages of the migration process, that is, not only the decision to migrate, but also the acculturation and adjustment to the receiving society. In fact, the objective conditions existing there, such as job opportunities, housing, salaries, educational facilities and the like, as well as norms, beliefs and values which characterize the urban society and its component social groups, will exercise a profound impact on the reception of the migrants and their integration.

Finally it must be stressed that the several elements so far indicated do not operate atomistically: on the contrary they are closely interdependent. The emphasis on analytical distinctions should not lead us to forget the basic fact that, in the empirical process to be observed, those elements constitute a specific configuration rather than a mere collection of isolated traits.

Nature and aspects of assimilation

This broad conceptual scheme must now be focused on the specific problem of the assimilation of migrants in urban areas. It is well known that this concept is rather ambiguous. On the one side we have a series of terms which refer to the same or related phenomena;[1] on the other, quite often, the same term has different meanings. This is not the place for a terminological and theoretical discussion on this topic; we will rather start by distinguishing a minimum number of notions which will allow us to identify the most important phenomena and processes, relevant for the study of assimilation in urban areas: adjustment, participation, acculturation.[2]

ADJUSTMENT

The notion of adjustment refers to the manner in which the migrant performs his roles in the various spheres of activity in which he participates. Here the

1. See, for instance, M. J. Herskowitz, *Acculturation*, New York, J. J. Agustin Publ., 1938.
2. Eisenstadt, op. cit.

interest of the observer is focused on the migrant himself: it is his personal adjustment which is studied, that is, his ability to perform the roles without excessive or unbearable psychological stress. There are, of course, a variety of ways of defining adjustment: what must be stressed here is the need to distinguish as clearly as possible this particular aspect from all the others.

PARTICIPATION

With the concept of participation we assume the standpoint not of the individual migrant but of the receiving society. Here we must distinguish again at least three different dimensions. In the first place we may ask about the extent and degree of his participation: how many and which roles is he performing within the institutions, social groups and various sectors of the urban society. This interest will include participation as well as non-participation, and participation in non-urban structures: for instance, how much is he still connected (that is, participates), with his original community? Or, very often—and if he is participating in institutions and social groups located ecologically within the boundaries of the urban area in which he is living—to what extent do these belong to the urban society proper?[1] In the second place we may inquire about the efficiency with which roles are performed, efficiency to be defined from the standpoint of the receiving institutions and groups and the values of the receiving society. Thirdly we may be concerned about the reception given by the urban society: how its social groups and institutions react with regard to the migrants and their participation. Here we may be confronted with situations of accepted, non-accepted and conflictual participation. Perhaps we could speak in this respect of integration, referring specifically to the degree of accepted and/or non-conflictual participation. This distinction means that a group of migrants could be participant in a particular urban structure, without being integrated into it, if the group is performing roles within the said structure, but such activity is resisted or non-accepted by other relevant groups in the same structure (the common cases of racial and political conflicts).

ACCULTURATION

By acculturation we indicate the process (and the degree) of acquisition and learning by the migrant of urban ways of behaviour (including roles, habits, attitudes, values, knowledge). As noted by anthropologists, such

---

1. The term 'amalgamation' sometimes indicates intermarriage. See the discussion of the term 'assimilation' by C. Tilly, *Migration to an American City*, duplicated copy, 1963.

process will not take place without having some influence on the receiving society. This aspect must be remembered, even if it is not always considered very important from the point of view of a study chiefly concerned with the assimilation of the urban migrants. Another observation is more in order. Acquisition of new cultural traits may occur in different ways: it may consist of relatively superficial learning, or it may penetrate deeply into the personality. It may be more or less internalized and the subject may feel more or less involved in the new behaviour pattern. By internalization we mean the process by which the trait becomes part of the personality of the individual, in which case a completely internalized behaviour pattern would be experienced as a spontaneous expression by the subject himself. Through the normal socialization and learning process within the family, during childhood, the migrant has internalized the culture of his society of origin: in the new urban setting he is confronted with the need of acquiring new roles, new knowledge, and also new attitudes and new values. But in such re-socialization, he may achieve sometimes a sufficient, but not deeply experienced knowledge of the new behaviour patterns; and sometimes he may achieve a deeper level of internalization. In the field of attitudes and values the re-socialization may lead to a deep involvement and identification with the new urban pattern, to a very superficial acceptance, or to a more or less complete rejection.[1]

The recognition of such different forms and degrees of acculturation is sometimes of paramount importance. Intellectual learning is easier than the acquisition of traits where the emotional and affective components dominate, such as attitudes, values, or behaviour patterns associated with given fields of interpersonal relations. It is well known that the rural migrants are able to acquire with relative speed new technical skills; at the same time, however, their acculturation to new types of modern industrial social relations in the factory or in the union will usually require much more time, and may not be achieved so completely.[2]

There are some further observations to be formulated in connexion with the three notions of adjustment, participation and acculturation. All of them refer both to a certain state of affairs at a given moment, and to a process in time: in this sense the interests of the research may be centred on one or the other, or both. One may want to assess which is the degree of adjustment, participation, etc., as it may be observed at a certain period,

1. P. Mayer describes three types of acculturated migrant: 'the double cultured', who ·can come and go freely between rustic and urban circles always retaining the other set of patterns in a latent state', the 'rustic' who continues to behave as such even when in town, and finally the migrant who has become a 'turncoat in a cultural sense'. See P. Mayer, *Townsmen or Tribesmen. Urbanization in a divided society*, Capetown, Oxford University Press, 1963, pp. 10-11.
2. See, for instance, the report of J. R. Brandao Lopes, 'Adaptation of rural migrants in São Paulo', in: P. Hauser (ed.), *Urbanization in Latin America*, Paris, Unesco, 1961 (Technology and society)'

and/or one may want to study the process by which the migrants are adjusting to the urban conditions. This distinction seems obvious enough, and different techniques will be employed in each case. Furthermore the three processes are not necessarily simultaneous and associated in the same group or in the same individual. This, of course, is the primary reason for introducing such distinctions. Also, a given degree of adjustment (or participation, or acculturation) may be achieved in one sphere of activity, and not in another. A person may be (or feel) quite adjusted with regard to the concrete technical tasks required in his job, and be unable to bear the psychological stresses introduced by the impersonal human relations. Acculturation to certain traits does not involve acculturation to others, participation in given urban groups may be performed with insufficient acculturation, etc. It is true that, at least with regard to certain spheres of activity, adjustment, participation and acculturation will usually go together, but incongruities between different spheres of activity may be quite frequent.

Concerning this possibility it must be noted that while most migrants will be able at least to perform a number of roles, which are the minimum required to continue to live in the urban areas, they will remain nonetheless segregated or alien to a number of other activities, which on the contrary may be considered normal for the native urbanite of the same education and socio-economic status. For instance, they are likely to have a job, to use public services, to buy goods, etc., and in this sense they must have acquired the knowledge needed to carry on these activities and perform the various roles involved in the corresponding social situations. At the same time, however, the same persons may well continue to live in an encapsulated neighbourhood formed by migrants of the same origin, maintaining or trying to maintain the same culture of their village or place of origin, and close interpersonal relations with friends and kin groups still residing there. While living physically in the city, and even participating in a number of urban activities, these migrants remain partially or totally alien to other important sectors of the urban life, such as certain forms of leisure, union participation, politics, voluntary association and the like.

The origins of the migrants and their motivation to emigrate: data and analysis

The preceding two sections will have suggested to the reader the complexity of situations characterizing migration and acculturation and the variety of factors which may condition such processes. While it would be impossible to give a complete and coherent survey of them, not only because of the limited scope of the present chapter, but also on account of the still very imperfect state of our theoretical and empirical knowledge, we will attempt to indicate the kind of data the researcher should look for in a study devoted to migration of emigrants in urban areas.

In the present section we will be concerned chiefly with what we have called the first two stages in the process: decision to migrate and actual transfer; we will thus examine the kind of data needed for such analysis and, in particular, data on: (a) characteristics of the place of origin; (b) characteristics of the migrants before migration; (c) motivation to emigrate; and (d) circumstances of the transfer.

PLACE OF ORIGIN

While it is unusual to find studies on urban migration which include systematic surveys actually conducted in the place of origin, and on the migrant groups previous to migration, most of them gather information on both topics, either by analysis of secondary sources, or by direct inquiry on the migrants after migration. Knowledge about the place of origin is necessary not only because its characteristics will deeply influence the type of migration but, also, because the degree of similarity or the difference between the place of origin and the place of destination (that is, the cultural distance), is an important factor in itself in conditioning the incorporation of the migrant to the urban way of life.

On the other hand, for purposes of comparison with changes subsequent to migration, the information on the place of origin (and the characteristics of the migrant groups) should be fairly well detailed. For instance, a general description of the main institutions—family, work and economy, religion, politics, education, etc.—and their functioning constitutes very important background information against which the observations made on the migrants in the city could be compared. Of special importance will be the data related to degree of economic development and of cultural modernization and the particular aspects which may characterize the place of origin from the point of view of the transition from less modern to more modern or more traditional to less traditional structure: forms of land tenure, degree of concentration of land ownership, extent of monetary or subsistence economy, degree of the integration of the area into the national market, kind of social relations prevailing in the field of work and economy, as well as in other orders of life.

Unfortunately, the researcher will seldom find previous studies or even primary data on such essential topics. However, it would not be advisable to restrict oneself only to the material gathered through the migrants interviewed in the city, and efforts should be made to have at least an approximate picture through other sources or even personal acquaintance.

One conspicuous example of thorough analysis of the society of origin is the classical study on the Polish peasant by Thomas and Znaniecki.[1] It is well known that these authors included in their book on the assimilation of the Polish immigrant in America a deep analysis of the Polish peasant society, its main institutions and the process of individual and social disorganization. Their study was based on collections of letters, newspapers, biographic material complemented by ethnographic sources, other systematic studies and their own knowledge of the Polish society. In those developing countries in which an indigenous population still lives in folk or tribal societies, there may exist an important body of ethnographic and anthropological studies which may contribute a great deal to a complete picture of the nature of sending societies, of their present degree of integration, and of the characteristics of the groups from which the migrants are drawn. Such are, for instance, the cases of Africa and the Indio-mestizo countries in Latin America. In most cases the authors do not perform specific analyses of the place of origin, but employ their knowledge of other information about it mostly for comparison with the receiving society and as a basis for inference as needed when studying problems of acculturation.[2]

Sometimes, summary comparisons between place of origin and place of destination may be quite useful in giving the general context within which a more detailed analysis may be conducted.[3]

Often, the most readily available information relevant to some of these general topics is found in census data and other analogous statistics. City size and non-agricultural employment are two of the best known indicators

1. W. I. Thomas and W. I. Znaniecki, *The Polish peasant in Europe and America*, Vol. 1, New York, Dover Publications Inc., 1958.
2. See, for instance, the report by J. Matos Mar, 'Migration and Urbanization. The Barriadas in Lima', in: P. Hauser, op. cit. Many examples may be found in: International African Institute, *Social Implications of Industrialization and Urbanization in Africa South of the Sahara*, Paris, Unesco, 1956 (Tensions and technology).
3. R. N. Textor, 'The Northeastern Samlor Driver in Bangkok', in: R. B. Textor *et al.*, *The Social Implications of Industrialization and Urbanization. Five studies of urban populations of ... southern Asia*, Calcutta, Unesco, 1956.

of modernization and economic development. However, even though both are often associated with such processes, it would be quite misleading to rely exclusively on them. Not only for theoretical, but also for empirical reasons, they must be considered as different processes. In fact, we have both modernized rural areas and traditional cities. In some of the more advanced countries, rural-urban differentials—with regard to demographic, social, cultural and psycho-social characteristics—have diminished considerably. In such cases, the cultural distance between modernized rural areas, small and large cities, may be not very large or non-existent at all. An analogous situation of reduced cultural distance is often found in those developing countries where traditional patterns still prevail both in urban and rural areas. However, considerable internal discontinuities in degree of modernization will be quite normal in most developing countries and not uncommon in developed ones. According to the previous indications, city size and proportion employed in non-agricultural activities should always be completed with other data regarding areas of emigration, such as fertility, general mortality and infant mortality rates, size of family, proportion employed in factory industry, size of plants, *per capita* income, proportion of middle socio-occupational strata, literacy and other educational rates, proportion of voters, proportion of union affiliation, newspaper circulation, radio and television sets in operation, etc.[1]

In addition to indicators relevant to degree of modernization, what we could call degree of disintegration of the traditional order should be explored. Attitude change, new expectations, partial refusal of old values, beliefs and obligations, and other kinds of innovating behaviour could be inferred often from the degree of modernization assessed on the basis of demographic and other indicators suggested above. However, especially in the early transitional stages, psycho-social changes most relevant to migration—i.e., spread of attitudinal deviations from predominant values and norms—may well precede the kind of changes likely to be detected by the said indicators.

Size and composition of in- and out-migration from the area of origin should be carefully analysed if possible, not only to assess the demographic characteristics of the migrants, but also in relation to the nature of the migration and of the sending society as a whole. For instance a high rate of out-migration from an otherwise traditional setting would suggest the hypothesis, worth exploring, of the advanced disintegration of the old order,

1. On indicators of economic and social development and on modernization, see, for instance: United Nations, *Report on the World Social Situation*, New York, 1961, pp. 49-62; W. K. Deutsch, 'Social Mobilization and Political Development', *American Political Science Review*, Vol. LV, 1961, pp. 493-514; P. Hauser, 'Demographic Indicators of Economic Development', in: *Economic Development and Cultural Change*.

or perhaps of the existence of overwhelming push factors; the selectivity of the migration should be rather low. On the contrary, a low rate, in a society at an equivalent traditional stage, should be interpreted as highly selective, and probably not related to disintegrating processes.

CHARACTERISTICS OF THE MIGRANTS BEFORE MIGRATION (AND OF THE CATEGORIES, GROUPS AND STRATA OUT OF WHICH THEY WERE SELECTED)

Information on the society in which the migrants were born and lived before migration is not sufficient to ascertain the various factors which may intervene in their decision to migrate, producing different propensities and various kind of motivations, and in their subsequent behaviour in the city.

We may distinguish two types of characteristics: socio-cultural (including biosocial or demographic) aspects, and individual attributes.

Among the first, the most known and universal are age and sex: most migrations are characterized by such differentials, various kinds of societies and configurations of conditions will originate different propensities among the various groups of age and also will induce different proportions of family or individual migration. But not less important than these are education and occupation which will be highly important in themselves and, also, for the fact of their close correlation with other variables, such as standard of living, income, housing or, in more general terms, socioeconomic status which usually is taken to include all of them together with occupation and education.

Intelligence and other psycho-social traits related to the propensity for innovating attitudes, high aspirations, leadership and the like, are among the most prominent individual characteristics.

It may be seen that the distinction among the two types of characteristics is not very clear: on one side all the socio-cultural characteristics are expressed—empirically—as individual attributes, no less than those labelled as individual and psychological. On the other side, the latter are not (or not always) independent from the socio-cultural aspects (e.g., intelligence, etc.) and may be differentially distributed among the various socio-economic strata, etc. The reason for the distinction will be made clear, once we analyse the role it has in the analysis of motivation, adjustment and acculturation. The socio-cultural characteristics affect individuals, not *qua* individuals, but by the fact of their belonging to a certain category, social group or social stratum. Females are not only a category defined by biological characteristics, but also by a specific *status*, defined by a set of norms and values: it is precisely this status which will forbid, make difficult or facilitate migration. And, of course, such status is part of the social structure of the society.

The same can be said of the other categories and of those defined by the socio-economic strata, a category which may be thought of as combining occupation, education and the other variables indicated above. People belonging to the same socio-economic stratum are exposed to analogous conditions, which will facilitate or prevent migration, determine the kind of migration, facilitate or make difficult adjustment and acculturation. This can be seen quite easily with regard to economic conditions: unemployment or low wages affect some socio-economic strata, not others; forms of land tenure or land-population ratio impinge only on given categories of peasants, etc. But the same considerations may be made with regard to values, norms and attitudes; socio-economic strata may constitute to a certain extent specific 'sub-cultures' characterized by different normative frameworks and, consequently, endowed with different propensities to migration and eventually to assimilation. More than that: in transitional societies, the different biosocial and socio-economic categories may be differentially exposed to the process of disintegration of the old order and to attitudinal changes. While the conditions which affect one given stratum may have left it unchanged, so that most of its individual members still feel and behave according to the traditional pattern, in another stratum this may be impossible because of modifications in the objective conditions, or because of changes in attitudes perhaps as a result of differential exposure to communication media. A given socio-economic group may feel so frustrated that it may, even in a society which forbids or discourages migration, resort to it.

'Individual traits' operate within the general framework set by the categories as defined by socio-cultural characteristics. Even if a considerable proportion of the younger people or the women, or the labourers want to emigrate (or actually do emigrate) there will be others who prefer to stay. There is always a selection, and the factors which condition such selection, within the socio-cultural category, must be sought precisely in differences in intelligence, needs for achievement, etc. Under given conditions it will be the more intelligent, or the high achievers who will emigrate, or who will be more readily acculturated.

It must be noted that the two categories of attributes are employed as explaining factors in the motivation to migrate and in their subsequent behaviour: however, they do not exhaust all the causation, in both aspects. A third series of factors may and do intervene: these we could call purely random factors, such as idiosyncratic traits, biographical accidents and the like. We have not included them in the categories to be taken into account because the research is focused on discovering regularities, on determining the given probability of occurrence of certain behaviour in a category of individuals and not on predicting individual behaviour as such. It could be further noted that sometimes what in most situations is considered a 'biographical accident' turns out to be, under different circumstances, a common condition affecting all the persons classified in a given category. But in such cases it is precisely because of its nature of common condition, affecting a whole stratum, age group, etc., that it will be not considered by the researcher, as an individual, biographical occurrence.

Sources of data for the characteristics discussed so far are approximatively the same as those indicated with regard to the place or area of origin, and similar difficulties and limitations are likely to arise in this respect. Usually the census will give at least a modicum of information which may offer a picture of the demographic characteristics of the migrants, for instance, age and sex groups, often by place or area of origin. Such data may allow a comparison to ascertain to what extent are they drawn disproportionately from certain categories. In some cases such comparisons may be extended to other attributes, such as education. In any case, however, most information can be obtained from the migrants and the comparison must be based on this group as against data regarding the population of the place of origin.[1] As for intelligence and other psychological characteristics, usually a special study will be required, if one includes in the research design this kind of attributes.

THE MOTIVATION TO EMIGRATE

The study of motivation is a strategic point in the whole research: on the one side, to understand it correctly, all the data discussed so far must be meaningfully integrated and used as a basis to interpret whatever direct information one may obtain on the individual decision to emigrate; on the other side, types of migration (e.g., permanent or transitory), types of motivation and types of migrants are closely related aspects which represent one of the basic keys to understand adjustment, participation and acculturation.

Data on the character of the migration and its motivation are generally obtained through the migrants by means of questionnaires, interviews, etc.; in some cases other kinds of personal documents may be used. Surveys

---

1. An example of use of census data to characterize region of origin and migrant groups may be found in M. B. Deshmukh, 'Delhi, A Study of Floating Migration', in: Textor *et al.*, op. cit. Comparison based on the same kind of source between migrant and non-migrant population, born in the same place of origin, may be seen in F. Zaccone de Rossi, 'L'Inserimento nel Lavoro degli Immigrati Meridionali a Torino', in: [various authors], *Immigrazione e Industria*, Milano, Edizione di Communità, 1962.

at the place of origin on attitudes or propensity to migration are much more scarce: their interest, however, is very high because they illuminate the total socio-psychological context which is conducive to the decision to migrate or to stay. One may also attempt to reconstruct such context by questioning the migrants contacted in the city.

Relevant literature reveals that, in an overwhelming majority, 'economic' motives are imputed to migration: thus direct answers by the subjects seem to confirm the analysis made in terms of push and pull factors. We have seen, however, that migration is the outcome of a very complex process, in which the so-called 'economic' as well as other pressures or attractions are mediated through the peculiar values and norms of the society and the social groups to which the migrant belongs, as well as through his attitudes. As indicated earlier, though we are not concerned with discovering the peculiarities and complexities of individual motivations and decisions as such, we do emphasize the need of ascertaining the nature of the migration in so far as it is related to the social context of the place of origin and to adjustment and acculturation in the city. From this point of view we may indicate some aspects of motivation which should be explored:

1. Manifest motives, which may be reported and analysed in the usual terms of economic (low salaries, unemployment, lack of land, etc.), domestic (i.e., wish to rejoin other members), educational, and other reasons (wish for new experiences, escape from traditional setting, higher aspiration and mobility, etc.).[1]
2. Manifest intention of the migrant regarding the temporary or permanent character of the migration.
3. Nature of the decision, which could be analysed in terms of degree of deliberation, such as from high rational choice to sheer impulsivity, in which no conscious stage of deliberation could be detected.

There are, of course, many other aspects to be added to those just indicated. However, the scheme of analysis should be designed according to the specific purposes of the research and also in relation to the particular circumstances of the migration which is being studied. Some examples drawn from the literature may illustrate this possibility.

Touraine,[2] for instance, distinguishes between *déplacement* (displacement), where the migration is not an expression of a personal and matured design, but the result of fortuitous circumstances, occasional pressures or

1. See examples of such classifications of motives for migration in Matos Mar, op. cit.; G. Balandier, *Sociologie des Brazzavilles Noires*, Paris, Colin, 1955, pp. 40-3; G. Germani, 'El Proceso de Urbanización en la Argentina', *Revista Interamericana de Ciencias Sociales*, Washington, Vol. 2, 1963. pp. 287-345.
2. A. Touraine and O. Ragazzi, *Ouvriers d'Origine Agricole*, Paris, Aux Éditions du Seuil, 1961, Chapter I.

attractions (as when an industrial job is offered to the migrant, without deliberate effort on his side to look for one); *départ* (departure), where at least this intention exists and it is conscious enough; and finally *mobilité* (mobility), where the migration is motivated by deliberate aspirations to higher social status. It is important to note that the three modes are related to the process of assimilation in the city. In the first case the migration is likely to be transitory or, if permanent, the acculturation will be lacking or incomplete participation in urban structures, as a consequence, may be very restricted, and the probability of maladjustment higher. On the contrary, in the case of *mobilité*, assimilation to urban life will be easier and more complete.

Another typology of mobility orientations,[1] takes into account the connexion between occupational status and mode of decision. Here the hypothesis is advanced that the higher the status, the more frequent the 'purposive-rational' mode of decision, and vice versa, the lower the status, the more frequent the 'short-run hedonistic' orientation. The former will be conditioned by life-long goals, while the latter is determined chiefly by situational factors of the moment. It could be suggested that this typology should be related not only to the social stratum, but also to the degree of modernization and development in the place of origin as a whole; the more advanced the cultural modernization of this society, the more frequent 'rational-purposive' decisions, while 'short-run hedonistic' ones, will be more likely in traditional areas.[2]

Furthermore, types of motivation are not independent of the degree of disorganization and change of the traditional order. Emigration may be a substitute for revolution; in any case it is an expression of social mobilization and, as it has been frequently observed, propensity to emigrate is correlated with refusal of the traditional order.[3]

Finally it has been suggested that types of decision may be also determined in part by the relative position of place of origin and place of destination as to prestige, and by their cultural distance: when the place of origin is still accepted, highly valued by the individuals (an indication of good integration in this society) and the cultural distance with place of destination very large, if there is migration at all, it will more likely be transitory, and the migrant will tend to isolate himself from the host society, participating in it as little as possible, and achieving little acculturation. When the cultural

1. J. M. Beshers and E. N. Nishiura, 'A Theory of Internal Migration Differentials', *Social Forces*, Vol. 39, 1960, pp. 214-18.
2. Of the migrants studied in a survey in Buenos Aires, 62 per cent said they had decided to emigrate 'on the spur of the moment'—G. Germani, 'Inquiry into the Social Effects of Urbanization in a Working Class Sector of Greater Buenos Aires' in : Hauser (ed.), op. cit. (The tables are to be found only in the duplicated United Nations/Unesco document E/CN/12/URB/10.)
3. J. Galtung, 'Componenti Psicosociali della Decisione di Emigrare', *Immigrazione e Industria*, op. cit.

distance is smaller, the place of origin less valued than the place of destination, and the degree of integration in the former is rather low, the migration will tend to be permanent and the acculturation easier.[1]

This scheme seems adaptable to many situations in developing countries, as in Africa and in Latin America, and the existence and degree of a demonstration effect between place of origin and place of destination could be used in the construction of interesting working hypotheses. Still other situations may affect the mode and type of migration. For instance, we could compare situations of mass migration with isolated migration: in the first case it may be suggested that selectivity will be low, and the decision will tend to be of the 'short-run hedonistic' type; the opposite tendency should be observed in the case of isolated migration.

CIRCUMSTANCES OF THE TRANSFER

The most important aspect to be included here is the nature of what we could call the 'channel' through which the transfer takes place. As for all other aspects, it is not an independent feature of the process of migration. In this regard, the distinction has been made between work-related channels and kinship and friendship channels.[2] A typical and 'pure' case of the former is the migration of the executive or other employees of a corporation or public administration, who move from one place to another, along the lines of the 'organizational network'; similar cases are the migrations of professionals and persons in other occupations which one may speak of as an 'occupational contact network',[3] that is, a system of communication which supports the ecological mobility.

Kinship and friendship channels are best illustrated by the typical migration chains, which are so commonly found in many countries; the in-flow of migrants occurs along the chain established by the pioneers who settle in the city: friends, relatives and neighbours will then follow, finding support for location and work, as well as a powerful mechanism of adjustment to the new situation. It may be observed that these two modes of transfer are closely connected with the mode of decision and with motivation. On the other hand they are related to the process of adjustment and acculturation: it is worthwhile to mention here that the chain of migration facilitates incapsulation and alienation from full participation in the urban culture, even though, as indicated, it may give psychological support. Another important aspect related to the circumstance of the transfer, is the distinction between family and individual migration. By family we understand here

1. Alberoni, op. cit.
2. This distinction is suggested (in different terms) by Tilly, op. cit.
3. F. E. Katz, 'Occupational Contact Network', *Social Forces*, Vol. 37, 1958, pp. 52-5.

the nuclear or conjugal family only. Information on this aspect, as well as on the kind of channel mentioned earlier, may be of great importance in analysing motivation and subsequent processes of assimilation in the city.

The process of assimilation: data and analysis

As indicated in a previous section the assimilation of migrants may be analysed in terms of three processes: adjustment, participation and acculturation. Such processes may be observed in the various spheres of activities of an individual, and in relation with the different institutions, groups and sectors of society. How deeply one goes depends on the scope and the comprehensiveness of the study, the inclusion of specific spheres and the omission of others. The literature reveals a great variety of topics: anthropological inventories[1] can in fact give an idea of such variety. Most of the studies, however, restrict the field of observation to a number of subjects defined according to main purposes of the research. There are, of course, some topics which are very frequent, and rarely omitted, even if different emphasis is given to them: family and kinship, work (technical, social, and psychological aspects), location and neighbourhood (material culture and social relations), mass media and other contacts with the larger society, informal participation (especially political participation), education (formal and informal, special types such as technical and professional), customs and habits (clothing, food), language career patterns and social mobility (both intra- and inter-generational). Factual information on occurrences, overt behaviour, and on aspects of the material culture, as well as information on attitudes and other psychological aspects are usually included in the surveys.

Whichever may be the particular interest of the research, and the particular aspect which is emphasized (work, family, political participation, etc.), it is convenient to take into account the possibility stressed in a previous section that the same person may not achieve comparable degrees of assimilation simultaneously in all the spheres of behaviour, and that this lack of congruence may be highly important when it is not a merely idiosyncratic expression of an isolated individual, but affects whole categories—social strata, social groups—of subjects.

Each of the various aspects of assimilation (adjustment, participation,

---

1. See, for instance, the *Outline of Cultural Materials,* published in 1950 by the HRAF Press, New Haven, Conn.; and the *Notes and Queries on Anthropology,* of the Royal Institute for Anthropology

acculturation) will require specific indicators to be selected within the spheres of activity which have been in the research. The study of adjustment is also conducted at a more general level, by means of psychological tests, not necessarily related to behaviour or attitudes in specific institutions (or else including samples of many possible situations, in various areas).[1]

The choice of indicators should be guided by the criterion of maximum discriminating power between the 'assimilated' and 'non-assimilated' behaviour (and attitudes). This, of course, involves an operational definition of 'assimilation' for each of the specific items being observed. As is well known, the determination of the validity of the indicators is one of the crucial problems in social research and one whose solution is quite arduous. Here the researcher may decide in favour of a pragmatic criterion. For instance, the model or the average behaviour of the native urbanite is taken as the model against which the migrant is compared. Of course, such comparison must be restricted to what is really comparable: consideration of age, sex and socio-occupational level must be taken into account. Degree and extent of political participation of the migrant unskilled worker only may be compared with the native unskilled worker; attitudes towards the unions, or types of interpersonal relationships within the family are likewise compared, taking as a criterion the equivalent categories among the native urbanites. Many a research assumes explicitly, or implicitly these kinds of pragmatic criteria.[2]

There are, however, other solutions: the criterion may be not set by an empirical but by a theoretical model. In this case a 'type' must be constructed, and this should be made in accordance with a specific theoretical background. An explicit and theoretically founded definition of the 'industrial man' or the 'modern urbanite' (with all the specifications for age, sex and socio-economic strata) could be used as a criterion for comparison with the various empirical types observed in the research. It must be said that such an explicit construction is rarely found in research on urbanization and migration. More often the model is implicit and, when it does not coincide with the empirical model offered by the local urbanites, may take as a basis for comparison the examples offered by the urban society in more advanced countries. For instance, while studying the rise of 'working-class consciousness' among workers of rural origin in a developing country the research may compare it with the present situation or sometimes with the historical situation in Europe and the United States. Now, this is a

1. An illustration may be found in the study of mental health in relation to urbanization by H. Rotondo, in: Hauser (ed.), op. cit.
2. Natives and migrants of different length of urban residence were used in the comparisons by Germani, op. cit.

perfectly adequate approach, provided the relevant historical differences are duly considered.[1]

Comparisons with the criterion assumed as the model for 'assimilation' are not enough: a 'base-line' against which to measure or compare the changes which have occurred since the migration took place is likewise necessary, not only in explanatory studies, but also when one simply wants to describe the process. Such 'base-line' is offered by the description of the society at the place of origin and by the characteristics of the migrant, before migration. Usually here, it is not the same concrete group of migrants which is being compared: the migrants found at present in the place of destination are compared with the corresponding group observed at present in the place of origin. Such procedure has its risks, but very often it is the only one available to the researcher: in any case it should be complemented by additional data concerning possible changes which may have altered the situation at the place of origin, since the departure of the present migrants. Also, allowance for the selectivity of migration and other precautions to be taken are obvious enough. As indicated earlier, present respondents in the city and at the place of origin may report on previous situations and subsequent changes.

Final observations

In the present chapter we have restricted our task to the discussion of the conceptual scheme and other analytical problems involved in a research on migration and assimilation of migrants. Such restriction leaves out a variety of problems: scope and limit of the research, choice of techniques, etc. These, however, have been dealt with elsewhere and the reader is referred to the literature.

---

1. This kind of approach may be found in a series of articles devoted to workers and unions in Latin America and which deal with the problem of assimilation of the migrants by A. Touraine, F. H. Cardoso, A. Simao and J R. Brandao Lopes, *Ouvriers et Syndicats d'Amerique Latine*, special number of *Sociologie du Travail*, No. 4, December 1961.

9   Social and personal disorganization

Judah Matras

General considerations

The process of urbanization is very widely believed to be accompanied by mounting social and personal disorganization presumably caused by, or at least associated with, the nature, conditions and tempo of urban life. Whether or not this is the case is, of course, a matter of empirical study and analysis.

In this chapter the concepts of social disorganization and of personal disorganization are reviewed, some examples of actual studies of social and personal disorganization in urban areas are considered, and some problems of research and investigation of social and personal disorganization are examined.

Social disorganization refers to impairment of the functioning of a social system or inability of a social system to attain its goals due to conflicts, inconsistencies or absence of co-ordination among the elements of the system, group or institution. For example, a family whose major bread-winner is unemployed is unable to look after the welfare and sustenance of its members, and hence is said to be disorganized. Another example is that of the union whose officials accept bribes from employers, rendering the union unable to promote the interests of its members and hence character-ized by disorganization. The club which cannot meet for lack of space, or athletic group which cannot carry out activities for lack of facilities, or community which cannot perform essential services for lack of leadership . . . are all social systems characterized by social disorganization. Thus, a society or social system experiences disorganization when the parts of it lose their integration and fail to function according to their implicit purposes.

Personal disorganization is a term applied to individuals rather than to groups or social systems but, nevertheless, is defined in terms of the individual's behaviour with reference to the values and norms of his social group. The individual who cannot accept the values or does not follow the behaviour norms of the social group of which he is a member is said to be characterized by personal disorganization. The unemployed individual, the delinquent, the homeless man, the prostitute are examples of individuals characterized by personal disorganization.

Social disorganization is usually viewed not simply as a characteristic of groups and of neighbourhoods and communities, but rather as a social process. Neighbourhoods and communities are said to become disorganized as conflicts between component groups and social sub-systems, e.g., between home and school, or between church and neighbourhood club or peer-group, develop and intensify. Families become disorganized as other social groups make conflicting demands upon members, and so forth.

In reverse fashion social reorganization has reference to a social process operating to diminish conflict, increase social solidarity within a given social group, and to improve its ability to perform its functions and attain its goals. Similarly, personal reorganization refers to a process of diminishing personal conflicts and deviant behaviour, enhancing the individual's identification and solidarity with the larger social group.

Investigations and studies of social and personal disorganization may be classified according to whether they are comprehensive studies or focused studies. Comprehensive studies have reference to the sum total of disorganization characteristic of an area or community and attempt to identify and describe all the symptoms and aspects of disorganization prevalent in a community at a given time. By contrast the attention of focused studies is directed to a single specific type of social or personal disorganization, attempting to analyse its origins, consequences and variations.

The conduct of a social problem survey

Many social surveys derive from efforts of individuals and movements to effect social reforms in spheres such as housing, health, industrial wages and working conditions, penal institutions, mental and rehabilitation institutions, and educational institutions. In the last half of the eighteenth century John Howard collected and presented before a committee of the British House of Commons field data collected in his surveys of penal institutions to support his demands for their reform. In the first half of the nineteenth century Frederic Le Play, a French economist and social reformer, conducted surveys of family budgets both to determine standards of living and to make inferences concerning family and social organization, and also to describe stratification and class differences. Le Play's investigators were instructed to obtain data by direct observation, by personal interviews with family members and by interviews with non-family members regarding the families being studied. In the latter half of the nineteenth century and in the early decades of the present century numerous other social surveys were carried out in Europe and North America, also primarily in connexion with social reform movements. Probably the most famous of these was the study in London by Charles Booth, carried out and published over a period of close to fifteen years. Booth hired a staff of social investigators and employed a variety of methods including house-to-house canvassing of districts studied; analysis of census materials; participant observation; conferences and interviews with key personages such as employers, political figures, businessmen and clergy; presentation of charts, graphs, diagrams, maps, drawings and photographs in addition to his own descriptive comments; and he employed quantitative measures such as rates, distributions, averages, etc., in order to characterize and compare the populations and districts studied. Booth studied various aspects of family, economic, religious and neighbourhood life in London, including descriptions and classifications of occupations and trades, labour disputes and their causes and modes of settlement, work rules and industrial abuses, foreign groups and their national and cultural organizations, second generations of the various ethnic groupings, religious work and church doctrines, missions and rescue work, police and municipal institutions, and property characteristics and housing conditions.

The methods employed in collection of data for comprehensive and for focused social problem surveys may include techniques such as field observation, the case-study and the sample survey. Field observation is the first-hand observation of the persons, groups or institutions which individually or collectively comprise the subject of the inquiry. Field observation may be 'controlled' or 'non-controlled'.

Non-controlled observation is the scrutiny of real-life situations without the use of measurements and instruments of precision and with no attempt to check for accuracy in the phenomena observed. Non-controlled observation may be participant observation or non-participant observation. In participant observation the investigator joins and takes part in the phenomenon being observed, i.e., lives in the community or tribe, participates in the club or gang, etc., being described, and often attempts to describe or relate the phenomenon from the point of view of a participant. Non-participant observation may include simple observation and recording of impressions, details, characteristics of the phenomenon studied, or use of informants, their descriptions and their accounts of the phenomenon studied.

Controlled observation may involve employment of mechanical tests or aids to accuracy, standardized conditions of observation and measures to obtain random samples or otherwise to take account of the sampling problem. Aids to accuracy include standardized formats for preparation of detailed field notes, use of photographs, maps and charts, use of interview schedules or questionnaires, design and employment of sociometric scales, and organization of observations in terms of predetermined units of analysis. Standardization of conditions of observation includes either restriction of observation to areas, situations or conditions conforming to some predetermined set of requirements or development of an exhaustive and mutually exclusive set of categories of conditions of observation. If each observation or set of observations can be assigned to its appropriate category, the influences of conditions of observation may be measured and controlled in interpreting study results. The problem of sampling is essentially the problem of the extent or limits to which results or conclusions of a particular observation or particular set of observations apply to, or may be extended or generalized to, some broader universe of similar phenomena. Judgement regarding the relationship of study results to a broader universe rests upon specification of the relationship between the phenomena observed or studied and the broader universe of similar phenomena, whereas without specification of this relationship no such judgement is possible. Accordingly, when the phenomena studied are chosen without clear reference to some parent universe of similar phenomena, the conclusions may not be generalized at all but, rather, must be restricted to those objects or phenomena actually observed. Specification of the relationship between phenomena observed and studied and the broader universe of similar phenomena is usually achieved either by random sampling or by comparative analysis of characteristics of the sample of objects or phenomena studied with those of the broader, more general universe of similar phenomena.

The case-study is one of the oldest methods of social scientific research It was probably introduced by Frederic Le Play as a supplement to his statistical studies of family budgets, was used by Herbert Spencer, and extensive use of case-studies in a modern field-study was made by W. I. Thomas and F. Znaniecki in their monumental study, *The Polish Peasant in Europe and America*. A 'case' may be regarded as a set of data depicting either a phase or an entire life process or cycle of a unit, where such a unit might be an individual, a family, a social institution or system, a community, a nation, etc., as the investigation might require. The case-study method involves collection of facts concerning elements of a social situation and their combinations and interrelationships and, by comparison and classification of such social situations, development of generalizations or formulation of principles governing such situations. In other words the case-study, far from being descriptive only, is intended to serve in formulation of principles and generalizations describing or governing the class of phenomena being investigated.

Case-studies thus seek to compile data throwing light on the processes, causal factors, and rate and direction of change in characteristics of the unit studied in addition to being an accurate and comprehensive description. Life-records and histories, diaries, letters, personal accounts and interview materials may all serve in preparation of case-studies of individuals. Similarly, combinations of such materials may serve for case-studies of couples, families or groups; and in addition materials bearing upon the group activities, characteristics and changes are appropriate.

Development of case-study materials, both for individuals and for groupings of all sizes, very often use standardized formats and study-aids, e.g., questionnaires and interview schedules, checklists of documents and materials, etc. The chief limitation of the case-study is that it is usually very difficult to specify its exact relationship to a broader universe of cases and, hence, to ascertain the extent to which conclusions of its analysis may validly be extended or generalized.

A sample survey is the study of characteristics of a part or fraction of a specified population, the part or fraction ordinarily comprising persons (or households, families or other-sized units) chosen from the parent population according to principles of random selection or probability sampling. One of the most important characteristics of a sample so chosen is that its relationship to the parent universe or population is known, and the range of accuracy or reliability of inference or imputation of sample results to the parent population may be calculated and assessed on the basis of mathematical principles. Usually, though not always, sample surveys are conducted through use of questionnaires administered to persons chosen in the sample, the questionnaires eliciting information on personal characteristics, behaviour, attitudes, possessions or histories of the respondents. Sample surveys have been used, for example, to obtain information on church attendance, educational levels, consumption patterns, health and morbidity, political activity and preferences, attitudes to community problems, and so forth. A large number of texts and manuals dealing with sampling and sample surveys are available. In addition a comprehensive United Nations manual covering all aspects of household surveys, their design and their analysis is at present in preparation.

The procedure in conducting a sample survey calls for translating the research problem into an interview instrument or questionnaire. Ordinarily the manner in which responses to the questionnaire will subsequently be classified, tabulated and analysed is determined in advance, although sometimes such plans are altered in the light of the actual responses obtained in the field. Usually the questionnaire is also pre-tested on a number of respondents in order to determine if the questions are understood or typically elicit meaningful responses. A sample of respondents is chosen from the population to which the study is to have reference. The size of the sample chosen is dependent upon the amount of detail required in analysis of results, the extent of variability anticipated in the responses, the degree of precision required in relating sample results to the total or parent population. Interviews are then conducted with the respondents chosen, results are recorded, responses are coded in terms of predetermined standardized set of categories, and results tabulated, analysed and interpreted.

The processes and phenomena studied in social problem surveys may include elements of personal disorganization, elements of social disorganization and problems of specific groups. Studies of personal disorganization may have reference to juvenile and adult delinquency and crime; vice, including prostitution, narcotics addiction and trade, etc.; mental illness, including both admissions to institutions or other illnesses receiving treatment and mental illness not being treated; and suicide. Studies of personal disorganization include two broad types of investigations: analysis of correlates, causes and consequences of personal disorganization for the individual so affected; and analysis of rates of delinquency, mental illness or other personal disorganization characteristic of a community, of an urban area, of a nation or of sub-areas or sub-groups of the population.

Investigations of social disorganization include studies of family disorganization, of community problems, of industrial strife and problems, of political corruption, and studies of mass disorders and mob violence. Again, such studies may focus upon the structure, the origins, the consequences of family disorganization, of industrial strife or of other types of social disorganization, while others may consider especially the prevalence or rates of occurrence of the phenomenon in different types of areas, of population groupings or economies, etc.

Study of the problems affecting specific groups in the population include those of youth, problems of children, of aged persons, of women, of handicapped or mentally ill persons, problems of persons living in slum, tenement or shanty-town communities, and problems, social organization and culture of persons, neighbourhoods and areas characterized by poverty. More or less elaborate studies of this type have been carried out in the past in connexion with almost every movement for social reform, and the very origins of factual and empirical social research rest with such studies.

The major steps in conducting a social problem survey consist of statement or formulation of the specific problem or objective of the study, specification of the study design, collection of the data, analysis of the data, interpretation and presentation of conclusions. The United Nations manual on household survey methods should be referred to in the planning of such a survey. Formulation of the research or study problem should both indicate the relationship of the problem to similar problems previously investigated and provide the guidelines with reference to which all subsequent steps should be planned and carried out. Formulation of the problem properly indicates the bearing of results of previous investigations upon the problem at hand and indicates the origins of the need for additional investigation.

Specification of the study design must indicate the exact bearing the data to be collected are expected to have upon the problem formulated in the initial step, and how analyses of the data will have reference to the problem. To this end it is necessary at this step to spell out all the sources of data, the techniques for their collection, modes and techniques of analysis of the data and, in a general way, the guidelines or rules for interpreting the data after they are analysed.

The remaining steps call essentially for implementation of the design of the study, i.e., for actually collecting the data, for analysing them, and for interpreting them. However, ordinarily no study design can anticipate all the problems encountered in data collection, analysis or interpretation.

Collection of data may sometimes be complicated by problems arising in the field, problems of interviewing, co-ordination of field operations, quality of personnel and costs of operations. Problems of non-response, or of non-co-operation of respondents, may arise; or investigators may not be permitted to observe the phenomena to be studied and recorded. Very often decisions and changes in the design must be made in the field.

Analysis of data usually requires the use of some set of categories which are useful and meaningful with reference to the problem originally formulated. Sometimes dichotomous classifications, e.g., disorganized-not-disorganized, delinquent-non-delinquent. etc., suffice; but more often more elaborate classification schemes are necessary. The scheme or set of categories employed in some earlier study is often very useful and promotes comparability of results and conclusions. Sometimes, however, entirely new sets of categories must be devised.

Aside from counting and other technical manœuvres, analysis of data is essentially a process of plotting, measuring or testing relationships between variables. Usually, though not always, the choice of variables whose relationships are to be described and measured is implicit in the formulation of the problem. Nevertheless, many important relationships are seen only in the course of analysis, and it is in part the task of the analyst or of the investigator *qua* analyst to pose possibly interesting relationships between variables.

A quite large repertoire of techniques is available to the analyst for describing, measuring and testing relationships between variables. Included among these are frequency counts, distributions, analysis of correlation and regression, and analysis of variance.

One of the most frequently encountered problems in social problem surveys is the measurement of change in time. It is very often of crucial importance to be able to determine if delinquency has increased or decreased in time, if the incidence of mental illness has changed, if the severity of poverty has diminished, and if the corruption of public officials has become more or less frequent, has increased or decreased in seriousness, has changed in form or retained previous patterns. Two types of change in time should, accordingly, be distinguished: quantitative change and qualitative change. The question of quantitative change is that of frequency, and of incidence or relative frequency. The question of qualitative change is that of severity, intensity, seriousness or form.

Analysis of quantitative change is, at least conceptually, the more straightforward of the two. The frequency of a given phenomenon or example of social or personal disorganization is simply the total number of instances of the phenomenon. If it is possible to count the total number of instances in a given interval of time, if the definition of an instance of the phenomenon in question does not change, and if it is possible to count the total number of instances in a second interval in time, the comparison of frequencies follows. Similarly a rate is simply a quotient, the numerator ordinarily comprising the number of instances recorded and the denominator usually giving the average number of persons or objects exposed to such a phenomenon during a given time interval. If the definitions of numerator and denominator remain constant, and if it is possible to count both instances and persons exposed for the two time intervals, then comparison of the two rates derived does in fact indicate the direction and amount of change.

Analysis of qualitative change is primarily a matter of sensitivity and precision of categories of the phenomenon in question and precision of the measuring or observation techniques. If the categories are sufficiently detailed, and if the measuring techniques are sufficiently precise, then changes in the distribution of instances of the disorganization by qualitative categories offer one type of measure of qualitative change. Sometimes other types of measures of qualitative change are also available, e.g., measures of personal or community costs of instances of disorganization, measures of time, measures of resources committed to corrective action, and other such measures.

Examples of studies

A number of studies of social and personal disorganization in urban areas are reported in Unesco publications. For example, a Latin American study of social and personal disorganization reported in a collection of studies of urbanization is the focused investigation of H. Rotondo concerning psychological and mental health problems in Peru. In this study two populations, an urban slum quarter of Lima and a rural coastal village not far from Lima, were compared with respect to mental health and emotional life indicators and symptoms. Household samples were drawn based upon census results and a health questionnaire was administered.

Persons in the urban sample were about 2½ times as likely (26.6 per cent of total) to indicate trembling during an examination or questioning as were those in the rural sample (11 per cent); and the urban-dwellers were about twice as likely (29.9 per cent, compared to 15.4 per cent among rural respondents) to answer affirmatively to the question regarding nervousness, fear or trembling upon the approach of the employer or 'boss'. These results are interpreted by the investigator as indicating that those in the urban community more easily 'go to pieces' under conditions of stress than do those in the rural community.

More than half the respondents in both urban slum and rural village replied in favour of always having someone close by who could advise and help make decisions. About 17 per cent of the urban dwellers admitted feeling lonely and unhappy on holidays, compared to 12 per cent of the rural sample. Almost a fourth (24.2 per cent) of the urban slum sample avowed that they had 'nothing to hope for in life' and 17.6 per cent stated they 'sometimes wished they were dead', with similar answers given by 17.7 per cent of the rural sample in the first instance and 12 per cent in the second.

Anxiety symptoms were found to be fairly frequent, and about equally so in both groups. Almost a third, 32.4 per cent, of the urban group, but only about a fourth of the rural group, showed timidity and difficulty in entering into relationships with others. About half the urban respondents indicated readiness to take offence, compared to only a fifth (20.9 per cent) of those in the village.

Slum dwellers interviewed in the city were very likely to express distrust of each other (about 50.2 per cent stated that they always felt distrust, even among their friends). The investigators found little sociability among those in the urban area, but much more in the village. People in the urban slum have a poor opinion of one another, even though they are not well acquainted, and anti-social acts committed by a few are blamed on everybody. The study also reports findings in the areas of aggressiveness, susceptibility to fatigue, chronic illness and alcoholism. In the urban area, much tension, friction, feelings of failure, racial prejudice and tendencies to take refuge in family life were found. In the rural community there was found to be widespread insecurity, concern to protect property and feeling of inadequate opportunity, but ample sociability, group homogeneity, high degree of stability and a strong spirit of solidarity.

A 'social survey' carried out by K. A. Busia dealt with a number of characteristics and social problems of the city of Sekondi-Takoradi. The study was carried out in 1947-48 and presents results bearing upon housing; occupations and earnings; occupational associations; married life; educational activities; municipal government; religious, social and political associations; and 'social failures', including juvenile delinquency, crime, collapse of sexual morality, bribery and corruption, quarrelling and fighting, unemployment, destitution, and disease and death.

The origin of the statistical material, the nature of the samples and sampling methods employed and the basis for choosing households for study are quite obscure. Nevertheless several of the findings and conclusions are of considerable interest. Overcrowding of housing units is evidently chronic, with more than half the houses studied in the investigation characterized by 'over-crowding'. Forty per cent of the total number of persons in the investigator's sample belonged to families living in a single room. Large numbers of men do not earn sufficient wages to support their households, and the overwhelming majority of wives engage in petty trading or some gainful employment to supplement the household's income. The number of dependents increases with rise in salaries and incomes, a relationship which can ordinarily be accounted for by additional relatives tending to join and claim support in the relatively affluent household. Many families live in 'secondary poverty', a state in which total earnings could suffice for survival and physical efficiency were it not for the fact that some considerable part is absorbed by useless or wasteful expenditure on prestige items of clothing, display, etc., in connexion with marriage, puberty rites, funerals, church parades and other public functions.

Marriage in Sekondi-Takoradi is beset by some fundamental ambiguities and contradictions, and it tends to be unstable and very expensive. There were two ways of getting married in the city: under native customary law and under the civil marriage ordinance. Marriages under the ordinance account for only 4 per cent of the marriages contracted annually. Such marriage is usually accompanied by payment of the customary gifts—but much more expensive—and most of the girls married this way are educated, with parents demanding not only higher sums of money in respect to the usual marriage payments, but also expensive public celebrations. Accordingly ordinance marriages are typically substantially more expensive.

About 30 per cent of the marriages surveyed were intertribal. Since partners often are said to feel attachments to different tribal areas, such marriages tended to be particularly unstable. Typically there would be few personal relationships between families, and sometimes differences in languages and customs. Another problem is that of rules of inheritance, the latter sometimes conflicting in the different tribes and almost always conflicting with inheritance rules under the marriage ordinance.

European ideals of monogamy, expressed in the marriage ordinance forbidding polygamy, conflicted with the not infrequent practice of polygyny, permissible under native customary law. The European marriage ideal further calls for strengthening of bonds between husband and wife, while in many matrilineal societies husband and wife owe their separate matrilineages separate sets of obligations.

Two studies of social effects of industrialization, carried out in South-East Asia present data on adjustment of industrial workers to new occupational and residential settings. The first refers to industrial workers migrating from rural areas to the city of Bombay. (India) and was completed in 1955; and the second refers to a survey undertaken in 1953-54 of factory workers and rickshaw drivers in factories and village in the immediate area of Dacca (Pakistan).

In the first study, census data for the city of Bombay are reviewed showing the composition of the population by place of birth, and it is seen that about 72 per cent of the 1951 population of the city came from elsewhere in the Bombay state, from other states in India, or from other countries. The survey covered a sample of some 523 respondents, all members of the Marathi-speaking population, and all migrants to Bombay from the various surrounding districts. Migrants from the different areas were chosen in about the same proportion as found in the population. The study reviews the main socio-economic features of the areas of origin and considers then the socio-economic causes of migration. The latter are inferred from general considerations, including comparison of characteristics of the areas of origin with those of the city, and from analysis of age composition and educational level of the migrants. But the objective of the study is investigation of the extent and type of influences that city conditions have exerted on the lives of the migrants.

Although the overwhelming majority of the workers were said to be content with their job situations, some 88 per cent said they took the city jobs because there was no apparent alternative, and some 71 per cent indicated that they would prefer to return to agricultural work if it were available. Reasons for disliking present job included low wages, strenuous or troublesome work, or temporary nature of the job.

A large number of immigrants to the city reported owning property in the village, 71 per cent reported at least one close family member left behind in the village, and more than two-thirds reported sending money home to the village. Further questions related to health, recreation, family structure, attitude toward the city, opinions about women's activities, social participation and religious observance.

The second study was reportedly carried out in three stages. In the first stage a preliminary investigation of seven selected factories in the Dacca area was carried out using questionnaires administered to factory employers, employees and villagers living in close proximity to the factories. Nineteen factories in East Bengal were chosen in a sample out of a total of 512 factories registered with the Labour Directorate, and 417 factory workers were interviewed. In addition, ninety rickshaw drivers in the city of Dacca were interviewed with the same schedule.

In addition to the interviews with the 'statistical schedule', a number of case studies were made through interview, discussion, and observation. In all sixty-eight case-studies and five other 'miscellaneous interviews' were made. Characteristics and problems investigated included housing of workers, employment background, methods of recruitment, age, sex and marital status, religion and religious observance, language spoken and literacy, wages, length of service, consumption and dress patterns, health and access to medical services, family relationships and visits to village, marriage and family planning, recreation, undesirable habits and attitudes toward education, women, their occupations and employers.

Certain similarities occur in the findings of the two studies, the one in Bombay and the other in the Dacca area. Large proportions of the workers are new to industrial employment; extreme housing congestion is the rule rather than the exception; almost all urban workers have strong family and often economic ties to the village; industrial workers are much more often literate than is the case in the population generally. Arrangements for marriage tend to be similar in the city to those obtaining in the village. Religious practices are observed in the city to a considerable extent, though somewhat less than in the village. Drinking, gambling, prostitution are common in the city, though said to be virtually unknown in the village. Health is evidently adversely affected by city conditions and industrial employment, as large numbers of workers report themselves in poorer health in the urban situation than previously. Wages are low, and the vast majority of employees would prefer non-factory employment, including agricultural employment if it were available. Workers and their families are evidently less attracted to the city than pushed there by the extreme poverty and near starvation of the villages. The joint or extended family is found in the city as well as in the village, but is declining in the city, the emerging pattern being that of nuclear families.

Thus a quite extended tradition of social scientific research concerned with social and personal disorganization continues and is expanded geographically to areas of relatively recent beginnings of urbanization. Continuing trends of urbanization will surely generate increasing interest in and concern with problems of personal and social disorganization; and it may be hoped that steady improvement in research techniques and ever-broadening acquaintance with them and proficiency in their applications will combine to yield a body of relevant knowledge based upon empirical research and available to planners, educators, administrators and all who are concerned with diminishing the stresses, strains and costs of social and personal disorganization.

Bibliography

ADORNO, T. W. *et al. The authoritarian personality*. New York, Harper's, 1950.
CHAMPION, Y. *Migration et maladie mentale*. Paris, Arnette, 1958.
DRAKE, St. Clair; CAYTON, H. R. *Black metropolis*. Rev. ed. New York, Harper & Row, 1962.
DURKHEIM, E. *Le suicide, étude sociologique*. Paris, Alcan, 1897.
FARIS, R. E. L. *Social disorganization*. New York, Ronald Press Co., 1948.
GOLDHAMMER, H.; MARSHALL, A. *Psychosis and civilization*. Glencoe, Ill., The Free Press, 1949.
HAUSER, P. M. (ed.). *Urbanization in Latin America*. Paris, Unesco, 1961. (Technology and society.)
INTERNATIONAL AFRICAN INSTITUTE. *Social implications of industrialization and urbanization in Africa south of the Sahara*. Paris, Unesco, 1956. (Tensions and technology.)
LEWIN, K. *Resolving social conflicts*. New York, Harper's, 1948.
MYRDAL, G. *An American dilemma*. 2 vols. New York, Harper's, 1944.
PARROT, P.; GUENEAU, M. *Les gangs d'adolescents*. Paris, Presses Universitaires de France, 1959.
SZABO, D. *Crimes et villes*. Paris, Éditions Cujas, 1960.
TEXTOR, R. B. *et al. The social implications of industrialization and urbanization. Five studies of urban populations . . . of southern Asia*. Calcutta, Unesco, 1956.
THOMAS, W. I.; ZNANIECKI, F. *The Polish peasant in Europe and America*. 2nd ed. New York, A. A. Knopf, 1927.
THRASHER, F. M. *The gang*. Chicago, Ill., University of Chicago Press, 1963.
UNITED NATIONS DEPARTMENT OF SOCIAL AFFAIRS. *Report on the world social situation*. New York, 1961.
VIELLE-MICHEL, A. *Études de socio-psychiatrie*. Paris, Institut National d'Hygiène, 1955.
YOUNG, P. V. *Scientific social surveys and research*. 3rd ed. Englewood Cliffs, N.J., Prentice-Hall, 1956.

10 Research on urban plant and administration

Z. Pioro[1]

Introductory observations

The understanding of many social processes and structures of urban communities is impossible without concomitant knowledge of the immensely intricate and ever-changing material tissue of any city. The urban way of life is formed in close interdependence with urban technology. Urbanites become more and more dependent upon functioning of the technological basis of a city. On the other side, the physical structure of a city forms itself under the influence of the economic and social organization of the urban community and its historical development. A considerable influence upon the spatial configuration of the city, however, has been the physiographic features of the land which is occupied by the community.

Thus each research project which aims at a comprehensive analysis of human behaviour within the urban community should include in its programme a study of the physical structure of the city and all pertinent factors moulding its size and shape.

The city administration has an important role in the efficient functioning of the elements of the city's physical structure as well as the city's social life. An analysis of all pertinent factors of urban community should therefore include the structure and functions of city administration also.

A precise and up-to-date knowledge of the physical urban machinery is indispensable to rational city management. City authorities should possess

---

1. In collaboration with: Stanislaw Dziewulski eng., senior planner, Chief of Planning Section of Warsaw Metropolitan Area, Chairman of the Standing Commission for Transportation of UIA; Bohdan Jastrzebski eng., director of City Engineering Bureau, Warsaw; Jerzy Moloniewicz eng., director of Water and Sewage Designing Bureau, Lublin; Bohdan Skaradzinski eng., planner, City Engineering Bureau, Warsaw; Maria Wyganowska eng., senior planner, Town Planning Office of Warsaw Metropolitan Area.

a good, i.e., comprehensive, reliable and dynamic inventory of every architectural structure and every public facility within the city. It must know their number, their location and their functioning in order to be able to provide a plan for their modernization and development. The aim of the inventory is to know which elements of the city plant are 'sound' and which ones are 'unhealthy'; and to determine which parts of the city have potential possibilities of further development.

The general scope of research into urban plant should cover the manner in which people coming together in cities utilize land, the activities that proceed on the land, the structures that are erected to accommodate these activities and the spatial arrangements of these activities and structures along with the streets and open spaces. But since cities rarely remain static, an understanding of the ways in which they change and the causes of these changes becomes vital if urban man is to shape his environment intelligently.

From the theoretical point of view the range of problems to be analysed should be so wide as to permit an understanding of the mutual relations between the world of artifacts and the behaviour of man.

To maximize its usefulness, research on urban plant should strive: (a) to help recognize the qualitative and quantitative level of satisfaction of human primary needs; (b) to point out the most urgent wants and the obstacles to rational community development; (c) to define the possibilities of future development.

The main sources of data are: municipal inventories, censuses, maps, registers, etc. When no data are available or reliable, it is necessary to make sample surveys or comprehensive studies. This chapter will stress the specific problems of urban plant and administration, their role in urban life and the general scientific approach to them.

Physical problems

THE NATURAL BASIS—GEOGRAPHIC ENVIRONMENT

Climate, geological structures and water resources are dominant factors affecting the form of human settlement, land usage, lines of transport, system of water supply and sewage; and people's health and other components of any community. Therefore the research into the world of urban artifacts should be preceded by an inquiry into its natural basis—geographic environment.

Comprehensive study of the natural urban environment—called physiographic research—makes possible an analysis of the ecological structure of a community as well as rational town-planning. The knowledge thus acquired helps to determine the means of improving existing urban conditions and to point out the natural obstacles to and favourable factors in the development of a city.

The aim of physiographic research is to obtain data which permit an analysis of the structure of the geographic environment of the city and the changes going on in it. The subject matter of such research usually deals with the following problems: division of the urban area and its surroundings into isometric and geomorphological spatial units; characteristics of the fluvial system, natural water reservoirs, water conditions of the urban area; characteristics of the climate (including temperature, rainfall, wind and inversion areas) and air pollution caused by industry; the amount of drinking and industrial water; characteristics of agricultural land use; natural resources; reservoirs of nature requiring protection.

This inquiry should be made by specialists, mainly geographers, and its results are usually presented in the form of maps with elaborated legends and explanation.

LAND USE

Concern about the use of land is not a new thing; it is as old as humanity itself. Nearly every human activity requires functionally individuated space. In modern urban communities 'friction of space' reflects an awareness that the proper use of urban land can mean the difference between success and failure.

The analysis of actual land use and its historical development is a springboard for every ecological study of the urban community. There is intense competition for land in every city throughout the world, and this is what lies behind the concept of land use and its practical application. The urban community must define and set limits upon the uses that are to be made of the limited amount of land within its borders, and it must assign land uses in such a way that the future needs of the community will be met. Before this can be done, however, one must find out what purposes the urban land is being used for today. This is the role of land-use maps and surveys.

The value of such a map lies in the information about the usage of properties which is gathered and represented on it—and this requires some form of land-use survey.

The goal of a land-use survey is to discover these uses, catalogue them and classify them. The purpose of a land-use map is to display graphically the kinds of land use and their distribution within the area studied. In essence, a land-use map reveals the mosaic pattern of a community's physical development.

The scale of a map depends on the use to which it will be put and on the scope of the land-use study. It is advisable to have a basic map prepared in two different scales or sizes in order to meet the many different demands. Suggested scale ranges might be: a large scale of 1 : 2,000 or 1 : 5,000 and a small scale of 1 : 10,000. The final choice will depend on the size of the community and particular needs of the study.

According to the practice of Polish town-planning, land uses have been organized into thirteen classifications, each of which has a distinctive colour or outline to identify it. These classifications are: 1. Industry; 2. Warehouses and yards; 3. Agriculture and forestry; 4. Building industry; 5. Administration; 6. Housing; 7. Services; 8. Green spaces; 9. Traffic and transport; 10. Water supply and waterworks; 11. Sewage and refuse collection system; 12. Power industry—electricity, gas, heating; 13. Miscellaneous uses.

This classification is used also to make land-use plans and town-planning programmes. The amount of detail shown within each land-use classification depends on the scale of the map which is to be prepared.

If historical maps of the city are available it is advisable to make one or more supplementary maps illustrating the dynamics of the city land-use development. A chronology of changes depends on the particular history of the city. Nevertheless it might be useful to accept this classification: (a) the pre-industrial period; (b) first stage of industrialization; and (c) a period after the Second World War.

HOUSING

Adequate housing conditions are of basic interest to a single man, to a family and to a community. From the beginning of the industrial revolution and the concomitant process of urbanization many social and political groups have raised questions about the problem of housing shortages and about the poor condition of dwellings for the working class and its biological and moral consequences. The post-war period did not bring visible improvement of the situation. Slums, shanty-towns, squatters' settlements instead of being liquidated are spreading throughout urban areas. Urban concentration makes the problem more and more acute.

The most significant factors that have contributed to the housing crisis in urban areas in the period following the Second World War throughout the world are as follows:

1. The waves of migration to cities, unprecedented in their volume, accelerating urbanization.

2. Mass destruction of homes in wartime.
3. The disparity between the people's income and the cost of adequate housing according to modern notions of comfort.
4. Comparatively slow progress in the housing industry.
5. Lack of adequate municipal or national housing policy and building regulations systems.
6. The opposition of vested interests, e.g., real estate proprietors, to building houses for low-income families and to slum clearance.
7. Material deterioration of houses by reason of inadequate maintenance.
8. Abuse of property by uneducated in-migrants—usually from the country.
9. The blighting effect of housing conditions from industry and heavy traffic.
10. Difficulty in the democratization of dwelling space by reason of discrimination on the basis of race, class or wealth. If the relevance of the above-mentioned factors is accepted, it follows that any comprehensive urban research must take into consideration the housing problem in its physical and socio-economic aspects. Before undertaking the research one should know the main legal factors determining the development of home-building in the city, past and present.

Housing policy

Adequate housing depends basically on a policy stating: (a) who should build houses; (b) what is the possible limit and degree of intervention from administration authorities into building processes; and (c) what are the protective spatial and technical norms and standards.

Land-use policy

Many urban communities have grown without planning and control. The land-use plan is a relatively new device for rational city development. According to *laissez-faire* policy commercial, industrial and residential structures were built whenever the owner desired. The law of land rent has created the tendency to overcrowd those sections of the city which were well equipped in modern facilities, while other parts of the land remained undeveloped. In this way the housing problem was aggravated by the inequalities of land values, and real estate speculation was a serious obstacle to adequate housing.

It is of the utmost value to obtain information about what were and are the rules governing land-use policy and zoning regulations in the city, and to gauge their effects on housing conditions.

Housing industry

Since under the capitalist system each private enterprise engaged in building is organized to promote its own interests, private construction may often distort housing developments from a social standpoint. Thus information about the organization of the housing industry and its practice is necessary to help to interpret properly the housing problems of the community. Similarly, since under centralized control problems of resource allocation and synchronization of activities may create serious problems in meeting housing demands, research should include the study of the organization and functioning of central bodies charged with housing developments. Researches should include study of architectural design and town-planning services, if any.

Housing inspection

Municipalities usually have building inspection bureaux to detect and report to the authorities possible violations of building regulations, fire hazards, necessities of repair, etc. There is general underestimation of the fact that conservation and modernization of houses reduces the housing problem as well as the social costs of biological and social pathology. The knowledge of actual inspection ordinances and efficient work of supervision building inspectors is very helpful in comprehensive analysis of a housing problem.

House financing

Many potential house owners, private or co-operative, do not have the required funds to build a house or housing estate outright. Loans are obtained from banks or loan companies. All the regulations concerning loan-taking have substantial influence on building processes and consequently on housing problems in the city.

System of building regulations

In some countries all the above-mentioned particular regulations are codified into one system.

In Poland, for example, the system of building regulations creates the general basis for building activities. It includes all matters connected with the process of building investments, starting with making a programme and ending with a delivery of completed structure for use. Moreover, it regulates the activities designed to maintain buildings in a proper state.

The building code, also, has rules regulating the work and duties of investing agencies, architectural designing bureaux, building industry units, building supervision agencies, and basic duties of owners and managers of structures.

Therefore, to know the major factors influencing housing problems one should use as a springboard to further research the specific system of building regulations and its supplementary clauses and provisions or, in the case of its absence, the particular ordinances regulating in some way the development of housing in the city.

Housing research

The aim of housing research is to give a scientific basis for a sound housing policy and for an objective frame of reference for analysis of human behaviour and certain social processes. It should provide information about the number and condition of housing units, the housing industry, rents, cost of house management, physical decay, need of repairs and the social needs of housing.

The object of housing research may be either the existing housing plant, its size and value, its physical state, or ways of using the housing by people; i.e., social relations created by the distribution of houses on the basis of social stratification in the community. According to the purpose, the scope of housing research may be changed and the main stress may be put either on existing housing volume and its material factors or upon its social aspects. The evaluation of the level of housing conditions in the city demands joint analysis of both aspects: physical and social.

Housing research may be static, when its main purpose is to study a single characteristic of existing housing volume at a certain time. But by its repetition one may trace the dynamics of changes going on in the number of units, in their physical quality, in the housing conditions of the population, etc.

Sources of information

To collect data concerning the quantity and quality of housing and to explore housing conditions one may use the following sources of information: housing and population censuses; inventories of existing housing volume; statistical data concerning building investments, the housing industry, management of houses—repairs, modernization, merger, etc.—as well as data concerning population movements based on current municipal records and reports; housing surveys.

As regards the method of gathering data one can use comprehensive or sample techniques. The latter may be applied to each of the above-listed sources and they permit deeper and wider study with less effort.

Housing research problems

As regards the physical aspects of housing, the aim of a housing inventory is to define the building system, the size of houses and dwellings, house sanitary equipment, physical condition of structures and other specific features characterizing the quality of the city housing volume. The analysis of inventory data should encompass the classification of quantitative data in specific categories and the computation of average and structural indices. Architecture may be analysed by means of division of the urban area according to the size and height of buildings and their situation. Estimation of the technical and economic value of buildings depends, in general, on various sources of information, and usually it is advisable to employ experts to make the evaluation.

When approaching the problem of sanitary equipment one should have a map of the network of public utilities: the reticulation of conduits of water, sewage, gas, electricity and central heating systems. With the aid of the map it is possible to find out which houses are included in the central water, sewage, heating, gas and electricity system, and which are left out. For the latter one must find out what substitute facilities are made for the convenience of inhabitants. Functional analysis of dwellings usually includes the following points: (a) the distribution of dwelling units by size—the number of dwellings with different number of rooms; (b) the sanitary equipment of dwellings.

The rational use of housing

Inquiry into the rational use of housing aims at the determination and analysis of quantitative relations between existent housing plant and its users.

Thus the research endeavour should go in the direction of establishing the proportions of persons per room in every size and type of dwelling unit and the proportion of dwellings with full and partial sanitary equipment. A starting-point in this kind of research is a comparison between the number of housing units and the number of its users—the number of dwelling units in relation to the number of households or families; also the total floor space in relation to the number of inhabitants.

But average indices for the whole community are not sufficient to get a detailed analysis of housing usage. The inquiry into the problems of the dwelling unit use should be concentrated on the analysis of dwelling-users, taking into consideration at least the following factors: household and

199

family structure, the family growth cycle, social status and demographic components. This structural approach permits the determination of the number of multi-family dwellings, the number and kind of people living in each structural category of housing conditions, the relations between family housing needs and their actual satisfaction.

While conducting a housing study it is necessary to accept or to determine some criteria for measurement of the actual state of housing conditions. They fall into the following categories: health conditions caused by microclimate, hydrogeological characteristics of the environment and land use (e.g., the harmful influence of industry), sufficient insulation and ventilation of houses, the standard of sanitary equipment, material condition of buildings, quality of building materials.

Dynamics of changes in housing

Housing volume and housing conditions are not static; they are in constant fluctuation. A single housing study based upon census data and a general housing inventory, even if periodically repeated, does not give insight into all the changes which have occurred in the meantime. Execution of a housing policy and planning demand continuous observation of the changes in housing conditions in the community. An increase of housing supply is caused by the following factors: building new houses, modernization of existent structures, conversion of buildings of different previous use into dwellings.

The decrease of housing supply may arise from: losses caused by the demolition of structures which are dilapidated, or those whose demolition was determined by town-planning regulations; losses brought about by elemental disasters (fire, floods, etc.); and losses made by changes of use (i.e., if dwellings are converted into other use or if merged).

A researcher studying housing conditions is interested in changes in the size of the population living in an investigated area. These changes are caused by two factors: natural growth of population, births and deaths, and migrations.

In addition to these changes, which one may call 'real', there are others called 'apparent'. These are changes brought about by the extension of a city's administrative boundaries.

The above type of research may be called quantitative. Qualitative study is concerned with changes in the housing infrastructure, the reticulation of water, sewage and gas networks, and in the physical and sanitary equipment of houses.

The sources of information for these aims are to be found in the statistics of the building industry and in municipal housing reports. More detailed study of housing changes, e.g., economic and social differentiation of housing are possible only through field studies on a sample basis.

INDUSTRY AS A FACTOR IN AN URBAN PATTERN

Industry is a fundamental factor in urban growth. In most urban areas industry, through its land use and its connexions with other domains of city life and its influence upon other kinds of land use, is a powerful factor in determining the physical structure or land-use pattern. Industrial areas constitute from 5 to 15 per cent of built-up areas of numerous cities. Thus industries are important competitors for urban space. Not only are they highly dependent on various forms of transport and transit, but often their needs helped to determine the location or extension of these facilities.

Industry has widespread connexions with and influence over other branches of the economy: transport, wholesale and retail trade, international trade, storage space, labour. It often determines the location of substantial amounts of housing.

Problems to study

The problems to be studied may be grouped as follows:
1. The general characteristics of the location of industry of a city: e.g. concentration or dispersal.
2. What kinds of industries prevail in each category.
3. For dispersed industry:
   (a) causes of dispersal—(spontaneous growth, land rent, conditions of geographic environment, land-use policy);
   (b) functioning of scattered industrial plants—routes of transport, mutual co-operation between industries, infrastructure (communal or local);
   (c) the influence on neighbouring areas—noise, air pollution, belts of isolation, occupation of areas suitable for other uses (housing, services);
   (d) restricted possibilities of extension, restrictions in the management of the lot;
   (e) needs and possibilities of liquidating or removal of dispersed industry (from economic, physical or sanitary reasons), the scope of the problem.
4. For concentrated industry—industrial quarters:
   (a) main reasons of the rise of industrial concentrations—a historical view (kind of industry, land-use policy, physical planning policy);

(b) forms of industrial concentrations in a city—size, character (one or many kinds of industry), branch specialization;

(c) spatial distribution of industrial concentrations in a city—relation of areas of industrial concentration to the function and physical pattern of a city;

(d) transportation routes and infrastructure;

(e) possibilities of development, or advisability of liquidation or removal, total or partial.

The best way to collect data on these problems is to send questionnaires to specific factories and to analyse the land-use map.

Air pollution

Tendencies towards urbanization and greater industrial concentration result in more severe and widespread contamination of urban atmosphere. Man must have fresh air to live. This need exceeds man's consumption of food and water. The pollution of air that man breathes by industry and its by-products has reached alarming heights in many communities. In such cities there is need to know what are the sources of air pollution, their spatial influence (reach area), the gradients of pollution, the health conditions in such areas, the means to counteract such influence or to eliminate the sources.

GREEN SPACES IN URBAN AREAS

Green spaces—'the lungs of a city'—fulfil various functions, some of which are detailed under the sub-headings below.

Biological and climatic function

Conditions of physical environment (among others: temperature, moisture, air composition) strongly affect the life of man. Powerful technical means now under the control of man exert powerful influences on this environment, especially in cities and industrial areas. On the other hand, the development of natural sciences provides an adequate basis for defining optimal environmental conditions for human life.

The aim of physical planning is to guarantee these optimal conditions to the people. The role of open spaces in urban areas is to counteract unhealthy influences in the environment; this role is carried out through their appropriate location in different parts of the city and through their proper development.

Social function

Green spaces in a city are places of recreation in the open air in various forms. A sufficient amount of leisure is a necessary condition of regenerating the physical and mental strength of man. Number, location and management of green spaces in a city and its environs determine the quality and universality of rest and recreation of the urban population.

An aesthetic function

Living in ugly surroundings has a bad effect on the psychical balance of man. Having green trees and grass around is good for the mind and increases susceptibility to beautiful things. Emotions felt in viewing a beautiful landscape as a combination of fine architecture, green space and water are among the strongest experiences enriching man's personality.

Economic and technical functions

Investments made by man have material consequences which directly or indirectly influence the elements of the natural environment in a way often unfavourable, causing disturbances of biological and economic balance. Green spaces rationally spaced reduce harmful influence (for example green belts of isolation around industrial areas).

Green areas in a city are divided, according to Polish town-planning theory, into five groups according to their functions: (a) areas influencing natural conditions (usually large forests); (b) public green areas (parks, playgrounds, cemeteries); (c) areas for sports; (d) complementary green spaces in housing areas, streets around public buildings, etc.; (e) horticultural areas supplying food for the city.

An inventory of green areas should supply data concerning their size, location and development. But to establish how they are utilized by diverse social groups, field studies on a sample basis should be made.

WATER SUPPLY

The mechanization of the modern man's life and the higher standard of living combine steadily to increase the demand for water. Water is used for cooking, washing and other household needs. The amount of water used for household needs oscillates from 20 to 50 litres per person for 24 hours according to the standard of equipment in houses. Industrial plants are important consumers of water. They use water both for consumption and for technological needs. In many cases the industrial demand for water considerably exceeds the household one and determines the size of water-supply installations.

The amount of water for industrial needs is limited by technological norms suited to the requirements of different industries and different methods of production. It is usually measured in cubic metres per production unit.

Moreover, in a city water is also used to meet the needs of public institutions, for watering trees and lawns in the parks, for street cleaning, for decoration, and for protection against fire.

The sum total of these separate elements indicates the total consumption of water in a city and is usually calculated in cubic metres per 24 hours. All matters connected with the water supply and sewage system are usually under the management of city authorities, who supervise the exploitation of the sanitary installations and make proper investments.

The progress of urbanization and the growth of new industrial plants and new kinds of industrial production combine considerably to increase the demand for water. The growing urban organisms must seek more and more abundant sources of water, often reaching for them to distant areas. Difficulties are increased by the fact that surface waters are often polluted by communal and industrial sewers. For that reason some waters are unfit to be used as sources of the central city water supply. Of necessity distant sources of ground water are reached for. It is imperative to observe the rational exploitation of such distant sources so as not to spoil the general balance of ground waters.

Basic characteristics of the city water supply are:

1. Points of water intake for central city waterworks. Surface and ground waters are basic founts of water intake for waterworks. According to the size of a city and abundance of a fount, there may be one or more points of water intake in a city.

   A parameter which denotes the size of a water intake place is its output measured in cubic metres per 24 hours.

   Water derived from these places, especially surface water, is subjected to suitable treatment to meet the sanitary requirements set for drinking water.

   One of the basic problems connected with the exploitation of water intake construction is the provision of sufficiently extensive intake areas free from habitation to protect the founts of water from pollution.

   In new water intake construction it is desirable to ensure the possibility of their future extension on neighbouring grounds, because building water intakes in distant places complicates the reticulation of water pipes.

2. Pumping stations. The water suitably treated in filtering works is con-

ducted to the city network by means of pumps, whose size and location depend on the size of a city, on land configuration, on the accepted system of aqueducts. The pumping apparatus must be so selected as to guarantee the proper water pressure in the most distant and highest parts of the city.

3. In the initial stages of work of the city aqueduct the network of water-pipes covers only a part of the habitation area. In the course of its development the water network covers farther sections, and in optimal cases the whole urban area. But it happens more often that certain quarters are not included in the central water supply, and are forced to use local aqueducts based on individual wells. This local apparatus is gradually abandoned as the central network extends its reach.

In Poland, at the present time the average percentage of urban population who have the benefit of central or local water supply is between 60 and 80.

4. The supply of water to industrial plants is a separate question. Small factories, scattered in the city area, usually take water for their consumption and technological needs from the central city network. But big plants, whose demand often exceeds the possible output of the city water intake points, must organize their own water supply by building industrial water intakes. In such cases it is possible to use water of poor quality for industrial needs.

Materials illustrating the problems of water supply in a city are:

1. Concerning water intake points: a technological schema of water intake construction, hydrobiological and hydrogeological data, statistics of exploitation of water, prices of water.
2. Concerning the water network: an inventory of the networks, the percentage of urban area covered by the water network, the percentage of users of the water network, the amount of losses through leakage.

When presenting the results of the analysis of the condition of the city water-supply apparatus it is necessary to give:

1. A map of the city area indicating the location of water intake places and of main water conduits, and showing the approximate limits of reach of the city water network.
2. Statistical data concerning: the output of water intake places, the general output and sale of water, the approximate percentage of population using the city water installation, other sources of water supply.
3. A general estimate of needs and possiblities of development of the water facilities in the city.

SEWERAGE AND DRAINAGE

The rational drainage of sewage and storm water from the city area is one of the fundamental factors in maintaining good sanitary conditions of the community and one of the most expensive city facilities. Thus water and sewage are of the highest concern to the city administration.

The flow of sewage in sewers is generally by gravity and sewers are virtually underground covered channels. The layout of a sewage system is therefore dependent on the topography of the area. The location and level of the point at which the sewage is disposed has fundamental influence upon the structure and shape of a city.

If sewage and storm water flow in the same channels, then the system is called a combined system. In separate sewage systems there are separate drains for household and industrial sewage, and separate pipes for rainwater drainage. Which of these basic sewage systems is employed depends on local conditions; often both are working in one and the same city.

The majority of city sewers conduct sewage by gravity towards the lowest parts of the city, where treatment works are usually located. Streams running through the lowest parts of the city are the usual receptacles of sewage discharge, previously suitably treated in treatment works. It is not always possible to canalize the whole city area by gravity towards one point. When this is the case local pumping stations must be installed to pump sewage up from the lower parts of the city.

To protect the natural river vegetation and biological life of a river, sewage must be delivered to treatment works before it is discharged into a stream. Steadily increasing size of a city and industrial sewage discharged into streams pollute the water, kill fish, deform the natural exterior of rivers, and prevent the use of surface waters as sources of city water supply.

For protection of streams men build special treatment works, working through mechanical, biological and chemical processes. In some cases sewage, after preliminary treatment, may be taken to a sewage farm where it soaks into the ground. This frees the streams completely from pollution.

The most important characteristics of the city canalization are:
1. Sewage installations collecting sewage from all points of the city where it is produced. The reach of these installations develops with the growth of the city and in optimal cases covers the whole city area.

    It is necessary to provide areas without drainage with a local sewage system, with sewage discharged into the ground or disposed of by sanitation columns.

    With the growth of a central sewage system, houses are gradually joined to city sewage, and local installations are liquidated.

In Poland on the average 60 to 80 per cent of the city population use the city sewage facilities.

2. Sewage treatment works receive sewage from city drains and after treatment discharge it into receptacles.

The size and system of treatment works depends mainly on the size of the city, on the quality of sewage discharged, on the power of flow in a receptacle and its ability of self-cleaning.

The size of treatment works is usually determined by its exploitation capacity, measured in cubic metres of sewage treated per 24 hours.

Materials illustrating the problems of city sewage disposal and treatment are:

1. Concerning the sewer network: an inventory of sewage pipes, the percentage of urban area equipped with sewage installations, the percentage of urban population benefiting by the city sewage facilities.

2. Concerning the treatment works: a technological scheme of treatment works, the degree of treatment attained, statistical data on utilization of treatment works.

A presentation of the results of the analytical study of a city sewage system must contain:

1. A map of the city area indicating the location of main sewers and treatment works, and showing the approximate limits of reach of the city sewage system.

2. Statistical data concerning the number of sewers joined to a city sewage system and treated in city treatment works and the number of people using the local sewage system.

3. A general evaluation of needs and possibilities of development of sewage facilities in the city.

Refuse disposal

Refuse produced by a city is generally collected and disposed of by the city department of sanitation. It is taken in special trucks to central points beyond areas of habitation, called refuse heaps.

Refuse may be utilized in compost mounds where, through heat, fermentation may be attained and a high degree of mineralization of the organic compounds contained in refuse. This process produces a compost fertilizer used in agriculture. Data obtained about refuse disposal should concern the characteristics of the accepted system, the number and kind of vehicles, the places of disposal, the use made of refuse, and the costs of disposition of refuse.

We watch in the cities of today a gigantic growth of the means of transport and, at the same time, we witness that as rapidly as they grow they become overburdened. This phenomenon signifies the heightened spatial mobility of city-dwellers—the cause of the huge flows of traffic, difficult to control. Even in cities equipped with the most modern means of transport, everyday mass passenger movements (mainly to work and back) is one of the chief vexations of city inhabitants.

The opinion that private car ownership would solve the transportation problem proved quite false. It became evident that if in a middle-sized city every third family owned a car, the streams of car traffic became so enormous that they not only paralysed their own progress but, also, seriously impeded mass transportation. The concentration of traffic arising spontaneously in a modern city requires study of the causes of mobility to find means of dealing with them.

The causes of movement may be divided into three groups: trips to work, trips to shops and different purpose trips, trips to recreation areas. Each of these groups requires separate studies.

Trips to work

The first step in this research must be the location of points of destination—which means that we must find out where in the city area are concentrations of places of employment. In the second place we must discover from which parts of the city this passenger movement originates. It is important to draw the borderline of areas where the intensity of trips to work is the greatest. These areas have become extended considerably in recent years.

Nowadays cities tend to become centres of agglomerations from which mass passenger movements originate to go to work towards the city centre. They originate also from many rural communities of the suburban zone. The latter can be explained both by the development of the means of transport (chiefly individual cars), and by socio-economic changes going on in rural districts.

The next step is to consider the routes of travel; we must establish from which places of residence to which concentrations of places of employment people travel most often. Studies on this question allow us to state that the mutual proximity of places of residence and employment is only one of many motives (and not always decisive) of choosing either one or the other. The knowledge of reasons why members of a certain community do not seek work in the nearest accessible quarter, but often travel to the farthest end of the city, and the discovery of certain regularities (if any) in this domain, could perhaps lead to measures to shorten the distance between places of work and residence.

The problem is complicated and not easy to solve either in theory or in practice. We must realize that different factors are active here, for instance: professional specialization, tradition and habit, personal preferences, aspiration, the amount of wages and, lastly, the convenience and cost of transportation.

Besides the location of trips to work in space there is the question of their location in time. For that purpose we must study the hours at which work in different institutions begins and ends; whether and at what time there are breaks for lunch and whether or not people travel home to meals during breaks. When we have proper data, we can provide against excessive flow of traffic by changing the schedule of hours of work and luncheon breaks.

We shall also need data concerning distance, time and mode of travel. It is necessary to know what is the percentage of people travelling to work in private cars to specific work places and what factors are involved.

Shopping and different purpose trips

The methods of studying trips to work can be applied in a degree to studies of other groups of trips. But each group has its specific features which must be treated separately.

A study of shopping and different purpose trips must begin with establishing which shops, workshops, restaurants, theatres, medical centres, etc., people have in their neighbourhoods or close to the place of their work, which are within walking distance, and which are farther removed.

The next stage of the study is to establish how often people go to these places from home and how often from work. Distance, time and mode of travel are also important.

Trips to recreation areas

In an introductory stage of research it should be established what percentage of the population undertake trips to recreational areas and in what rhythm such trips occur.

Do weekend trips prevail or are weekday trips as frequent? At what rate do they occur during a month, a season, a year?

We must study the location of recreational areas, especially those much frequented, and establish the reasons for their popularity. Is it their natural beauty (lakes, rivers, forests) or facilities for sports and rest, or good transportation, or proximity to certain habitation quarters?

As in previous studies, we must find out how many people seek recreation in areas nearest to their homes and how many go to areas which they consider more attractive, even if they are situated far beyond the outskirts of the city. How far do the borderlines of recreational areas around the city towards which the population travel reach? Are the farthest points to which people travel by cars situated at a decidedly greater distance from the city than the farthest places accessible by train, street-car or bus?

This short description of the most important social and technical problems of the city traffic points to the types of data and indicates the methods by means of which a contemporary town-planner tries to cope with the problems. The planner must deal with problems of rational distribution of places of employment and of services and consider among other things the decentralization of institutions hitherto localized in the centre of the city, or in large industrial quarters. He must also plan the distribution of recreational areas. Furthermore, he must also consider the proper size and extension of the urban agglomeration itself.

Study of the transportation system requires two groups of data: the first group consists of the usual statistical data concerning individual and collective vehicles of transport, the amount and quality of bases of technical service (garages, repair workshops, filling stations, etc.), the total length of routes of transport, frequency and regularity of the transit service, the speed of vehicles, the spacing of stops, the length of walking distances to shops, etc.

The second group of data consists of indices showing the extent to which needs are satisfied in the field of transportation, with proper differentiation of the central and peripheral parts of the city. Included among the useful indices frequently used by specialists are: the network of routes of individual vehicles expressed as kilometres per square kilometre of city built-up area, the volume of moving vehicles for every 1,000 inhabitants, isochrones of trips to the centre and other points of the city that attract the inflow of people, the number of sitting and standing places (when vehicles are properly loaded) and its relation to maximum and average flows of traffic and, lastly, the number of transfers in journeys to work.

In studying the transport of goods it is necessary to have data on the volume of goods transported by type of vehicles (railways, trucks, boats, pack-animals, etc.) and chief routes and destination points.

THE POWER INDUSTRY

Nowadays one cannot even imagine the organized life of men without energetics. Energetics supplies drive to machines; it is also an integral component of numerous technological processes. It enables efficient transfer in space of people and goods. Through media of mass communication it makes possible instantaneous forwarding of news and cultural achievements and makes them accessible to practically unlimited numbers of people.

Energetics gives heat and light to houses and streets and makes our work, rest and movements independent of sunlight. It lightens considerably many household tasks. There are two energetic systems in cities: centralized and decentralized.

Centralized energetics consists of the electric power industry, the gas industry and central heating stations (or thermal-electric power stations).

With technologies applied today, centralized energetics, i.e., a system of collective production and distribution of power, has as much supremacy over individual systems (each consumer for himself) as has modern industrial production over handicraft. Energetics permits the satisfying of consumer demand for power at a low social cost.

An analysis and evaluation of the actual energetic systems in a city may be conducted by comparing it to a model or optimal system for that city. Such a model system assumes a definite branch structure of production and consumption, that means an optimal participation of all branches in supplying total demand. The model system is different for every city and depends on various factors such as climate, size of a city, kinds and scale of industry, etc. The proportional share of every branch is determined by a calculation of economic and technical effectiveness.

It is an accepted axiom that only a centralized energetic system fulfils optimal conditions. Generally speaking, in the framework of that system a demand for heat, light and power transmission ought to be supplied by a thermo-electric power station and a demand for gas by gasworks. In peripheral areas beyond the reach of these institutions, or where population is widely dispersed, it may be appropriate to replace them by local central heating stations and by distribution of gas in cylinders.

No separate figures or indices can present a true picture of power administration in a city. To get a comprehensive presentation one has to analyse a complex of numbers and indices. For instance, a total produced amount of power may camouflage a certain amount of waste. Besides, a total amount of production is conditioned to a considerable degree by kinds of industry in a city and by connexions of the city power industry with the power industry of a country. Data concerning the consumption of power provide more exact information. But this, in turn, depends on the general standard of living and of technical development.

When quantitative analysis of power industry problems in a city is completed, a qualitative analysis should follow.

An elementary index for this purpose is that showing the relation between the demand for power being met by centralized and decentralized energetic systems, or, in other words, showing the share of the centralized system in the total power balance of a city. The higher the share, the higher the development of the power industry of a city.

A high total consumption of power may be deceptive, as it may in a degree be the result of wasteful usage. So it must be established in what proportion respective demands are met by respective kinds of power. Deviations from 'ideal model', which will probably exist, will point to a certain underdevelopment of respective branches of the power industry. Most frequently underdeveloped is likely to be the gas and thermic-power industry.

It is useful to compare these data collected for one city with similar data for other cities at home and abroad, always remembering that the comparison is sensible only if general features of urban development in the cities are fairly alike.

ADMINISTRATION

The efficient functioning of the city as a whole is a necessary basis for securing satisfactory conditions of living to its inhabitants and for the proper management of its environs. This efficiency depends in great measure upon the chosen system of administration: the rationality of its methods and work and intellectual and moral qualities of the personnel.

Comprehensive knowledge of the city as a technological and social entity demands complementary studies of the following subjects:

1. What system of government is accepted in the city? Which constitutional provisions regulate this system? What are the historical traditions of municipal administration in the country?

2. In which way and for how long is the administrative authority chosen (or appointed)?

3. What is the scope of competence of the city administration? Which local institutions of government are not subjected to the city administration? What are the methods of control and co-ordination of the work of governmental agencies active in the city area?

4. What is the object of the activity of the city administration? (For example, to guard the laws, to protect private and social property, to safeguard the rights of citizens, to execute the civic and financial duties of citizens to the State, to co-operate with the State in functions of defence and security, to ensure safety and public order.)

5. Apart from bureaucratic functions, are there any relations of a social kind between the city administration and the citizens? Are there voluntary associations of citizens to promote city self-government? How do the city authorities respond to such an initiative?

6. What is the functional structure of the administrative system? What is the form of organization of the administrative system (a mayor and a city council; local councils in each quarter of a city; other agencies)?
7. What is the source and amount of the city budget?
8. What are the objects and the methods of city economic, social and physical planning?
9. By what technique is the city governed (meetings of the city council; committees; sessions of executive board). What is the competence of executive board and specified departments and sections?
10. What is the degree and method of control, if any, of city administration by the State government?
11. What are the qualifications required by administrative personnel, their morale, their wages and methods of advancement? What is the use of experts?
12. How is the work of the city administration judged by the citizens?

In conclusion it should be emphasized that urban research must include the study of problems relating to the urban plant and to urban administration. Such studies are of great importance in any effort to understand the problems of the urban complex and to deal with urban problems.

Bibliography

ANDRZEJEWSKI, A. *Polityka mieszkaniowa. Zagadnienia ekonomiczne i socjalne* [Housing policy. Economic and social problems]. Warsaw, 1959.

BURMEISTER, H. *Wasserwirtschaftliche Probleme grossstädtischer und industrieller Ballungsräume* [Problems of water management in larger industrial towns]. Bremen, 1955.

CHOMBART DE LAUWE, P. *Paris et l'agglomération parisienne.* Paris, 1952.

DAWIDOWICZ, V. G. *Planirowka gorodow. Inzenerno-ekonomiczeskie osnowy* [Town-planning. Engineering and economic principles]. Moscow, 1947.

DUNCAN, B.; HAUSER, P. *Housing a metropolis—Chicago.* Glencoe, 1960.

DZIEWOŃSKI, K. *Organizacja przestrzenna miast i jej kontrola* [Spatial structures of cities and their control]. Warsaw, 1951.

LEBRET, L.; BRIDE, R. *L'enquête urbaine. L'analyse du quartier et de la ville.* Paris, 1955.

MAGILL, A.; HOLDEN, F.; ACHLEY, C. *Air pollution handbook.* New York, 1956.

MALISZ, B. *Ekonomika planowania miast* [Economics of town-planning]. Warsaw, 1961.

MITCHELL, R.; RAPKIN, C. *Urban traffic. A function of land use.* Columbia University Press, 1954.

√ NATIONAL COMMITTEE ON URBAN TRANSPORTATION. *Better transportation for your city. A guide to the factual development of urban transportation.* Chicago, 1958.

OSTROWSKI, W. *Lokalizacja i planowanie terenów przemyslowych* [Localization and planning of industrial areas]. Warsaw, 1953.

PIÓRO, Z. *Ekologia spoleczna w urbanistyce* [Human ecology and town planning]. Warsaw, 1962.

PTASZYCKA, A. *Przestrzenie zielone w miastach* [Green spaces in cities]. Poznań, 1950.

SIMONDS, J. *Landscape architecture. The shaping of man's natural environment.* New York, 1961.

STRAMIENTOW, A. *Inżynieryjne woprosy planirowki gorodow* [Engineering problems of town planning]. Moscow, 1952.

WEISMANN, E. Grave deficit of dwellings in post-war Europe. *Housing and town planning bulletin,* vol. 7, 1953.

√ WOODBURY, C. (ed.). *The future of cities and urban redevelopment.* Chicago, 1953.